JUDGING POLICY

JUDGING POLICY

Courts and Policy Reform
in Democratic Brazil

MATTHEW M. TAYLOR

STANFORD UNIVERSITY PRESS

Stanford, California

Stanford University Press
Stanford, California

Printed in the United States of America on acid-free,
archival-quality paper

Library of Congress Cataloging-in-Publication Data
Taylor, Matthew M.
    Judging policy : courts and policy reform in democratic Brazil /
Matthew M. Taylor.
        p. cm.
    Includes bibliographical references and index.
    ISBN 978-0-8047-5811-6 (cloth : alk. paper)
    1. Justice, Administration of—Brazil—History. 2. Appellate courts—
Brazil—History. 3. Political questions and judicial power—Brazil.
4. Brazil—Politics and government—1985- I. Title.

    KHD2500.T39 2008
    347.81'012—dc22
                                                    2007039525

Typeset by Classic Typography in 10.5/13 Bembo

For Nácia

CONTENTS

Figures

Tables

ACKNOWLEDGMENTS

A project of this size cannot possibly be written without contributions from a large contingent of witting and unwitting collaborators. Although it is impossible to thank by name all the people who have contributed their immense understanding of courts and Brazilian politics to this book, a few stand out. Various ideas in this book were first inflicted on audiences at conferences held by the ABCP, ALACIP, APSA, BRASA, IPSA, LASA, and SPSA, whom I thank for bringing my arguments into focus. Articles that contributed to this book's arguments were also carefully reviewed and greatly improved by the editors and reviewers at *Comparative Politics*, the *Brazilian Journal of Political Economy*, and *América Latina Hoy*, as well as by Lourdes Sola and Laurence Whitehead, who invited me to contribute to their fantastic 2006 Oxford volume. Portions of the resulting chapters are gratefully reprinted with the publisher's permission.

The manuscript reviewers at Stanford University Press have been particularly generous. David Fleischer and Rogelio Pérez-Perdomo offered encouraging and constructive feedback. To his probable chagrin, Daniel Brinks agreed to surrender his anonymity as a reviewer and helpfully commented on some chapters repeatedly, drawing out the key arguments ahead. I have benefited throughout the editorial process from the guidance of the editors at Stanford University Press, and especially from David Horne's close editorial eye.

The research and writing of this book have been facilitated and enhanced by ties to a number of institutions: Georgetown University, a generous home for many years, where Kerry Pace, Maria Snyder, and Tatiana Mollazadeh were instrumental in keeping me afloat financially and somewhat organized in other regards; the Centro Brasileiro de Estudos e Pesquisas Judiciais (CEBEPEJ), where Kazuo Watanabe, Maria Tereza Sadek, and Marco Antonio Lorencini helped me find my footing early on; the Braudel Institute and Tendências Consultoria Integrada, two institutions filled with friends from my first stay in Brazil during the mid-1990s; the Fulbright Commission, which funded much of the early research, and the Fundação de Amparo à Pesquisa do Estado de São Paulo (FAPESP), which funded its conclusion;

the OAB and the AMB, whose members were so welcoming of my inquiries; the Department of Political Science at the University of São Paulo, where my colleagues have been consistently encouraging and welcoming of the *gringo* in their midst; and Lourdes Sola, the late Eduardo Kugelmas, Maria Rita Loureiro, and Moisés Marques, members of the FAPESP-financed working group that has provided me with a stimulating intellectual nest for several years. Other individuals who deserve special mention for helping put me on the right research track include Paulo Calmon, Rafael Favetti, Norman Gall, Eduardo Leite, Carlos Lopes, Jens Ludwig, Marcus André Melo, Naomi Moniz, Guilherme da Nóbrega, Nilson Oliveira, Carlos Pereira, Bill Prillaman, Marcelo Santos, and Bruno Speck.

The list of scholars who have read and commented on portions of this text is embarrassingly long, including Susan Alberts, Rogério Arantes, Zuleika Arashiro, Christina Bobrow, Maria da Glória Bonelli, Rachel Bowen, Ernani Carvalho, Luciana Gross Cunha, Lisa Hilbink, Taeko Hiroi, Andrei Koerner, Leany Lemos, Mary Fran Malone, Lesley McAllister, Cristina Pacheco, Tony Pereira, Tim Power, Dina Shehata, and Cliff Welch. Thanks to all, and my apologies and thanks to anyone I may have inadvertently overlooked.

Diana Kapiszewski and Julio Ríos-Figueroa have been especially pleasant, patient, and generous with their time and ideas, and much of the thinking in the pages ahead reflects their influence. Diana's help as an especially well-informed editor and hard-nosed critic of multiple iterations of the text was extraordinarily valuable, and greatly improved the ideas expressed here. My work with Julio on the comparison between Brazil and Mexico has helped to solidify and broaden the reach of many of the arguments laid out ahead. As always, although they should claim much of the credit, neither Diana nor Julio, nor anyone else mentioned here, carries any share of my blame for possible errors or omissions.

Four scholars without whom this book could not have been written are John Bailey, Gerald Mara, Arturo Valenzuela, and Linn Hammergren. Together they have coached me, broadened my intellectual approach, guided me to new findings, and otherwise driven me forward. Without wishing to withdraw merit from any of the others, John Bailey's continuing advice, counsel, and friendship—long after his formal responsibilities were officially dispatched—is a testament to why he is held in such high regard by students and colleagues.

It goes without saying, although it is worth saying nonetheless, that I'd never have set off down this path were it not for my mother and father, whose example is as encouraging as anything they've ever taught me. Finally, this book is dedicated to the woman who holds an inordinate share of the blame for my enduring interest in Brazil.

ABBREVIATIONS

ABI	Associação Brasileira de Imprensa
ACO	Ação Civil Originária
ADC	Ação Declaratória de Constitucionalidade
ADIN	Ação Direta de Inconstitucionalidade
ADPF	Argüição de Descumprimento de Preceito Fundamental
AGU	Advocacia Geral da União
AJUFE	Associação dos Juízes Federais do Brasil
AMB	Associação dos Magistrados Brasileiros
ANA	Agência Nacional de Águas
ANEEL	Agência Nacional de Energia Elétrica
ANFAVEA	Associação Nacional dos Fabricantes de Veículos Automotores
ANP	Agência Nacional do Petróleo, Gás Natural e Biocombustíveis
AP	Ação Popular
BNDES	Banco Nacional de Desenvolvimento Econômico e Social
CGT	Confederación General del Trabajo (Argentina)
CNBB	Conferência Nacional dos Bispos do Brasil
CNI	Confederação Nacional da Indústria
CNJ	Conselho Nacional de Justiça
CNT	Confederação Nacional do Transporte
CONAMP	Associação Nacional dos Membros do Ministério Público
CONTAG	Confederação Nacional dos Trabalhadores na Agricultura
CPMF	Contribuição Provisória sobre Movimentação Financeira
CPT	Comissão Pastoral da Terra
CTA	Central de los Trabajadores Argentinos
CUT	Central Única dos Trabalhadores
CVRD	Companhia Vale do Rio Doce

GCE	Câmara de Gestão da Crise de Energia
IBASE	Instituto Brasileiro de Análises Sociais e Econômicas
IMSS	Instituto Mexicano del Seguro Social (Mexico)
INSS	Instituto Nacional de Seguro Social
IPI	Imposto sobre Produtos Industrializados
MST	Movimento dos Sem-Terra
MTA	Movimiento de Trabajadores Argentinos
OAB	Ordem dos Advogados do Brasil
ONAJPU	Organización Nacional de Asociaciones de Jubilados y Pensionistas del Uruguay (Uruguay)
PCdoB	Partido Comunista do Brasil
PDT	Partido Democrático Trabalhista
PFL	Partido da Frente Liberal
PIT-CNT	Plenario Intersindical de Trabajadores—Convención Nacional de Trabajadores (Uruguay)
PL	Partido Liberal
PMDB	Partido do Movimento Democrático Brasileiro
PMN	Partido da Mobilização Nacional
PP	Partido Progressista
PPB	Partido Progressista Brasileiro
PPR	Partido Progressista Renovador
PPS	Partido Popular Socialista
PRD	Partido de la Revolución Democrática (Mexico)
PRI	Partido Revolucionario Institucional (Mexico)
PSB	Partido Socialista Brasileiro
PSC	Partido Social Cristão
PSDB	Partido da Social Democracia Brasileira
PSL	Partido Social Liberal
PST	Partido Social Trabalhista
PSTU	Partido Socialista dos Trabalhadores Unificado
PT	Partido dos Trabalhadores
PTB	Partido Trabalhista Brasileiro
PV	Partido Verde
Sindipeças	Sindicato Nacional da Indústria de Componentes para Veículos Automotores

STF   Supremo Tribunal Federal

STJ   Superior Tribunal de Justiça

TDA   Título da Dívida Agrária

TRF   Tribunal Regional Federal

UNE   União Nacional dos Estudantes

JUDGING POLICY

Chapter 1

Courts and Public Policy Reform in Brazil

Courts are playing an increasingly important role in shaping public policy in contemporary Latin America. In Brazil, the judiciary has molded policy initiatives governing everything from political party representation to privatization; in Costa Rica, courts have shaped policies ranging from telecommunications competition to fishing regulations; and in Mexico, courts have had a hand in fashioning policies ranging from public sector pension reform to industrial expropriation. In short, from the Amazon to the Rio Grande, and in nations in between, courts' ability to influence the definition of policy alternatives (Schattschneider 1960, 68) is an increasingly prominent facet of political life.[1]

Correspondingly, scholars of Latin America are increasingly analyzing the role of courts in policymaking throughout the region.[2] This recognition of courts' policy relevance builds on four previous waves of political science research on courts in the region (Kapiszewski and Taylor 2006, 1–2): a first wave focused on judicial reforms (for example, Hammergren 1998, 2007; Prillaman 2000; Ungar 2002) and courts effects' on economic development (for example, Buscaglia and Ulen 1997); a second wave focused on the justice-related legacy of authoritarianism (for example, McAdams 1997; Barahona De Brito et al. 2001); a third wave focused on courts' contribution to social justice (for example, Méndez et al. 1999; O'Donnell 1994); and, finally, a wave focused on judicial politics (for example, Chavez 2004; Hilbink 2007) and the "judicialization" of politics (for example, Gloppen et al. 2004, Sieder et al. 2005).

1

Despite this growing interest, the policy role of the Brazilian judiciary remains underanalyzed in the comparative politics literature. This is surprising given the multiple justifications for tackling the Brazilian case. First, the Brazilian judiciary has been an especially consequential policy actor in Latin America's largest democracy. Three examples illustrate the active role Brazil's courts played in challenging many of the executive-driven policy reforms implemented between 1988 and 2004, the period covered in this volume:

- On April 29, 1997, Brazil's largest mining company, CVRD, was to be sold in an auction that was expected to garner over three billion dollars and kick off a round of major privatizations. A wave of lawsuits filed by opposition political parties and their allies, however, led to a nail-biting sequence of injunctions that repeatedly delayed and rescheduled the auction. Even though the sale was eventually concluded, a number of suits contesting the privatization process remained pending, some to this day.

- Agrarian reform has been a major issue in Brazil for several generations, but it became an increasingly contentious political subject during the 1990s, with land seizures by landless groups and violent police repression gripping public attention. Between 1993 and 2002, over three hundred people are believed to have died in conflicts in the countryside. Forced to address the issue, in 1999 the government adopted a new policy that streamlined expropriation procedures but also constrained the landless movement's tactic of land seizures. The policy seemed to be a successful attempt at reconciling interests on both sides. Successful, that is, until the national bar association successfully challenged the policy's limits on monetary claims in high court, thereby rendering the new policy largely ineffective.

- On September 30, 1999, Brazil's highest court made headlines when it suspended a tax on civil service pensions, in response to a suit by the bar association. The government was shaken by the defeat, which followed a fierce legislative battle for fiscal austerity in the wake of the catastrophic January 1999 currency devaluation, and generated a budget shortfall exceeding one billion dollars. Markets were even more unnerved: the Brazilian currency depreciated by 2 percent the following trading day, and strong capital outflows drove Central Bank foreign currency reserves down by 6.3 percent in the ensuing month. To compensate for the judicial decision and reverse deteriorating market sentiment, the Finance Ministry was forced to announce an emergency package of spending cuts and tax increases.

As these examples demonstrate, the policy effects of Brazil's federal court decisions can be significant. On numerous occasions, courts have been called upon to evaluate decisions made by Congress or the president, and on a fair number of such occasions, courts effectively halted policy implementation and sent policymakers back to the drawing board, with effects that reverberated across the entire body politic. Less dramatic, but nonetheless significant, were the thousands of daily interactions between government and society in the courts that, in an accretive fashion, have played a role in defining the options available to policymakers. In sum, the evidence suggests that over the past two decades, during Brazil's dual transition to market economics and democratic government, courts at all levels of the judiciary have helped to define the alternatives available to policymakers, legitimating or de-legitimating certain policy choices.

In this sense, Brazil's courts directly challenge the prevailing regional stereotype of pliant judiciaries—a vision kept alive by cases such as Argentina or Chile, where courts have had a much less significant effect on policy outcomes in the post-transition era. More broadly, the Brazilian case offers a significant Latin American complement to existing research focused specifically on courts and public policy, which has predominantly addressed the experiences of more consolidated North American and European democracies and, more recently, the European Union and its own supranational courts (for example, Jackson and Tate 1992; Stone Sweet 2000, 2005; Volcansek 1992).

The Brazilian courts' role in the policy process, however, teaches us about more than judicial politics and power in a crucial Latin American case. It also illustrates what motivated policy actors may be able to achieve in a propitious judicial environment. Policy reform is difficult in most contexts, but it has represented a particularly great challenge in Brazil's new democracy due to the confluence of several factors: the country's sheer scale, the depth of the economic crisis bequeathed by the military regime, the breadth of the 1988 Constitution, and the difficulty of finding the super-majoritarian support needed to approve many reforms. Under these conditions, political opposition was bound to occur. What was not anticipated—and has been insufficiently analyzed—is policy opponents' selection of the *judicial* route to achieve their policy objectives, and how this choice has increasingly thrust the Brazilian courts into the vortex of policy debate.

Brazil is also a fitting case study because of the country's prominent place within the broader comparative political science literature. Brazil is a leading developing nation, with the world's fifth largest population and an economy that accounts for more than a third of the Latin American regional

GDP. This book, building on in-depth empirical study and on a wealth of new material on the Brazilian judiciary produced in Brazil itself,[3] seeks to integrate the courts into the excellent body of existing research in comparative political science on political institutions and policy outcomes in Brazil.[4]

I use the case of the full Brazilian federal court system, including the high court *and* lower courts, to develop a framework for understanding how courts are drawn into the policy game and how policy players use courts to advance their strategic political objectives. In so doing, this book speaks to broader debates surrounding judicial politics and the role of the judiciary as a crucial component of the gamut of institutions used to explain policy choice in Latin America's new democracies.

Courts in the Policy Game

Skeptics have posited many reasons why courts may not have significant policy effects.[5] First, courts are inherently reactive.[6] It is rarely reasonable to assume that the courts are "veto players" in their own right, much less that judges can or do actively seek out policies to influence along the lines of their normative preferences. Moreover, for policy players with access to many different venues, courts are frequently last on the list of institutions that come to mind when one considers the tactical options available to shape the public policy "game" and influence policy outcomes.

Further, given their close ties to governing elites and their general reliance on the elected branches of government for funding and survival, courts may be naturally cautious (see, for example, Dahl 1957). Because judges generally rule on specific cases, rather than general rules; because they can only act when called upon; and because they act as an arbitrator only when a law leads to dispute, on the face of it judges have little power to selectively influence policy. Despite significant evidence to the contrary, the analytical waters are further muddied by an enduring conception of courts as "neutral" institutions whose rulings are founded in legal rules rather than normative preferences (Friedman 2005). Finally, a weighty body of research questions the degree to which courts can be effective producers of social change except under exceptional circumstances (for example, Epp 1998; Rosenberg 1991; Shapiro 2004).[7]

And yet, these concerns notwithstanding, the evidence of courts' policy relevance cannot be disregarded. The potential for courts to have any policy relevance has two foundations. The first is that in a majority of nations, judges are given the right to found decisions on broad constitutional grounds, potentially imbuing them with "immense political power" (Tocqueville 1969, 99–101). The second is that even when they are not based on constitutional foundations, the results of court decisions build up over time in an accretive fashion: "Legal rules are never neutral. Every legal rule, or even principle, always prefers one interest, right, value, or group over another. . . . Thus, in the aggregate and over time, judicial decisions on such issues inevitably affect general public policy as well as economic development" (Murphy et al. 2002, 44). Partly as a result of these two foundations of judicial power, in U.S. academic circles by the 1960s there was an "open, childlike, acknowledgement of the obvious . . . courts were significant actors in American politics" (Shapiro and Stone Sweet 2002, 4). A similar epiphany has recently struck scholars of regions outside the more common European and North American case studies (for example, Gloppen et al. 2004), helped along in part by evidence of a growing "judicialization" of politics.[8]

That said, even if courts play a role in shaping the direction of policy possibilities, we do not really know much about how that role is determined. Why are some courts so much less relevant to policy outcomes than others? By contrast, when courts do play an important policy role, is their role essentially conservative, reinforcing the status quo, or are they effectively used to stake bold new claims?

The main reason to study the courts here, then, is to better understand how they are brought into the policymaking process, and the magnitude and direction of their effects. For those wondering how courts might gain policy importance in other new democracies, the evolution of the Brazilian judiciary over the past two decades offers an intriguing—but not unambiguous—case of judicial strengthening. For those interested in the policy role of courts, this book explores how it is that Brazilian courts are drawn into the policy game. More important, for skeptics who question the ability of courts to influence policy, it asks *why* they are drawn into the policy game, given that their expected impact is indeed only marginal in comparison to that of the elected branches. Finally, those who trust in the courts' potential as socially transformative institutions at the heart of new democracies will be interested in this book's discussion of the factors that shape policy actors' ability to achieve their policy objectives through the courts, the ways in which court structure influences the relative strength of different members of society, and hence, the types of social transformation courts permit.

The broad premise on which this book is founded is that the rules governing access to institutional venues for policy contestation matter significantly to final policy outcomes. The courts are no different in this regard from other political institutions, such as bureaucracies or legislative committees. Courts only act when they are called upon, but given that court decisions have an effect on policy because legal rules are never neutral, once courts are activated they can wield considerable policy influence. Hence, the question of

how they can be activated by different policy players is vital to understanding their importance in the policymaking process. For too long, analyses of
judicial behavior have attempted to explain judicial behavior while ignoring
the role and the motivations of those who trigger judicial intervention.

Engaging the judiciary to achieve one's policy ends is not a particularly
difficult task for any group that can afford a lawyer. Organizing a legal challenge is certainly no more difficult, and on occasion considerably easier and
less expensive, than attempting to shape the policymaking process in Congress or the executive branch. But much depends on how policy groups are
organized internally, and how this organization shapes the groups' ability to
implement coherent legal tactics that advance a broader political strategy.
Much also depends on the broader conditions of "legal enfranchisement,"
that is, the types of legal instruments available (either by law or in practice)
to any given plaintiff. Worldwide, it has long been a nostrum that not all
groups are equal before the courts. In many civil code systems, these different levels of legal franchise are written into the formal legal structure, with
some organizations, for example, given access to specific legal instruments or
to privileged forms of standing that are not available to others. Such differences are frequently grounded in constitutional texts and other founding
documents, and help to shape the tactics used to pursue policy outcomes in
the courts.

Further, courts are not exempt from strategic "venue-seeking"—that is,
policy actors' pursuit of the best possible institutional venue from which to
influence policy outcomes.[9] The tactical opportunities afforded by the courts
as a potential venue will vary based on formal institutional rules, such as
those governing standing or precedent; informal rules, such as tacit attitudes
within the legal community governing what types of appeals are permissible
or appropriate; and the overall administrative performance of the courts, as
reflected in judicial efficiency or practical access to judicial remedies.

The most significant impact courts can have on policy comes when a
judge or court, especially a high court whose decision cannot be appealed
and whose rulings may have effects that go far beyond the plaintiff and defendant at hand, issues a decision in a given case. Many studies have focused
on the factors that may influence such a decision, including the ideologies
or attitudes of judges (for example, Segal and Spaeth 1993); the strategic re-
actions of judges to the threats they perceive to themselves or to the court
(for example, Epstein and Knight 2000; Helmke 2005); the degree of societal support for the courts (for example, Staton 2004; Vanberg 2001); and the
trade-off judges and particularly high court justices face between making
broad constitutional decisions that could bring significant change but might
place the court in jeopardy, or smaller-scale, administrative decisions that

will bring little change in the short term but may build court power gradually over the long haul (for example, Roux 2004; Uprimny 2004).

As all of this research suggests, there can be little doubt that the study of judges' patterns of decision making is vital to understanding a given courts' effect on public policy. But academics worldwide have been so intent on explaining judicial decision making, especially by high courts, that they have often set aside the equally important, antecedent question of what policy issues the courts are in fact asked to decide, by whom, and why. Two core arguments may help remedy this situation; they are briefly presaged in the next sections.

ACTIVATING COURTS TO POLICY ENDS

Long before any judge makes a decision, several precursor factors play a crucial role in influencing the judiciary's overall effects on policy, by shaping litigants' views of whether the courts can and should be activated to policy ends. These dynamics are not unimportant, nor are they random. Without taking them into account, we cannot begin to understand how courts become relevant in the policy game.

My first argument is that three factors—policy salience, political environment, and the judicial institutional environment—have a significant effect in determining which public policies actually have their day in court (Figure 1.1). These factors influence policy contestation at several levels: they shape actors' strategies in the political system as a whole, drive the decision to activate the

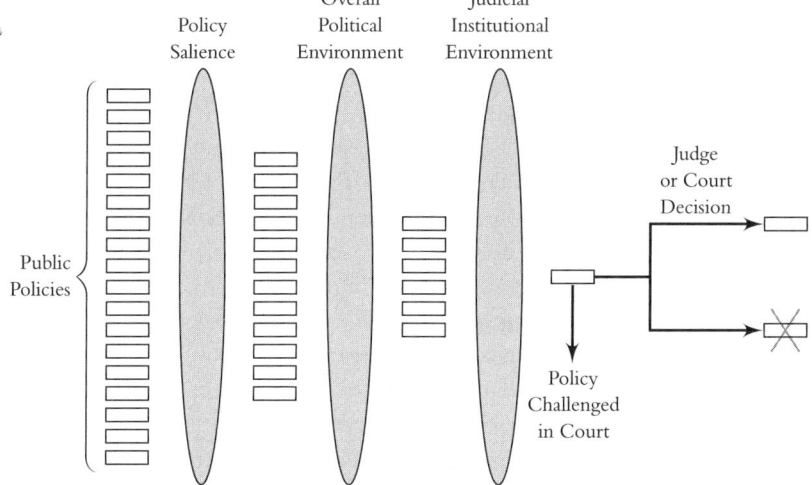

Figure 1.1.   Key factors in the activation of courts on policy questions

courts as a venue for policy contestation, and mold the legal tactics policy actors employ within the judicial venue.

The first factor is the salience of policy. Not all public policies are equally salient, and some are more likely to lead to contestation than others. Whether policy is contested in the courts or in congressional committee hearings, the degree of contestation is highly influenced by how the costs and benefits of policy are distributed, and, especially, by how this distribution influences the likelihood of policy "losers" organizing to fight against policy change (for example, Lowi 1964, 1972; Wilson 1995). Ultimately, however, salience varies greatly across members of society, and the only type of salience that matters to the argument here is the salience of a given policy to potential plaintiffs. This is determined by the concrete costs and benefits of the policy to a potential plaintiff's interests, as well as the rather less quantifiable costs and benefits to that plaintiff's beliefs and mores, which I aggregate under the label "ideas." In the case of organized policy groups, the path between these subjective perceptions of policy and actual political tactics is further mediated by the group's internal institutional structure, and, in particular, how it influences the tactical decisions made by the group.

The second factor is the overall political environment, which includes both fleetingly contingent political conditions and rather more stable (but not immutable) institutional rules governing the political regime.[10] Regarding the former, it is possible, for example, that some policies may benefit from such broad popular support that challenging them could be politically perilous for potential plaintiffs. In terms of the latter, institutional rules in the overall political system—which include such unwritten constraints as societal consensus on the proper role of legal contestation in the political system, as well as formal rules such as those governing judicial intervention in ongoing legislative deliberations—shape the place of courts in plaintiffs' overall political strategies. As a result, these institutional rules help to determine whether some policies will be challenged at all in the courts, or whether policy players will prefer to engage alternative institutional venues, such as regulatory agencies, civil service bureaucracies, or congressional committees. A number of different tactics may also be simultaneously employed in the service of a broader political strategy, meaning that a court suit may be filed in conjunction with other tactical efforts, such as lobbying in Congress, efforts to undermine bureaucratic implementation, or a public relations blitz.

Finally, the third factor that helps to determine whether a given policy actually goes before a court or judge is the judicial institutional environment, within which three features are of particular interest from a policy perspective: the structure of judicial independence, the structure of judicial review, and the administrative performance of the courts. Once a policy player decides to use legal tactics in the service of a larger political strategy, these tactics are shaped by the prevailing rules of the judicial system, which will in turn shape potential plaintiffs' analysis of whether policy contestation in the courts is a wise tactical option.

The first argument, to summarize, is that the use of the courts for policy ends is shaped by the salience of policy to specific policy actors and the way in which both the broader political environment and the specific judicial institutional framework shape the likely success of policy contestation in the courts, especially in contrast to (or in combination with) other potential venues of policy contestation. Court involvement in policy debates, in other words, cannot be studied in isolation from the broader strategies of political actors in the overall political system.

JUDICIAL TACTICS AND POLICY CONTESTATION

The second argument presented in this book is that the judicial institutional environment has a significant effect in shaping the legal tactics adopted by policy players. Once a policy has triggered opposition, in other words, the third factor in Figure 1.1 comes into play. Key to determining which actors are legally enfranchised to use the courts in strategically productive ways, and the tactics they use, are two sets of factors related to the judicial institutional structure: those governing judicial independence, as measured both in terms of the courts' independence from other branches and judges' independence from each other; and those governing the structure of judicial review, especially the accessibility of the courts and particular legal instruments to all potential policy players (Ríos-Figueroa and Taylor 2006). A court system dependent on the executive branch for its annual budget allocation, or a judiciary in which overtly political organizations have no special standing, will lead to very different patterns of policy contestation than those of budgetarily autonomous courts or courts in which political parties can contest policy directly in the high court. Such factors help to determine who the relevant policy players are within the court system; the location of veto points in the judicial structure; the array of possible tactics that may be used to challenge policy; and, as a result, the role of courts within the broader political system.

Again, not all opponents of policy will be motivated to contest policy in the courts. And those who are motivated may not be legally enfranchised to use the courts in productive ways. Furthermore, even among those policy actors who are legally enfranchised in ways that would allow them to productively contest policy in the courts, the legal tactics undertaken in pursuit of a broader political strategy may vary considerably, depending on the ideas that undergird their basic political objectives.[11] Given its deep professional interest in preserving constitutionality and the legal framework, the national bar association, for example, may use the courts in ways that differ from those of other professional unions, such as industrial federations or commercial associations.

In pursuing their policy objectives, policy actors may turn to courts as veto points that enable them to delay or disable policy or, alternatively, as opportunities to discredit policy, or declare their opposition. These four tactical objectives (delay, disable, discredit, declare) can be carried forward in ways that are premised both on solid legal grounds (a firm belief that a given law is unconstitutional, for example), and on purely strategic foundations (for example, an effort to appeal a policy decision despite clear recognition that the legal grounds for appeal are weak).

This last point deserves some fleshing out: legal tactics are not always chosen solely in expectation of achieving a favorable judicial decision. Policy players may indeed use the courts as a last recourse: if all else fails, the cost of challenging policy through the courts is not always great, and plaintiffs may even reason that a last-ditch challenge could lead to a surprising legal victory. But actors on the losing end of policymaking may also use legal tactics even when they realistically see little hope of a legal win. Defeated policy players may litigate to cast doubts about policy, draw public attention to supposed procedural miscarriages, or otherwise discredit policies bearing majoritarian support. By contesting policy in court, in other words, it may be possible to secure a political victory without ever achieving a legal victory. Legal tactics are therefore far more complicated than we often assume, and getting the "right" legal decision is not always the ultimate goal. In sum, the courts may be strategically productive in the larger political scheme of things, even for those who do not win the underlying legal battle.

The Road Ahead

To reiterate, two central questions are addressed in this book. First, in what ways have Brazilian federal courts been activated in policy debates, and why? Second, how do the salience of policy, the overall political environment, and the judicial institutional environment influence the manner by which key policy players engage policy in the courts? The answers to these questions will provide broader lessons about courts' effects on policymaking in complex and vibrant policy environments, in which both the economic situation and the rules governing the democratic regime are in flux.

These questions are tackled from a number of different perspectives over the course of this book. Chapter 2 describes a framework of legal tactical choice and looks more closely at how judicial structure may shape the tactical opportunities afforded to various potential policy opponents. Drawing on a framework founded in new institutionalism, I focus not only on the direct effects of the structures of judicial independence and judicial review on policy contestation but also on their indirect effects, which play out through the administrative performance of the court system. In the process, Chapter 2 provides the local knowledge necessary for understanding how the Brazilian federal courts influence the identity of the groups that can effectively challenge policy and shape the broad panoply of legal tactics available to them.

Chapter 3 offers case studies of eight key policy debates undertaken during the two-term Cardoso administration (1995–2002), demonstrating the frequent recourse to the federal courts during a period of intense reform. In addition to providing locally grounded evidence of the various policy uses of the federal courts, especially by minorities shut out of the governing coalition, this chapter illustrates how the combination of policy salience and the overall political environment guide the use of courts by policy opponents.

Together, these first chapters address the factors that shape policy opponents' tactics and overall patterns of court activation in the policy game. But they do not explain the differences between individual plaintiffs' tactics, which may vary significantly, even under similar institutional conditions. By focusing on one particularly prominent mechanism of judicial review, Chapter 4 illustrates first how the judiciary fits into the broader political environment and, especially, how institutional rules produce "veto points" within the judiciary that enable some policy opponents to effectively delay or defeat policies in areas in which they might otherwise have little or no leverage. This chapter also illustrates why it is that poor legal performance is not necessarily a disadvantageous political strategy: courts are frequently used as a tactical venue for voicing opposition, even when the judicial environment is not conducive to successful legal contestation.

Chapters 5 and 6 illustrate how organized political groups' legal tactics may differ, even under similar institutional rules and political conditions. Potential plaintiffs' ideas and perceived group interests, as well as their own internal decision-making structures, help determine which tactics they will use, and hence, the manner by which courts will be pulled into the policy game. These paired chapters compare the strategies and motivations behind the tactics of legal contestation used by a weak legal veto player, opposition political parties, and a strong legal veto player, the Brazilian bar association (Ordem dos Advogados do Brasil, or OAB).

Chapter 7 adopts a cross-national comparative perspective and shows how, under differing institutional rules, even very similar policy opponents facing comparably salient policy changes may be forced to adopt strikingly different tactics and different institutional venues. Drawing on a comparative case study of pension reform in four Latin American nations, this chapter illustrates how different institutional structures can lead to distinct patterns of court activation even in highly comparable policy debates. In the process, I offer a preliminary example of how the conclusions of this study of Brazil might be carried over productively to the policy literature beyond Brazil. Chapter 8 concludes with an overview of this book's lessons in terms of the courts' role in interest representation and policy reform in Latin American democracies.

Chapter 2

The Puzzling Policy Influence
of Brazil's Federal Courts

The policy role of the Brazilian judiciary should not be underestimated. As the examples of court intervention in Chapter 1 illustrated, Brazilian courts have reversed important decisions by powerful presidents, with effects that reverberated across the entire body politic. Like a handful of courts elsewhere in the region,[1] Brazil's federal courts thus offer an important counterexample to the stereotypical view of Latin American judiciaries, acting both dynamically and influentially to shape policy debates during the two decades of intense policy ferment that have followed the end of the military regime.

Further evidence of the courts' relative effects comes from the comparative record. While quantitative measures say little about the substantive significance of court decisions, the number of constitutional challenges upheld by the Brazilian Supreme Federal Tribunal (STF) is significant in comparison to its peers. Since its inception more than two centuries ago, the U.S. Supreme Court, for example, has ruled 135 federal laws unconstitutional (*The Economist* 1999). Mexico's high court, which is perhaps a better comparative example because it, like its Brazilian counterpart, operates in a federal nation with a civil code system, has ruled on the constitutionality of just over 600 state and federal laws between the judicial reform of 1994 and 2005, using two prominent review instruments.[2] In roughly a quarter of the cases, the court altered the underlying law, but of these, only 21 were federal laws (Guardado Rodríguez 2007). By contrast, responding to only one of many possible legal instruments (the *Ação Direta de Inconstitucionalidade,* or ADIN) in its first fifteen

13

years, the Brazilian STF debated the constitutionality of more than 1,000 federal laws and altered over 200 on constitutional grounds. Furthermore, at the lower court level, the picture is equally dynamic, with estimates that "no less than half a million cases have been brought every year against the federal government" (Arantes 2005, 237).

This important policy effect continues today. In 2005 and 2006, Brazilian courts have shaped policy on a number of fronts. To name just a few recent cases: the high court overruled a decade-old reform aimed at reducing the number of small political parties in Congress; federal courts overruled the CADE regulatory board to permit an R$600 million corporate acquisition by Nestlé; and the STF rejected Congress's effort to nearly double members' salaries. Most impressively, a November 2005 decision ruled that a 1998 increase in the pension contribution paid by businesses (known as PIS/Cofins)—implemented as Brazil was facing significant market uncertainty in the wake of the Russian financial crisis—was unconstitutional. Although the final effects of the decision are debatable, estimates of its cost range as high as R$26.8 billion, more than 10 percent of total federal government tax collections, or 2 percent of GDP.[3]

This is all by way of reiterating that on numerous occasions, courts have been called upon to challenge decisions made by Congress or the president, and on a fair number of such occasions, they effectively halted or altered policy implementation and sent policymakers back to the drawing board. Most important, compliance has been assumed, and governments have closely abided by these court decisions, despite significant costs to their policy agendas and their budgetary bottom line.

And yet, puzzlingly, the court system has two levels of performance: on the one hand it is strong, able to check the government, reverse policy, and ensure compliance with its rulings; on the other, the court system at the individual level functions poorly, providing few credible guarantees to the average citizen of rapid legal recourse against policy. The courts have enabled peaceful resolution of important policy disputes and incorporated opposition groups, such as political parties and social organizations shut out of the executive and legislative branches, in democracy-enhancing deliberations on policy. However, the manner in which the court system operates makes it extraordinarily difficult for individual citizens to effectively contest policy in the judiciary, and may thus temper their views of the effectiveness and even legitimacy of a major institution of Brazilian democracy.[4]

This chapter seeks to understand how the institutional architecture of the court system, and in particular this simultaneous combination of high-impact and low-functionality structures, shapes the tactical opportunities available to policy players. My focus is on the judicial remedies that courts offer against federal public policies, analyzed from a "new institutionalist" perspective, with its accumulated consensus that institutional norms and structures may affect political behavior by shaping the ability of political actors to advance their preferred courses of conduct.[5] In the next section of this chapter, I briefly outline the new institutionalism's application to the study of Brazilian courts, which informs much of my reasoning throughout this book. In the following section, I elaborate on a more broadly applicable framework that illustrates how the legal tactics of policy players may be influenced by institutional structure in Brazil as elsewhere. In the final sections, I apply this framework to the Brazilian case, looking more closely at how institutional rules have influenced the tactical perspectives of potential litigants in the policy game.

New Institutionalism and the Courts

The least common denominator of "new institutionalism" is that institutional norms, structures, or both may affect political behavior by shaping the ability of political actors to advance their preferred course of conduct. Three competing, if overlapping, variants of new institutionalism have expanded upon this theme (Hall and Taylor 1996; Koelble 1995). Rational choice new institutionalism places considerable emphasis on collective action and the strategic interaction between players, who are assumed to behave rationally within existing informational and behavioral constraints. Sociological new institutionalists are critical of the rational choice model's marginalization of cultural variables, and suggest that institutions "frame" behavior through cognitive scripts that shape not only individuals' strategic calculations but their very notion of group identity. Finally, historical new institutionalists fill the middle ground, emphasizing distinctions between political outcomes, power asymmetries, and the unintended consequences of institutional arrangements, while often drawing on culture as a transmission belt for the habitualization and internalization of norms (for example, Steinmo et al. 1992). Despite occasionally loud differences, the three schools share a common belief that institutions are not neutral in their effect on politics and society.

The Brazilian case offers a fascinating perspective on how the three approaches can be used in tandem to explain the influence of court structure on the legal tactics used to contest policy.[6] From a rational choice new institutional perspective, the structure of Brazilian judicial decision making is highly decentralized, even in comparison to other civil code systems. Judicial

decisions are tenuous in light of the widespread absence of binding precedent, their largely case-specific (rather than universal) applicability, and the
high degree of independence of judges from each other. The result is that
any given judge's individual decision on any given case is, for the most part,
less policy-relevant than the management of the nearly fifty-nine million
cases winding their way through the state and federal court systems (Cardoso 2007b). By way of illustration, Brazil's highest court is equipped with a
drive-through window in the basement, where lawyers can drop off cases
without leaving their cars; most federal courts have a full-time binding operation where functionaries sort, categorize, and bind incoming cases in a
color-coded system for justices to review; and most courts are equipped
with a machine resembling an automatic teller, with which lawyers can type
in case numbers to track their cases wherever they may be in the judicial
system. The implications of such a process-oriented system for public policy are indirect. But they provide strong incentives to policy actors to give
considerable tactical importance to the timing of suits and access to high
court hearings. Individual judges at all levels of the court system are granted
a good deal of discretion and power, but the importance of any individual
judge's decision is correspondingly deflated by the huge numbers of cases
and appeals that result from their autonomy.

From a sociological new institutionalist perspective, the culture of the legal profession in Brazil plays an important role in how the law is applied
and how the legal system fits into the overall political structure. Brazil was
once known as the "República dos Bacharéis," referring to the fact that over
half the presidents in the 1889–1930 Republic were drawn from the ranks
of lawyers. Although presidents are no longer as likely to be lawyers, the
narrowness of legal training and legal practice, the high societal and professional status accorded to legal organizations such as the Brazilian Bar Association (OAB) and the Association of Brazilian Magistrates (AMB), and the
strong adherence of judges and lawyers to the long list of rights enumerated
in the 1988 Constitution have an important effect on how legal decisions are
made, how legal processes are structured, and how government policy initiatives have been viewed by legal professionals. The judicial selection process
also plays an important role: only a small subset of federal judges are appointed by elected officials (the bulk are selected by entry examination), and
even among the political appointees, the fact that they are largely drawn from
within Brazil's own distinct legal culture means that judicial policy preferences
may have only tenuous parallels with the policy preferences of the appointing
executive. Justices imperfectly reflect the preferences of the presidents who
appoint them; the volume of cases heard is so great as to enormously compli-

cate attitudinal analyses of overall patterns of decision making; and even
where it is possible to divide conservative from liberal, these labels mean little in light of the many facets of policy being questioned daily in the high
volume of decisions made by the courts.[7]

Finally, from the historical new institutionalist perspective, the unique
pattern of political evolution from the military regime through the drafting
of the 1988 Constitution and into an era of "neoliberal" reform during the
1990s placed the judiciary in frequent tension with other institutions in society. The framers' opposition to military rule was evident in the institutional framework created by the 1988 Constitution, which guaranteed a
high degree of judicial independence, greater public access to the high
court, and the creation of new case types aimed at constraining executive
arrogation of power. Legal groups such as the OAB saw their opposition to
the military and their defense of democracy rewarded with new forms of
access to the courts. But as Steinmo et al. (1992, 9) have suggested, institutions may shape not only political actors' strategies but their very goals. The
Brazilian judiciary and the legal profession have thus frequently found themselves on a collision course with the executive branch's reforms at key moments over the past two decades, in light of the very important position of the
judiciary and lawyers in drafting the extensive democratic rights incorporated
in the Constitution, the related preferences these groups have strongly voiced
in years since, and the manner by which the courts have been used as a result.

In sum, the important role of the Brazilian courts in the policy process
should be less surprising to political scientists and policy analysts than has
all too frequently been the case, given the historical and cultural milieu in
which both judges and lawyers operate, and the manner by which the institutional rules governing the courts not infrequently lead to high-impact policy decisions despite generally high judicial congestion. In the next section,
I briefly couch these arguments in a more widely applicable framework, before returning in the final sections to the specifics of the Brazilian case.

A Framework of Legal Tactical Choice

The structures of judicial independence and judicial review are fundamental
to establishing the tactical value of courts to policy actors seeking to advance
their broader policy agendas, and thus help to determine how courts will be
activated in policy debates (Ríos-Figueroa and Taylor 2006). These structures
(summarized in Table 2.1) have both direct and indirect effects on legal tactics. Directly, they set the standards regarding who can contest policy, where,
and with what effect. Indirectly, the rules governing judicial independence

TABLE 2.1

Structures of judicial independence and judicial review

Variable	Brief Description
Judicial Independence	
Autonomy	The degree to which the judiciary's general structure and budget are regulated by the judiciary itself, rather than by other branches of government.
External Independence	The relation between individual Supreme Court judges and other branches of government; the extent to which individual judges can act without facing retaliatory measures (Iaryczower et al. 2002).
Internal Independence	The relation between lower court judges and their superiors in the judicial hierarchy; the extent to which judges can make decisions without taking into account the preferences of their hierarchical superiors.
Judicial Review	
Constitutional Arrangements	
Constitutional Rights	The breadth of the rights laid out in the constitution, which will influence the extent to which judicial review cases can be brought.
Original Jurisdiction	The degree to which cases can be brought directly in the high court; the breadth of original jurisdiction influences the extent to which the high court will be regularly activated to judge policy.
Scope of Juridical Power	
A priori or A posteriori	Whether a law can be contested prior to implementation or not.
Abstract or Concrete	Whether a concrete case needs to arise for a policy to be contested, or whether a law can be contested in the abstract, on its merits alone.
Bindingness or Universality	The degree to which a case decision is generalized to the broader judicial system; in other words, whether a decision has *erga omnes* effects, or is only applicable to that particular case or plaintiff.
Discretion	The ability of a judge or court to choose which cases to hear, how extensive a decision to issue, and when to issue that decision.
Standing	Whether all citizens are able to bring the same cases, or some groups have standing in some cases in which others do not.

SOURCE: Compiled, with minor alterations, from Ríos-Figueroa and Taylor 2006; Ríos-Figueroa 2006; and Taylor 2004.

and judicial review help to explain overall judicial administrative performance, determining the relative effectiveness of different policy tactics in terms
of both speed and definitiveness, and contributing to policy players' strategic calculus by influencing the tactical options available to them.

Judicial independence comprises three elements: the overall court system's independence from the elected branches of government (autonomy);
the independence of high court[8] justices from the elected branches (external independence); and the independence of lower court judges from their
colleagues on the high court (internal independence) (Ríos-Figueroa and
Taylor 2006, 743). The first two elements of judicial independence are obviously significant to whether the courts will be called on by policy opponents: a court that is not free to take decisions that contradict those set by
the elected branches is highly unlikely to serve as a reliable arena for policy
opponents.[9] Independence is a complex concept, and it has long been evident that courts are never entirely independent of the regime, as they are an
instrument of state power, used to impose state rules and interests on litigants (Shapiro 1981). Most conceptions of independence, however, share
the basic notion that judges' preferences and decisions should be identified
neither with the parties to the case nor with those of other interested parties,
including—most important when the subject is public policy—the government.[10] That is, while courts may serve the government by providing legitimacy to the application of regime rules, independent courts limit government
power along lines determined by a broad spectrum of political actors both
outside of government and within it.[11]

In a court system that has both high autonomy and high external independence, one can expect policy contestation to be effective, at a minimum,
on what the judge perceives to be strictly legal grounds. That is, courts that
are independent on both of these dimensions can be expected to serve as an
effective means for contesting clearly unconstitutional or illegal policies implemented by the elected branches. But these two factors tell us nothing
about the variance in opinions among courts or judges within the full court
system, or about the ability of lower courts to adopt decisions that differ
from those taken by high courts.

The third element of independence, the internal independence of lower
court judges from high court superiors, is thus highly relevant in determining
the breadth of tactics available to policy players. A highly centralized judicial
system in which lower court judges are beholden to the high courts would allow for few dissenting decisions and would tend to limit the policy game to
the high court. By contrast, a less homogenous system in which judges in

lower courts benefited from substantial internal independence would—other things equal, and assuming lower court judges availed themselves of such latitude—seemingly be propitious to venue shopping among various lower courts and judges.

The second structure, judicial review, helps to determine the potential differences between policy actors in the courts. In common law courts, the constitutional and legal rules that govern judicial review generally provide very little privileged recourse to any given judicial venue. In civil law systems, by contrast, such differences are a common feature. They are generally founded on the interaction between three broad elements: constitutional arrangements, the scope of juridical power, and the rules governing standing (Ríos-Figueroa and Taylor 2006: 747–755).

Constitutional arrangements includes two components: the breadth of formal rights outlined in the Constitution, and the original jurisdiction of the high court, especially whether or not the high court hears some legal instruments directly, rather than solely on appeal. The first component, constitutional rights, is important because the broader the formal rights incorporated in the constitutional text, other things equal, the more likely it is that the high court can be called upon for constitutional review. The second component, the original jurisdiction of the high court, refers not only to the types of instruments the high court hears directly (that is, not on appeal), but also to whether specific subjects are off limits, such as intervention in political questions or deliberation over certain types of political rights (Larkins 1998; Kapiszewski 2007). High courts hear cases based on a number of different legal instruments that reach them either indirectly, via appeals that make their way up through the judicial hierarchy, or directly, via specific legal remedies such as Brazil's *Ação Direta de Inconstitucionalidade* (ADIN, Direct Action of Unconstitutionality) or similar instruments, such as Mexico's *acción de inconstitucionalidad* or constitutional appeals to Costa Rica's *Sala IV.*

The scope of juridical power is the most complex of the elements of judicial review described here. Ríos-Figueroa and Taylor (2006) note three components of juridical power: the timing by which laws are judged (*a priori* versus *a posteriori*); the type of review (abstract versus concrete); and rules governing court decisions' bindingness and universality. To these I add a fourth: discretion, or the ability of a given judge or court to choose which cases to hear, how extensive or constrained a decision to issue, and when to issue that decision.

Most civil code systems generally subscribe to *a posteriori* timing, meaning that a law can only be judged after it goes into effect.[12] But in both Europe and Latin America, many countries impose time limitations on the referral of laws for constitutional review, which help to determine when policy contestation can take place. Second, both abstract and concrete review[13] are possible in civil code systems, because a plaintiff can petition for redress even if the plaintiff's interests are not concretely affected by the particular policy. But abstract review tends to have more significant policy effects. As Stone (1992, 45) notes, abstract review *"functions to extend what would otherwise be a concluded legislative process*—referrals in effect require the court to undertake a final 'reading' of a disputed bill or law" (emphasis in original). Third, two significant considerations regarding any decision are whether it sets a binding precedent on similar future cases and whether it applies to everyone affected by a given policy (*erga omnes*) or only to the parties to the suit (*inter partes*). Binding precedent is customary in common law systems, but the degree of bindingness varies significantly within any given civil code system: some cases have universally binding effects, while others will be relevant only to the plaintiffs to a case. Finally, discretion is somewhat derivative of the other components of juridical power, but merits discussion on its own, because the ability of policy players to draw courts into the policy fray depends in part on judges' ability to evade or rebuff difficult decisions, or instead to attract them to their court (Kapiszewski 2007; Kapiszewski and Taylor 2006; Wilson and Rodríguez Cordero 2006). While judges' discretion depends partly on the first three components mentioned here, it also is dependent on constitutional arrangements, previous jurisprudence, and less tangible factors such as the internal culture of the court system.

Together, the four components of the scope of juridical power help to explain the relative policy relevance of various legal instruments, as well as the identity of policy-relevant legal actors. The relative timing of cases helps to determine the extent to which courts can interfere in deliberations by the elected branches, and, especially, when the high court will be drawn into the policy debate. Second, the type of review used will be relevant to understanding the relative policy influence of potential litigants: other things equal, in a system with both abstract and concrete review, abstract review will be the more efficient and policy-relevant form of court activation, since in all cases it is carried out by the high court. The rules governing a particular legal instrument's bindingness and universality, and especially the way the sum of these rules influences the reach of courts' decisions on policy, clearly are important to policy players' venue selection, as well as to their choice of various legal instruments. Finally, discretion may influence the ability of policy players to successfully activate the court system, either by providing opportunities for judges to decline troublesome cases or, alternatively, by permitting them to take them up.

The third element of judicial review is standing: namely, which actors are legally enfranchised to file what type of suit, regarding what subjects, in what court. Standing plays a fundamental role in determining the range of tactics available to specific policy actors, and their likely use of the court system in politically productive ways.

Together these three elements of judicial review influence the degree of "coordination, uniformity and compliance" (Melnick 2005, 25; Shapiro 1981) within the judicial system, with a strong effect on the tactical options provided by the overall judicial structure. Drawing on the options made available by this structure, and taking into account both the salience of policy and the overall political environment, plaintiffs are able to choose the legal tactics that best suit their overall strategic objectives (Figure 2.1).

There are many variables in this framework, and thus it is worth emphasizing that it is not my intent that it should be used to produce a rigorously predictive model (either here or in an earlier iteration, in Ríos-Figueroa and Taylor 2006). Many other immeasurable intervening factors—ranging from

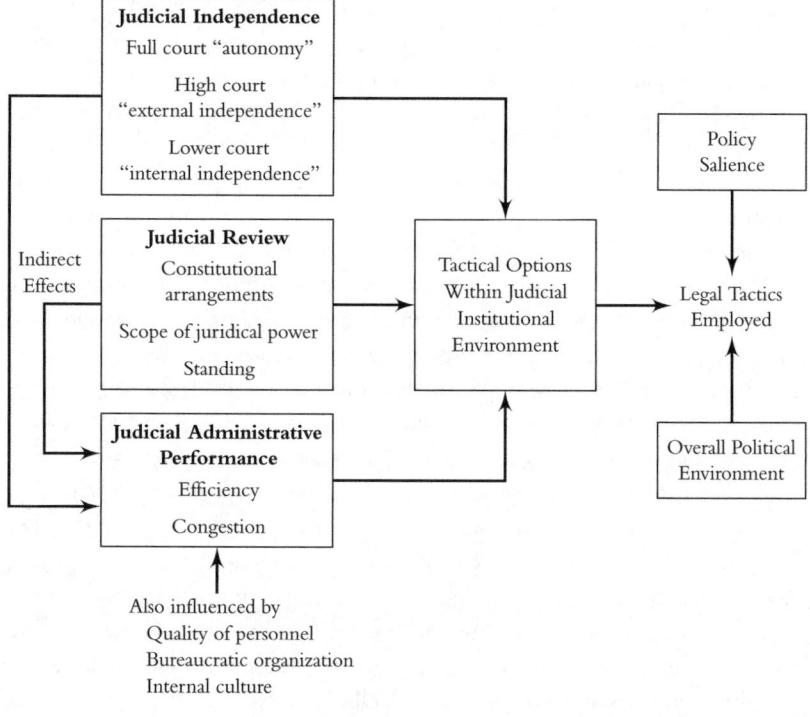

Figure 2.1.   Framework of legal tactical choice

the political climate to a lawyer's missing morning coffee—may influence policy players' tactical choices. The broader political context—including structural, cultural, and institutional factors—as well as the salience of policy to potential litigants, clearly matters to the relevance and prominence of courts in the policy game. And, of course, judges do not have complete liberty to impose their policy preferences within the boundaries set by the institutional framework: the law itself—and common interpretations of the law— also matter.[14] As a result, any attempt to use the framework in a positivist, predictive fashion would clearly run up against these problems of "context-conditionality" (Franzese 2003), as well as an extreme problem with degrees of freedom, given the number of component independent variables. Having said that, the framework provides a structure to the arguments that follow about the Brazilian courts' effects on policy players' tactical choice, framing them in a manner that can be applied without substantial readjustment to other civil code systems, in Latin America and elsewhere. With that in mind, I now turn to a brief description of the formal structure of Brazil's federal courts, before discussing the influence of the courts' recent history, internal culture, and administrative performance on Brazil's placement within the framework.

The Brazilian Federal Courts

INSTITUTIONAL ARRANGEMENTS

The Brazilian judicial branch is hierarchically structured in a federal system made up of both federal and state courts. Five courts sit at the apex of the full judicial system, each with different functional responsibilities: the Supreme Federal Tribunal (*Supremo Tribunal Federal,* or STF) is the key court for constitutional matters and conflicts between members of the federation;[15] the Superior Justice Tribunal (*Superior Tribunal de Justiça,* or STJ) acts as the court of last instance on nonconstitutional matters; and the Superior Military Tribunal, Superior Electoral Tribunal, and Superior Labor Tribunal act as the courts of last instance in their respective areas of responsibility.

Despite this nominal equivalence across all five high courts, in practice the Supreme Federal Tribunal is the highest court in the country, serving as the court of last instance for both state and federal cases involving constitutional law. Given the breadth of the 1988 Constitution—with its 245 articles and 73 transitional provisions—the STF's supposedly equal footing with the other Brazilian high courts means little in practice, since many rather banal cases, which on the face of it should have little constitutional merit, can be appealed on constitutional grounds to the STF. As one exasperated

STF justice, on hearing a constitutional case about a goat that had been bar-
bequed by the owner's neighbor, complained, "matters related to cows, but-
terflies and horses are all constitutional matters" (Morton 1998).

The legal procedures employed by the courts also influence the use of the
STF, with the breadth of constitutional arrangements generating a substantial
workload for STF ministers. As Stepan (2000) noted, the Brazilian judiciary's
use of constitutional review is much more diffuse than in the U.S. system, in
large part because of the absence of legal mechanisms that might limit such
review. Unlike that of the U.S. Supreme Court, the scope of the STF's juridical power is quite weak: it does not benefit from discretion-enhancing
mechanisms such as the *writ of certiorari,* which might allow it to reject some
cases; its decisions are largely not *erga omnes,* or effective against everyone; it
does not have broad powers of *stare decisis,* or similar forms of binding precedent; and there is no "political question doctrine" that might be used by the
STF to avoid entangling itself in political disputes that can be resolved in
the Congress.[16] Furthermore, given the possibility of direct constitutional
challenge at the STF, many cases are heard while they are in the thick of political debate, rather than a few years later, as they might be if they reached
the STF only after appeal. In the absence of such rules, STF docket control
is a question of sipping from the firehose, with no choice but to address all
of the cases thrown before it, albeit oftentimes after understandable delay.

The second most important court in practice within the federal court
system is the Superior Justice Tribunal. The STJ was created from scratch
under the 1988 Constitution, targeted in theory at reducing the case burden
on the STF by acting as the court of last instance in nonconstitutional cases.
The STJ does clear the decks of an enormous number of procedural questions: according to Castro and Ribeiro (2006), nearly 45 percent of all cases
in the STJ are decided on procedural grounds, as compared to less than 23
percent in the STF. In practice, though, the STJ's creation has had only marginal effects, given the fact that many cases can be framed as constitutional
cases and thereby appealed to the STF. But the thirty-three judges of the
STJ are charged with at least a first hearing on cases involving the states and
their governors, and appeals of decisions made by Federal Regional Tribunals (*Tribunais Regionais Federais,* or TRFs).

Figure 2.2 provides a diagram of the hierarchical nature of the federal judicial system in Brazil. Within the federal court system, the courts of first
instance are known as *varas.* Cases from the *varas* move up on appeal to the
TRFs, each of which covers a region made up of several states.[17] Appeals
from the TRFs rise to the STJ, and from there to the STF. A parallel judicial
hierarchy exists for the Labor Courts (1,109 *varas,* 24 regional courts, and

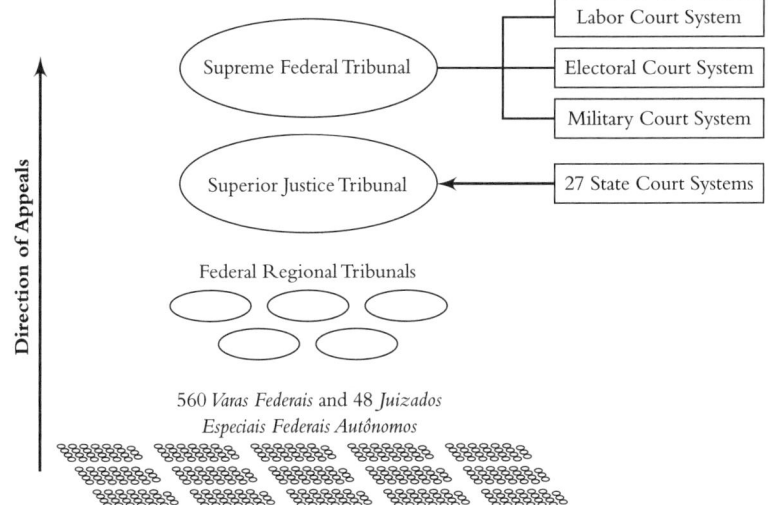

Figure 2.2.   Structure of the court system

N O T E : It must be stressed that the "federal system" as it is depicted here is an artificial construct: the STF and STJ are not, by the letter of the 1988 Constitution (Brasil 1988, Art. 106), a part of the Federal Judiciary, which formally is composed solely of the Federal Regional Tribunals and federal lower court judges. That said, because the STF and STJ have national jurisdictions as well as responsibilities for appeals from these courts (Art. 92, §2), they have a significant role in federal legal cases. My intent in using the phrase "federal court system" is (1) to separate the federal courts from their counterparts in the electoral, military, and labor court systems, as well as at the state level, and (2) to focus on the segment of the national court system that is most likely to be used to challenge federal public policies.

S O U R C E : Taylor 2005.

the Superior Labor Tribunal, TST); the Electoral Courts (2,884 electoral *cartórios,* 27 regional courts, and the Superior Electoral Tribunal, TSE); and the Military Courts (20 federal military *auditorias* and the Superior Military Tribunal). Each state also has its own judiciary, adding nearly 2,400 judicial districts and over 6,000 judges to the national total; cases from the state high courts can be appealed to the STJ.

RECENT HISTORY

Worldwide, courts are the least procedurally democratic of all democratic institutions. They are not representative, they are only remotely accountable to voters, and they are the most elitist of democratic institutions (barring perhaps central banks), employing a cadre of highly trained specialists responsible only to national constitutions and an amorphous concept often referred to as the "rule of law."

Brazilian history has provided two further, potentially delegitimizing, factors. The first is a long history of constitutional impermanence. With each of Brazil's seven constitutions, a new set of institutional rules was generated, while the sedimentary residue of past orders remained, requiring the repeated reconciliation of old institutions and new rules, as well as the reconstruction of both jurisprudence and judicial independence from the elected branches (Veiga da Rocha 2006, 8–9; see also Veiga da Rocha 2004). In Brazil's most recent experience with democracy, for example, the high court has relied heavily on historical standards set under the preauthoritarian 1946 Constitution (STF Minister Lewandowski, cited in Cardoso 2007a). The results have been confusing, especially at the outset of each new constitutional period, when judges have had latitude to make decisions based on their personal interests, political conceptions, or subjective theories of law and justice (Koerner 2006, 277).

A second potentially delegitimizing factor is the legacy of authoritarianism: under military rule (1964–85), governments often sought to cloak their actions in a mask of legality, and although judicial independence was significantly reduced under the military, courts continued to provide a pastiche of the rule of law, highly prized by the military government, throughout the authoritarian period (Pereira 2005; Skidmore 1988, 52–101). Courts entered the post-military period with few changes in procedure or personnel, despite the fact that the courts—like other democratic institutions—had been unable to uphold the democratic values often considered a *sine qua non* of the concept of the rule of law.

This authoritarian legacy provoked a vibrant reaction with the return of democracy. In one of the first significant institutional junctures after the military stepped down, much of the debate at the 1987–88 constituent assembly focused on addressing repressed political, economic, and social demands (Fleischer 1998). According to convention delegate Marco Maciel (who later served as vice-president, 1995–2002), "The Constitution was debated and voted on from a perspective in which the largest concern was not to look to the future, but to condemn and erase the past" (Nóbrega 2000, 102; translation mine).

Despite its laudable social goals and its strong democratic bent, the constituent assembly set in place a Constitution that was likely to make governance in Brazil from 1988 onward much less flexible. Much had been "constitutionalized," both in the economic and political spheres: the federal relations between center and states and municipalities were further rigidified, fiscal policy was largely constrained by constitutional mandates and transfers, and the electoral system tended toward the fragmentation of parties along regional, programmatic, and even personal lines. As Power (2000, 34) has noted, one outcome of the constituent assembly is that much of the post-1988 period has been devoted, ironically, to "unwriting" the Constitution. This is a process that necessarily has brought courts to the forefront of many policy battles: as Sadek notes, the Constitution represented an inflection point, launching the Judiciary into the "center of public life and conferring upon it the role of a leading protagonist" (1999a, 297; translation mine).

In regard to the courts' structure itself, while the 1988 Constitution kept intact many of the formal structures of preceding legal systems dating from the Constitution of 1891—including the civil code and the federal structure of the courts—the constituent assembly sought to incorporate new democratic guarantees within the judiciary. Critical to this objective was the establishment of rules highly favorable to judicial independence, especially from the executive branch (Castro 1997b), as well as the expansion of access to the courts (Prillaman 2000). The independence of judges under the new Constitution was assured by merit-based recruitment, by guaranteed life employment until age seventy, by "irreducible" judicial salaries, and by guarantees that judges can only be removed by a vote of their peers. Meanwhile, the courts themselves were guaranteed "administrative and financial autonomy" from other branches of government, as well as complete internal administrative oversight (Brasil 1988, Articles 93–100).

Access to the courts under the 1988 Constitution was expanded by creation of small claims courts (*juizados especiais*), as well as wider access to some legal instruments.[18] Perhaps most important, from a policy perspective, the Constitution expanded the possibilities for judicial review via a series of abstract review mechanisms including the *Ação Direta de Inconstitucionalidade* (ADIN, or Direct Action of Unconstitutionality). A narrow version of the ADIN mechanism had existed under the military, but was radically increased in importance under the new Constitution, allowing the constitutionality of a law to be directly contested in the STF by a broadened set of institutional actors: the president, the Senate, the Chamber of Deputies, the state assemblies, state governors, the prosecutor-general,[19] the Federal Council of the national bar association, political parties, and national "class or union confederations" (Brasil 1988, Art. 103).[20] As a result of the creation of this and other instruments of concentrated review, Brazil's system of constitutional review has been labeled a "hybrid system" (for example, Arantes 1997, 2000, 2006; Maciel and Koerner 2002), given that constitutional review is neither entirely diffuse like the U.S. system, nor completely concentrated, as in the

Austrian system. The presence of the ADIN mechanism and other types of constitutional review cases leads the STF to act as a "quasi-constitutional" court in a small proportion of cases; in the bulk of legal cases it decides, however, the STF is simply a last court of appeal.

In addition, the Constitution considerably strengthened the autonomy of the *Ministério Público,* a federal prosecutorial body with extensive powers and a degree of autonomy that have led some to call it the "fourth power" of government in Brazil. This newly autonomous prosecutorial body enabled a new set of policy actors to challenge the elected branches in policy matters including, of most importance, its own members—prosecutors—who have become active in policy debates, with special effect within the court system.[21]

For ordinary citizens using the lower courts, new mechanisms such as the popular suit (*ação popular*) were intended to offer similar recourse against government policies. But the complexity, cost, and duration of such cases have largely circumscribed their use, which has thus been dominated by the *Ministério Público* and other organized political actors (Werneck Vianna and Burgos 2002; Kerche 1999, 2003). More quotidian challenges filed in the lower courts by individual citizens have seldom carried over into policy because of the extraordinary delays engendered by the judicial process, and the particularistic, non-universal reach of the bulk of court decisions.

In sum, the new Constitution greatly increased judicial independence on all its dimensions. In terms of judicial review, increased access to lower courts has not translated into more effective legal contestation by common citizens. Thus the most important concrete effect from a policy perspective has been to expand the right to bring judicial review cases in the high court to a select (if broader) list of organized political actors. These newly legally enfranchised groups include political parties, the *Ministério Público* (as represented by its chief, the *Procurador Geral*), and many professional organizations, which have been able to obtain considerable policy leverage through their access to these legal instruments.

The collective effect of the changes introduced by the 1988 Constitution was thus extremely important to the judiciary's insertion in policy debates. Greater independence on all three axes of judicial independence was not matched, however, by countervailing mechanisms of accountability. Meanwhile, the expansion of judicial review has drawn the courts into the policy realm: the 1988 Constitution "included so many social and economic guarantees that virtually any type of social or economic interaction . . . quickly became a legal issue of constitutional importance" (Prillaman 2000, 76). As Ballard (1999, 276) notes, this "broad access to unfettered courts has increased the use of courts as political instruments." Furthermore, the indirect effects of these rules on judicial performance have been harnessed by policy players, who have been especially cognizant of the tactical opportunities provided by judicial delay.

RECENT REFORMS AND THE ROLE OF PRECEDENT

Partly as a result of these perceived problems, calls for judicial reform were persistent throughout the 1990s and the early 2000s, driven by perceptions that justice is slow and uneven, and by the increasing institutional conflict between the courts and their institutional counterparts elsewhere at the federal level. More than forty judicial reform projects were proposed in Congress between 1988 and the successful reform of 2004 (see Table 2.2 for the main reforms implemented during this period). The judiciary frequently reacted fiercely, escalating political disputes over these proposals and on occasion refusing to discuss them entirely. This was not an irrational response: in the past, efforts to change the judicial process have included rather direct assaults on the rule of law, such as efforts during the Collor stabilization plan to restrict lawsuits against the federal government.[22]

The degree of opposition to various judicial reform proposals, however, has not been uniform throughout the judiciary. There was some sympathy in the STF and STJ toward reforms that would introduce stricter rules of precedent and reduce lower court discretion. And many upper court judges with little sympathy for reform showed an unwillingness to be drawn into the institutional conflict surrounding reform proposals. Yet upper court judges represent a minority of the judges in the federal system (although they ultimately have the final say on the constitutionality of any reform), and even at the apex of the system, not all STF judges were receptive to reform. The result is that reforms have only been undertaken at the margins, including the broadest judicial reform of the post-military period, approved in December 2004.

One form of binding precedent, the so-called *súmula vinculante,* was strengthened by the 2004 judicial reform, but in order to go into effect, it will require proactive, case-by-case votes by eight out of eleven STF ministers. A second element of the reform, the *Repercussão Geral do Recurso Extraordinário,* significantly improves the discretion of the STF in terms of the types of cases it will be forced to hear, requiring plaintiffs to explain the broader implications of their appeal. Although the current president of the STF believes that the new *súmula vinculante* could reduce the number of new cases arriving at the STF by as much as 80 percent (Erdelyi 2006, 2007), and the new restrictions on appeals heard in the STF may ease its docket, it is unclear how

TABLE 2.2

Principal judicial reforms, 1988–2004

Reform	Principal Content
Constitutional Amendment 3 (1993)	This amendment was written as a response to the widespread use of the ADIN (Direct Action of Unconstitutionality) mechanism, which proved an especially effective means of challenging the constitutionality of laws. By creating the Declaratory Action of Constitutionality (ADC), this reform sought to give the government an equally swift means of establishing the constitutionality of a law, thus eliminating judicial uncertainty early in the policy process. It is worth noting, however, that the ADC has only been used nine times since its creation. One reason for this rather sparing use of the ADC is clear: the executive branch (or the congressional leadership) is unlikely to seek a test of the constitutional validity of its own laws: if the validity is evident, there is no need; if the validity is in question, there is little incentive to put the law into harm's way.
Constitutional Amendment 19 (1998)	This amendment was part of a larger reform of the civil service bureaucracy, and its effect on the judiciary was largely administrative. The reform created new rules for judicial salary setting—through agreement between the judiciary, the Congress, and the executive branch—but preserved judicial autonomy in how salaries were set; maintained the rule that judicial salaries are "irreducible" (that is, not subject to executive fiat); and upheld the rule that the judiciary has control over internal promotion decisions.
Constitutional Amendment 22 (1999)	This amendment fulfilled a constitutional mandate and created federal small claims courts (*juizados especiais federais*) to hear cases of relatively small monetary value, thus easing the burden on the rest of the federal court system. The reform also eliminated some appointed judges on the labor courts.
New Civil Code (2002)	After twenty-six years of debate, the new civil code was passed in 2002 and went into effect in 2003. The new code does not directly affect the judiciary as an institution, although the innovations proposed in the new code—such as changes in laws governing individual rights, and changes in property and contract laws—will undoubtedly influence new jurisprudence.
Constitutional Amendment 45 (2004)	Among the most important changes generated by this reform, two stand out: CNJ: The creation of the National Judicial Council (CNJ) may permit greater administrative and financial control over lower courts. Although the CNJ includes six external members, the other nine are all judges, meaning that despite judges' complaints, judicial independence does not seem seriously threatened by the new council. *Súmula vinculante:* Under the new rules, two thirds of the STF ministers can vote to make their rulings binding on other courts. While this still requires a proactive declaration of binding precedent, it could be used in future to prevent backlogs of similar cases from clogging the courts.

much the reforms will do to reduce unnecessary or repetitive cases lower in the court system. That said, as noted later in the chapter, the government has in the past been one of the worst offenders in terms of frivolous suits, and the reform does tie government lawyers' hands. Further, a second component of the reform, the *súmula impeditive de recurso,* may help the lower courts by allowing them to block appeals in cases in which the STF or STJ has already set a clear precedent.

The effects of the reform, however, lie largely outside the scope of this book, which covers the period from 1988 to 2004. Further, it is not clear how large an effect the reform will have: the reform has been labeled a "timid advance" by a leading scholar of the Brazilian judiciary (Sadek, in Vasconcelos 2004), and one former STF minister noted that it will "contribute very little to removing the true problem of the Brazilian Judiciary, which is the slowness [and] the delays in judicial service" (Velloso 2005, 11; translation mine). Further, much of the reform's effect will be felt in the STF and STJ, rather than the lower courts. This is of course beneficial, but may contribute to further increasing the relative importance of access to the high courts, at least for as long as it takes to resolve the problems of lower court congestion. Meanwhile, even with the reforms, precedent remains somewhat limited in its broad applicability to courts and judges at all levels of the judiciary. Until 2004, and possibly since then, these limits on the extension of the rules of precedent have provided Brazilian judges a *de facto* right of discovery at almost every level in the judicial system, in addition to encouraging a high volume of appeals to the apex of the judicial hierarchy.

The absence of precedent is not all that unusual, of course, for civil code systems, and most civil code nations find ways to circumvent its absence, as Shapiro notes:

> [I]f court decisions were not treated by judges themselves as announcing rules to be followed in future cases, thus at least constraining or limiting their future choices, then judicial lawmaking itself would dissolve into a series of completely arbitrary and unpredictable, case-by-case public policy choices. . . . Thus, even legal regimes that deny judicial law making and/or deny the practice of *stare decisis* in reality either do treat past judicial decisions as constraints on future ones and/or create alternative modes of creating judicial predictability . . . (2005, 293).

As Shapiro (2005) also notes, courts' decision making, like that of other political institutions, is incremental and path-dependent, building on past experience and historically constructed standards. But some systems may be more efficient than others at establishing the path to be followed and ensuring that current decisions pick up where past decisions left off. While they are not terribly different from many civil code systems, the Brazilian courts have not had an easy time in this regard, largely because of the various interruptions to regime stability over the past century, which have meant that the courts frequently had to simultaneously deal with their regular workload while racing to reconstruct the foundations of legal jurisprudence.

Further, prior to the 2004 reform and possibly to some extent afterward, the absence of system-wide binding precedent has been a defining feature of the Brazilian court system. The sheer volume of laws, combined with this lack of strict rules of precedent, means that in any given case the individual interpretation of the law may vary from judge to judge. Similar cases may thus be legitimately decided in a multitude of different ways by lower courts. True, they will ultimately find their way to the high courts, where those that are at significant variance with previous decisions will likely be overturned. But until such time, particularistic decisions are not only possible, but likely. This has resulted, systemically, in a high degree of congestion arising from the variety of possible interpretations given by judges at various levels of the court system, before these are overturned by the STJ or STF. In other words, "coordination, uniformity, and compliance" among lower-level federal courts (and also state courts) are weak, even though they are routinely imposed late in the appeals process.

Brazilian lower court judges, it must be said, are often loathe to rule in ways that vary significantly from their hierarchical superiors, especially because this may earn them a reputation-wounding rebuke. As a result, the internal independence of lower courts has not always led to such "atomized" decision making as Arantes suggested might be possible when he wrote, "A first consequence of this atomization of diffuse judicial consideration is that, at least potentially, there can be as many different decisions as there are judicial bodies activated" (1997, 33; translation mine). Perceptions of internal hierarchy, in other words, may function as a weak substitute for binding precedent. Further, there is considerable hierarchical and reputational control over judges within the five regions of the federal court system.

The crucial caveat, though, is that there is room for quite distinct patterns of decision making *across* the five regions of the federal courts; even though there may be uniformity within any given region, there is considerable room for divergence across judges at the same hierarchical level (for example, in the first instance trial courts) in different regional systems nationwide. As Sadek (1999a, 298, fn. 7) notes, this diversity of opinions is not limited to judges, but also exists across courts, including the federal regional courts (TRFs), which have not infrequently diverged on important issues. Second, there is a significant disconnect between the five regional court systems and the two higher courts (the STF and STJ), given their members' distinct origins. The result is that while lines of downward administrative control do exist, and may function as a substitute for precedent, these lines are multiple and not especially strong. Unlike the Chilean case described by Hilbink (2003), in which hierarchy has a conservative effect on judges who might otherwise have considerable internal independence, there is considerable play across the Brazilian regional court systems. Administrative controls are quite weak, although the 2004 reform did create a National Judicial Council (CNJ) (over the opposition of the Association of Brazilian Magistrates [AMB], which filed an ADIN against its creation). This is a significant new institution whose efforts to instill some downward administrative control of the court system will be worth following in coming years. In the short time it has been in existence, the CNJ has been somewhat successful in efforts to eliminate nepotism within the judiciary, but faced enormous difficulties in enforcing a cap it imposed on judicial salaries. The CNJ remains in a tenuous institutional position, and the drama surrounding its efforts to impose controls on lower courts offers a hint of the continuing strength and internal independence of lower court judges on both legal and administrative matters.

Further, the weak legal controls that do exist—including the new *súmula vinculante*—are not sufficient to prevent spurious cases or appeals from progressing in lower courts, and thus adding to overall congestion, even if these are often almost certain to be overturned upon reaching the STJ or STF. Opponents of stronger formal rules regarding precedent argue that judicial decisions are not meant to create rules of law—under a civil code system, that job should be left to legislators or presidents. As one STF minister framed this very common assertion in his comments during a constitutional case, "the constitutional review of normative acts by the Judiciary only allows the Judiciary to act as a 'negative legislator.'"[23] That is, the courts cannot change the original intent of the legislator by striking down select passages and changing the intent of legislation; they can only rule that a given law is constitutional or not. Binding precedent would undermine this principle by allowing more broadly founded challenges based on a law-like precedent.

Cynics have also suggested a counterintuitive reason why judges, particularly in the lower courts, have fought the introduction of binding precedent in the Brazilian context: judges want the freedom to grant individual rights to those who frequent their courtrooms, especially since they cannot guarantee collective rights to all.[24] Law-finding, in a civil system, is about the "application of legal propositions" (Weber 1978, 891).[25] But the immense body of laws adopted in Brazil—some 27,000 by one count (*The Economist* 2004)—provides a large and unwieldy collection of often confusing, sometimes mutually contradictory, legal rules.[26] STF Minister Marco Aurélio Mello described the discretionary latitude this provided him in making decisions: "First I imagine the most just solution. . . . only afterward do I seek support in the law" (Erdelyi 2006, cited in Amorim Alves 2006, 22; translation mine). The absence of a strong and broadly applicable form of precedent, combined with the internal independence of judges and an extensive body of laws, contributes to the flexible application of legal rules, as well as delays in ascertaining definitively how such laws should be applied.

INTERNAL LEGAL CULTURE

Legal culture has been defined as "the cluster of attitudes, ideas, expectations, and values that people hold with regard to their legal system, legal institutions, and legal rules" (Pérez-Perdomo and Friedman 2003, 2). Friedman (1975) previously had distinguished between the external legal culture of society at large, and the internal legal culture of lawyers and jurists within the judicial system. The internal legal culture is the focus of this section, with particular weight given to judges.

The internal legal culture of the members of the Brazilian judiciary has contributed to a new form of judicial activism and new types of conflict between the judiciary and the executive branch since the return to democracy. As Bonelli (2002) illustrated in her comprehensive work on São Paulo state judges, the profession has adopted the defense of societal well-being as a common professional virtue. Furthermore, the breadth of the 1988 Constitution and its commitment to social justice has charged "judges with the task of protecting vulnerable social classes" (Ballard 1999, 234), a responsibility that frequently plays out in the defense of particular rather than universal values. This ethos of protecting the vulnerable is communicated and implemented throughout the judicial branch by two key institutional factors: legal education and the independence of judges, both from the elected branches and from each other.

The dogmatism of legal education in the context of a civil law system has significant implications in terms of policy: judges are trained to focus on principles, rather than on consequences, and the focus of judges is on the law as it is written, rather than on the intent of legislators or on the broader consequences of any given decision in the nation at large. This tendency may be further exacerbated by the perception that most legal decisions have no widespread consequences, given the weak bindingness of precedent and the case-specific effects of most decisions.[27]

The education of judges further ingrains this legalistic bent, with its recurring aversion to thinking beyond the reach of a particular legal decision.[28] Under the governing legal statute, the Brazilian Bar Association (OAB) is responsible for regulating all law school classes, certifying their quality, and providing guidance to the Ministry of Education on all its decisions regarding law schools nationwide. As in most professions in Brazil, legal education is highly profession-specific, meaning that students have little exposure to disciplines outside their field which might speak to the broader implications of legal decisions. An above-average student graduating from high school, who does well on statewide examinations, could expect to enter a government-financed law school at age eighteen. For ten semesters, such a student would study everything from juridical sociology to the history of law to constitutional law to civil process. At a top-tier school such as the University of São Paulo (USP) school of law, the curriculum averages around twenty-five hours of class per semester. But over the course of five years of law school, a USP student is required to take only twenty to twenty-five hours of non-law classes on economics, sociology, or political science.[29]

As former Central Bank president Gustavo Loyola (2002) noted tongue-in-cheek, this professional orthodoxy has played out in two acts in regard to most economic stabilization plans:

> In the first act, which takes place during the implementation of the plan, economists become judges, "scribbling" the texts of the Executive Order with all the judicial knowledge they learned while getting their economics degrees. Later, much later, it is the judges who, using all the economic knowledge acquired during their law-school years, will rewrite the plan, distorting the intentions of its creators.

The rather narrow disciplinary training of judges has significant implications for how they rule: a recent study showed that 61 percent of judges and prosecutors thought that the quest for social justice justified decisions that violated contracts; only 7 percent felt that contracts should always be respected, regardless of their social repercussions (Lamounier and Souza 2002; see also Castelar Pinheiro 2003a and Sadek 1995b). In this worldview, consistency and the predictability of judicial decisions is subordinated to individual discretion and an emphasis on protecting the less fortunate, but in a highly case-specific manner.

Meanwhile, the University of São Paulo and its peers are an island of excellence in an ever-more-crowded field of study. The number of law schools more than tripled in the past decade to over one thousand schools, while the number of graduating law students taking the Education Ministry's "provão"[30]—a rough indicator of the number graduating from accredited law schools—almost doubled from twenty-six thousand to fifty-one thousand between 1996 and 2001 (*Consultor Jurídico* 2002). There has been acute concern about the number of lawyers, now estimated to total one million in the country as a whole (Nalini 2006), as well as about the quality of legal education, driving the Brazilian Bar Association to create a new ethics exam and, as of 1994, a bar exam. The numbers approved on the bar exam are shockingly low, ranging from state to state, but always remaining below 50 percent in both Rio de Janeiro and São Paulo. During one OAB examination in São Paulo during 2006, fewer than 10 percent of those tested were approved to practice law. The result may well be that "[s]oon Brazil will be a country with many graduated law students but fewer lawyers" (Junqueira 2003, 89).

The funnel continues to narrow as one moves from law students to lawyers to judges, who form a highly qualified elite at the pinnacle of the legal profession. Most federal judges are selected via a rigorous entrance examination, usually after several years as a lawyer or court staffer.[31] Lateral entry from other professions into higher-ranking federal judgeships is unheard of, except in the STF and STJ, whose judges are chosen from the ranks of the Justice Ministry, the *Ministério Público,* private practice, or lower courts. The judge's focus is thus highly theoretical, and usually devoid of professional experience outside the legal system, with important implications for how judges rule in the abstract. Nalini, a judge himself, notes that for the judge trained in this manner,

> The best decision is one aimed at resurrecting the past, that is, one that manages to return the situation to the *status quo ante.* This results in the total impossibility of the judge facing the future, of exercising a proactive stance, of evaluating the consequences of his or her decision for the parties [to the dispute], for the community, for the nation (Nalini 2000, 342; translation mine).

The strong bent toward particularistic decisions is further embedded by the absence of vertical downward control in the judiciary. Taken together, these factors suggest that despite an extensive catalogue of individual rights in the 1988 Constitution, protection of individual rights is almost always the exception, rather than the rule. As Pereira (2000, 222) notes, "The nonuniversal application of law gives rise to what might be called 'elitist liberalism,' a policy that justifies the granting of rights on a particularistic basis."

The training of judges and the autonomy of the various component members of the judiciary have implications in terms of what is to be expected from the courts. The broad-based 1988 Constitution was written in the hopes of reversing the worst abuses of the military regime. But despite judges' widespread sympathy toward the protection of rights, the achievement of the impressive list of expanded rights laid out by the Constitution is undermined by the failure of the court as an institution to perform efficiently, and especially by the possibility of particularistic appeals for justice. The next section addresses some of the potential bottlenecks that arise as a result, in terms of the efficiency and accessibility of the courts.

ADMINISTRATIVE PERFORMANCE

Administrative performance plays an important role in the policy impact of Brazilian courts. On the budget front, the Brazilian judiciary has considerable autonomy and is well funded as a whole, with the highest budget in purchasing power parity terms per inhabitant of all the federal systems in the Western hemisphere.[32] While some of this large budget allocation may be explained in part by the fact that the judiciary was making up for low investment during the military regime and the necessary expansion of the judiciary in the intervening years, the budget allocation is large even in comparison with other democratic institutions within Brazil.[33] The judicial branch received on average 4.3 percent of the total annual federal budget (after debt payments and constitutionally mandated transfers) between 1995 and 2000, or, on average, three times more than the budget allocated to the Congress during the same period.[34] Judges' salaries are quite good, with the purchasing power parity value of STF ministers' wages nearly one-third higher than that of their counterparts on the U.S. Supreme Court, while federal trial judges earn roughly 40 percent more than their U.S. counterparts (Júlio Brunet, cited in *Agência Estado* 2006).

Although Brazil has a relatively high number of judges per capita, the number of unfilled judgeships in Brazil is also a perennial source of concern. There were nearly two thousand unfilled judgeships in the federal and state judiciaries in 2003 (an unexceptional year), for an 18 percent vacancy rate nationwide, with a 14 percent vacancy rate in the federal courts of first instance and regional federal tribunals (Supremo Tribunal Federal 2005). Although the number of judges per 100,000 population (5.5, excluding labor court judges) is mid-range for comparable systems—somewhere between the 10.2 in France and the 1.02 in Peru or 0.65 in Chile (Dakolias 1999,

19; Supremo Tribunal Federal 2005)[35]—the number of cases per judge is also high, making unfilled judgeships a continuous worry. In part, the unfilled spots are due to the high hurdles to becoming a judge: only a small percentage of candidates pass the entrance examinations. Incumbent judges continue to push against any relaxation of the stringent entrance examinations, with obvious repercussions in terms of the availability of justice, even if these are correctly balanced against concerns about the quality of that justice.

On the case front, the number of cases in the system has increased significantly since the end of the military regime. The number of cases distributed among judges in the federal court system (excluding labor, military, and electoral courts) has mushroomed, from 339,000 cases in 1989 to 2.1 million in 2001 (Supremo Tribunal Federal 2005). On average, within the judiciary as a whole, this is not an especially large number in comparison with the more than 12 million cases currently working their way through state courts.[36] But rates of congestion—the relation of unresolved cases to cases outstanding in a given year—have consistently remained at 70–80 percent in the trial courts and 60–70 percent in the TRFs (Hernández 2006, 102). In other words, more than three-fifths of cases in the lower courts are not disposed of in any given year, with the absolute number of new cases continuing to rise sharply in the federal first instance trial courts, as Figure 2.3 illustrates.

The one positive element seen in this figure is the fact that new caseloads in the TRFs have fallen off and may soon drop below their 1997 levels,

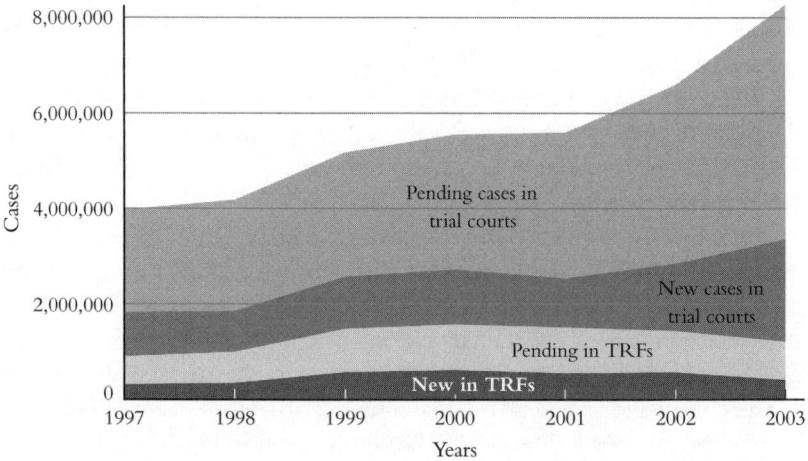

Figure 2.3. Caseloads in federal trial courts and TRFs
SOURCE: Hernández 2006, 108.

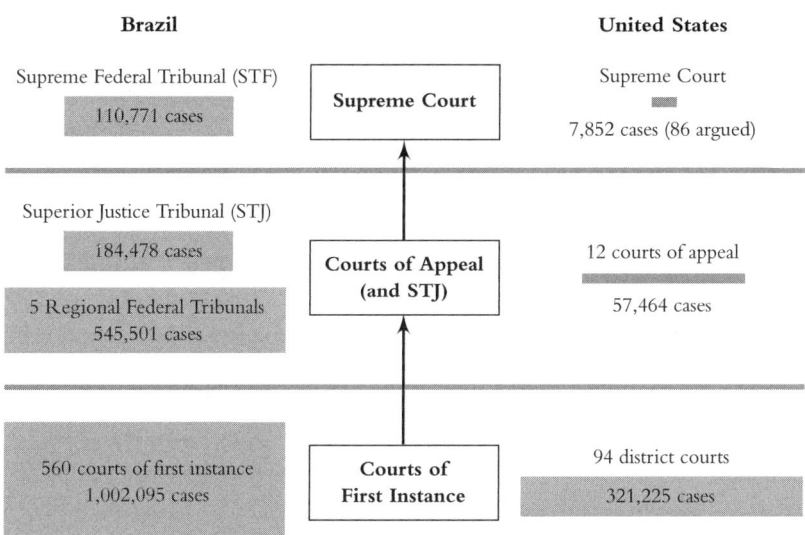

Figure 2.4. Comparison of Brazil and U.S. federal judicial caseloads
NOTE: The size of the shaded boxes is proportional to the number of cases in each court.
All data except the U.S. Supreme Court cases (which are from 2000) are from 2001.
SOURCE: Taylor 2006b. Data are from Supremo Tribunal Federal 2006 and
Rehnquist 2002.

in large part because of the creation of the new workhorse of federal judicial activity—the *juizados especiais* (Ministério da Justiça 2004, 40). Because these small claims courts do not allow appeals to the TRFs, they help to remove an incredible burden in the middle of the federal court system.

Having said that, the caseload remains heavy and—after temporary improvement—is once again rising at the higher reaches of the federal judiciary. Figure 2.4 compares the new cases arriving in the Brazilian federal courts with those facing the U.S. federal courts, to illustrate differences both in initial caseload and in the progression of cases from lower courts upward. Although differences between civil code and common law systems explain much of the disparity in the number of cases at all levels of the court system, the most interesting finding here is the proportion of cases found in each nation's high court: the Brazilian high court (STF) receives 11 percent of the volume of cases heard in the Brazilian federal courts of first instance, against fewer than 2.5 percent in the U.S. case.

Although the different legal systems mean that there is no equivalency between the number actually argued in the U.S. Supreme Court (86 cases) and the number "judged" (*julgado*) in the Brazilian STF (109,692 cases), the difference in magnitude is telling. Even considering all cases filed in both high courts, rather than only those argued, there were 872 cases filed per U.S. Supreme Court justice, against 10,070 per Brazilian STF minister. In the Brazilian STF, even though only a minority of cases actually go to a hearing before the full STF on the merits, all cases must be judged by at least one minister, and the decision approved and signed by that minister. This is very different from the United States, where a decision not to grant *certiorari* means that the pre-appeal decision stands, and justices are thus freed of any further deliberation or administrative processing.

The congestion in the upper reaches of the Brazilian judiciary can be largely attributed to public sector litigation, with state companies and governments at all three levels (federal, state, and municipal) accounting for 79 percent of all litigation in the STF during the period 1999–2003.[37] The federal government alone accounts for 64.8 percent of this caseload, with much of this burden due to appeals by the National Social Security Institute (INSS), the *Caixa Econômica Federal* bank, and the Central Bank of cases related to the seven economic stabilization plans implemented between 1986 and 1994 (*Folha de São Paulo* 2004).

A considerable share of the blame for this predicament falls on the federal government, which has historically preferred to challenge and appeal all suits against itself for as long as possible.[38] The costs of the government defending itself are quite small in comparison to the potential costs of some of the suits it faces: judicial debts represent a significant skeleton in Brazil's fiscal closet. The 2001 federal budget, for example, included outstanding liabilities from over forty thousand judicial debt sentences, totaling over R$500 million (Mendes 2002). The yearly budget proposal also includes a long appendix listing potential risks to the budget from judicial cases that are awaiting STF decisions. The three largest as of this writing are cases related to the inflation readjustment of home mortgages under the 1990 Collor Plan (estimated potential cost, R$87 billion); losses incurred by sugar farmers and mill operators in the wake of the 1986 Cruzado plan (R$40–R$50 billion); and losses to the airlines under the same plan (R$7–R$26 billion) (Fleischer 2004; Santafé Idéias 2004, 2007).

The history of Brazilian hyperinflation has meant that there has been what I label a substantial "judicial Tanzi effect": the longer cases remained in hearings, the more likely the real value of the underlying debt would be eroded. With inflation largely controlled by the Real Plan, this calculus shifted, with increasing importance given to the fiscal results; the result, however, is similar, leading governments to attempt to push off any decision that might weaken the fiscal balance. The proportion of cases involving the federal government thus increases the higher one looks in the judiciary. Given this endless appeals process, it is not unusual to hear the government described as a "bad faith" litigant, or to hear of government defenses in intermediate appeals that are, in the Brazilian phrase, *para inglês ver* (roughly translated, "just for show").

As Figure 2.5 illustrates, cases on the STF docket ballooned over the past decade, from 20,000 in 1987 to a remarkable 160,000 in 2002. As a result of the use of appeals to the highest level, the STF frequently ran a "deficit"— in other words, cases that it simply did not have time to rule upon, whether for dismissal or judgment. This situation was dramatically improved in 2003, partly as a result of the Cardoso government's efforts to reduce its own use of the courts.[39] But there is still an enormous workload in the STF. In 2006, the Supreme Federal Tribunal received more than 127,000 new cases, and judged an impressive 124,000. Even with this impressive performance, the dog continues to chase its tail. The glut of cases in the STF and STJ includes not just appeals from lower courts but also appeals of decisions already taken in the upper courts. According to a former vice president of the STF, almost 80 percent of cases in the STF are repeat cases (Velloso 1999, 35), and the STJ's case figures in 2002 showed that, like the STF, 78.8 percent of its cases were a result of two such appeals.[40] As one STF minister, Sepúlveda Pertence, noted, the STF does not judge new cases, it judges repeat cases: "Equal sentences were approved in equivalent cases, in which the [STF] ministers acted merely as paper stampers for cases that had already been judged" (Gondim 1998, translation mine).

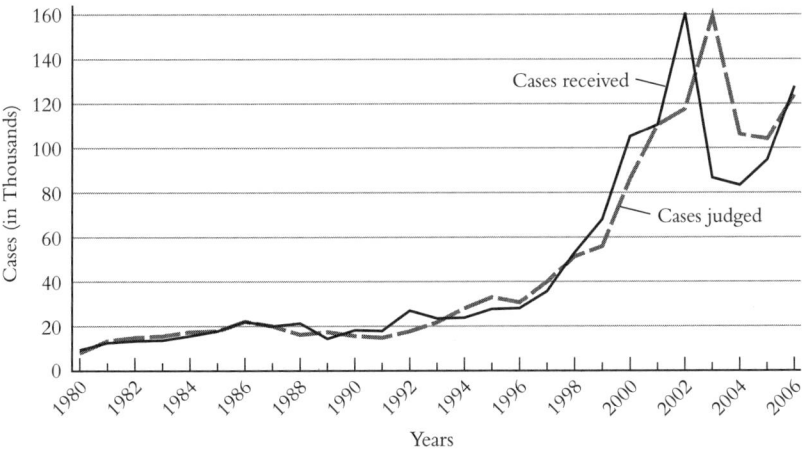

Figure 2.5. Court cases referred to the Supreme Federal Tribunal (STF)
SOURCE: Data from Supremo Tribunal Federal 2006.

And yet, although the Brazilian high court deals with considerable case overload, it is not that inefficient, especially because so much of the caseload can be relatively easily disposed of on procedural grounds. Former STF president Nelson Jobim noted that the ten thousand opinions he rendered annually dealt, in reality, with only twenty-five conflicts (Jobim 2003, cited in Hammergren 2006, 7). As Hammergren notes, on sheer numbers alone, it would be hard to reconcile the supposed burden facing high court justices with their long vacations, speaking tours, and hours spent teaching law school classes. Some figures, then, may illustrate how STF ministers deal with this superhuman workload: of the 124,000 cases decided by the STF in 2006, nine in ten went to judgment, while the remaining one case in ten was filed away after the plaintiff (in the vast majority of cases, the government) decided to suspend appeal. Of the cases that went to judgment, however, most were dealt with perfunctorily; just under 10 percent of these actually were decided by a collegial body of ministers, via *acórdão*. Having said that, this percentage represents more than eleven thousand cases per year, so while it is not an impossible figure, it is nonetheless a sign that delays in the STF are somewhat inevitable. Yet it also suggests that it is far better—if possible—for a plaintiff to leapfrog the appeals process in lower courts to obtain a definitive result via one of the case types heard directly by the STF. Recent reforms, if anything, seem likely to increase the relative importance of the STF by improving its efficiency relative to lower courts.

Public dissatisfaction with the speed of justice remains acute. This was best illustrated by one student protest against the STF's failure to hear a case against a state governor, which featured a giant papier-mâché turtle dressed in a judge's toga; in another case, a plaintiff rented a billboard to make a public plea for the courts to hear his case four years after he had filed it. In a 1995 poll, 40 percent of respondents listed slowness (*morosidade*) as the major problem of the federal judiciary (the second and third complaints were "elitism" and problems of "access," which registered 35 percent and 24 percent, respectively; Nascimento and Nunes 1995).

Cases not resolved through accord are estimated—on the basis of polls of businessmen—to take thirty-eight months on average to get through the common state justice system, and forty-six months in the federal courts (Castelar Pinheiro 2000, 187). A retired STF minister guessed that a *typical* case that started at the bottom of the judiciary and worked its way through appeal up to the STF would average between eight and ten years from start to finish. Most tragic is the fact that in most cases, the high court upholds the decision made at the outset.[41] Although Brazil may be better off than many of its neighbors in terms of court delays and congestion, the existing congestion does undermine the possibility of rapid policy contestation in the lower courts by individuals.

A final point regards the administration of court bureaucracy. Although Brazil has an estimated 33,500 staff members working in the federal courts (Supremo Tribunal Federal 2005; this figure excludes labor, military, and electoral courts), unlike many countries, it does not have a formal profession of court administrator. This puts judges in the ambiguous role of both hearing cases and negotiating contracts with local governments for the rental or purchase of properties and other administrative tasks. Many have noted the undesirable nature of this arrangement: not only is the staff not centrally trained to a uniform pattern of administration, but judges are frequently charged with carrying out administrative tasks that may place them in a conflict of interest (Dipp 2001).

Lower courts have a good deal of flexibility both in how they spend their budgets and in the rules they establish for their own operation, contributing to internal independence. This flexibility has had curious effects, especially on wage questions, when the lower court judges have vociferously pushed for higher wages against the public (and occasionally legal) opposition of higher courts. Perhaps as a result, Brazil has an unusually even ratio between high court and low court judges' salaries, at 1.17 to 1.[42]

On occasion, loose hierarchical controls and judge-led court administration may also have contributed to corrupt or questionable practices. Notable recent examples of questionable practices include the hiring of STF and STJ ministers' children to file cases before the courts; accusations of nepotism in hiring staff for the lower courts; the questionable freeing on bond of unsavory characters such as Salvatore Cacciola, a banker who was awaiting trial for embezzlement (and who promptly fled the country); and injunctions freeing the eleven members of a group of tax collectors convicted for massive corruption in Rio de Janeiro. Accusations of directly corrupt behavior include the alleged sale of *habeas corpus* decisions by a minister of the STJ; wholesale corruption in the construction of a new labor court in São Paulo;[43] and convictions obtained against a group of judges in the high-profile *Operação Anaconda,* a federal sting operation that found evidence of the sale of decisions over the period of more than a decade.[44] Alongside other prominent examples of corruption, these revelations have undermined public trust in the courts[45] and led to repeated calls for greater external control over the judiciary, culminating in the creation of the CNJ in 2004.[46]

Revisiting the Framework

This chapter began by expanding on a framework (originally laid out in Ríos-Figueroa and Taylor 2006) for thinking about how the federal courts shape policy outcomes through their influence on the tactical options available to policy actors. I close here by summarizing the implications of the placement of Brazil's federal court system within this framework.

JUDICIAL INDEPENDENCE

Largely as a result of the formal rules laid down by the constituent assembly, and subsequent adherence to the letter of these arrangements, Brazil's federal courts are strongly independent of the elected branches. Judicial decisions are made without undue concern for the executive or legislative branches' reaction; compliance with court decisions by public bureaucracies is largely expected; and recent history suggests that no retaliation is to be expected in terms of court budgets or general administrative freedom. As in most democracies, there are occasional shouting matches between the branches of government and efforts by one branch to shape the others to better serve its preferences, as in the 2004 judicial reform. But these have not undermined the basic autonomy of the courts nor the external independence of the high court. Meanwhile, the "internal independence" of the lower courts is considerable in terms of judges' ability to take decisions freely, without undue fear of disciplinary or budgetary ramifications.

As a result, courts at all levels are able to take decisions without giving undue consideration to their extra-legal implications. The federal courts are largely considered as venues within which decisions can be taken freely on legal and constitutional grounds, and thus are perceived by policy players outside the courts as potentially relevant venues for policy contestation. There are some countervailing forces that limit the dispersion and variance among judges' opinions—such as jurisprudential norms, the internal legal culture of judges, and the hierarchy within each of the five regions of the federal courts—but these do not enforce a strict hierarchy uniformly across the full federal system.

JUDICIAL REVIEW

The first element of judicial review, constitutional arrangements, has significant effects both because of the breadth of formal rights laid out in the Constitution and the breadth of the STF's jurisdiction. Together with greater access to the court system, and nonjudicial factors such as a series of failed economic plans, the extension of new constitutional rights has led to a rapid and constant rise in federal court use since the transition. Meanwhile, the increased original jurisdiction of the STF in many case types and its relative efficiency means that it is favored as a site for constitutional review.

The federal courts present a mixed picture when it comes to juridical power. Laws are judged *a posteriori,* but as a result of judges' discretion, there is great variation in the time to judgment, meaning that any given case's policy implications can be considerably postponed (but not necessarily). An even more complicated effect comes from the "hybrid" system of review. The political effect of these new rules has perhaps been best expressed by STF Minister Gilmar Mendes, who as both a prosecutor and judge has been an active participant in many of the battles they triggered:

> [Coexistence] between diffuse and concentrated control produced . . . a judicialization of politics with consequences unknown to mature democracies. Defeated in majoritarian arenas, political minorities seek to overturn in the Judiciary the decisions of the majority. The politicization of judicial actors created the current environment, in which more than a million injunctions are in effect (Maciel and Koerner 2002, 117, fn. 9; translation mine).

Leaving aside Mendes's implicit opinion of the counter-majoritarian role of the courts, this quotation suggests that Brazil's "hybrid" system of constitutional review has led to policy contestation at all levels of the courts. In the absence of strong and binding forms of precedent, and with only weak downward administrative control, the pyramidal structure of the federal courts means that upward appeals are likely, given that policy issues are seldom definitively resolved in a broadly applicable manner until, or unless, they reach the high courts.

Discretion is considerable, which tends to accentuate the problem of definitive resolution both in the high courts and lower courts. Discretion relates to whether to accept a case, and thereby commit to making a decision, but also to how broad a decision should be issued, and the timing of that decision. Federal judges have little discretion in terms of accepting or rejecting the cases that come their way. However, their control over both the breadth of decisions and their timing is almost unconstrained. There is enormous variance in times to disposition in all courts, including the STF, and decisions range from narrowly applicable temporary injunctions by lower courts to universally applicable decisions on the merits by the high court. Further, because judges' training tends to emphasize the restoration of the *status quo ante* in any individual case, rather than being focused on the overall impact of their decisions, or of the judicial process, on society as a whole, the policy implications can be considerable. On the downside, although individual judges are granted a good deal of discretion and power, the importance of any individual judge's decision is correspondingly deflated.

The final element of judicial review is standing. Aside from cases heard on appeal, individuals only have standing in the STF in *habeas corpus* cases.[47] This is a common feature of civil code systems, and limits direct constitutional suits by individuals. The policy relevance of individuals' constitutional challenges that are carried up the judicial hierarchy via appeals is further weakened by the fact that in all but the rarest cases, individuals cannot successfully produce *erga omnes* effects in constitutional cases, even if the high court rules in their favor.

Having said that, the number of group actors with standing to bring constitutional review challenges is arguably broader than in any civil code system in Europe or Latin America, save Costa Rica or Colombia. Political actors who are given the special privilege of using these case types—including the government, the *Ministério Público*, political parties, and corporatist professional groups—have special policy influence, especially in comparison to ordinary citizens, who face an altogether more daunting legal process.

ADMINISTRATIVE PERFORMANCE

The administrative conditions under which judges work contribute to the slow pace of judicial appeals. Although budgets are ample, there is perennial understaffing and a large case load. Judicial decisions are tenuous in light of the weakness of precedent (or an administrative substitute with effects across the full federal court system), the largely case-specific (rather than universal) applicability of most decisions, and the independence of judges from each other. Although there is considerable uniformity in decisions by high courts, this consensus tapers off as one moves down the judicial ladder, introducing a considerable degree of congestion. The result is that judges' decisions are to a certain extent less important to the overall functioning of the courts than the management of the huge congestion of caseloads.

Conclusion

The implications of this system for public policy contestation are indirect, but lead policy actors to give considerable tactical importance to the timing of suits and access to high court hearings. Three effects stand out: the great play in the system before a definitive decision can be reached; the likelihood of considerable delay, measured in years, before any ordinary court case comes to definitive resolution; and the fact that few decisions made by the courts, including—even after the 2004 reform—a majority of case types heard by the STF, have formally binding or universally applicable effects. This raises the question of why the courts are of any use at all in the policy process. Clearly, the courts offer a much longer and more circuitous route to policy change than the legislative process, after all.

The answer is twofold. At the level of the lower courts, these factors suggest that policy players will use Brazil's lower courts either to delay a probable legal defeat or to seek a venue that will provide a temporary symbolic victory—even though this will, in all likelihood, eventually be overturned. Although lower courts are not a site used to push policy forward, they are a good and likely place for policy players to thwart potential policy change, however temporarily.

High courts, meanwhile, will be a useful site to gain visibility, but very few litigants are legally enfranchised to bring review cases with broad and binding effects directly in the STF. The groups that do have such standing will be well-placed to exert pressure and gain leverage over policy, even if they are relatively unimportant to, or unrepresented in, policy debates in the elected branches of government. The veto point provided by standing in constitutional review cases, in other words, may well provide some players with policy relevance they would not otherwise have. The relationship between these judicial veto points and their effect on the identity and relative strength of veto players is discussed in greater detail in Chapter 4. But first, Chapter 3 turns to some practical case studies of court use in Brazil, illustrating how the salience of policy and the overall political environment have influenced policy players' decisions to push policy into the court system, and the various pathways they have found to do so effectively.

Chapter 3

Policy Type and Judicial Contestation

How have Brazil's federal courts been drawn into the policy debate during the post-constitutional period in Brazil? Long before judges' attitudes, legal tactical choices, or even the structures of judicial independence and judicial review come into play, the characteristics of policy influence its salience to policy actors and their willingness to engage in collective action, including by contesting policy in the courts.

This chapter has two objectives. The first is to explore the ramifications of the argument just posited, namely, that the raw material entering the court system may be significantly affected by the characteristics of the public policies being implemented. The second is to provide illustrative examples of the different ways in which the structure of the *full* federal court system has been used in policy debates, focusing less on the concrete decisions made by courts or judges and more on the patterns by which policy has been contested in the venue provided by the full federal court system.

This chapter relies on a small number of case studies—four comprehensive primary case studies and four brief supplementary case studies—to illustrate the broad patterns by which political actors used the Brazilian federal courts to contest policies adopted during the two-term Cardoso administration (1995–2002).[1] Rather than providing a large-N study of the use of a single legal instrument or a single plaintiff's use of the courts, then, these case studies were selected "for the purpose of understanding a large class of similar units" (Gerring 2004, 342)—namely, episodes of the contestation of federal public policies in the federal court system.[2] Case studies do not yield the probabilistic models that some readers might prefer. That said, they provide a thick description of the patterns of policy contestation that constitute the first step—court activation—in the long sequential chain that ends in a judge's decision. Further, as George and Bennett note (2005, 19), case studies can be extremely helpful in developing new hypotheses, explaining causal mechanisms, and describing situations of causal complexity. The case studies here thus lay the groundwork for deepening our understanding of the federal court system's effects on policy contestation and policy outcomes in the broader political system.[3]

A second reason to analyze case studies based in specific policies is that they point to the full toolkit used by policy players to contest policy in court. Policy opponents frequently used complex, multilevel tactics that would not be visible if we were to focus solely on the high court or on a single legal instrument. If, for example, I were to describe policy contestation in the courts solely on the basis of a large-*N* study of cases in the high court (a technique common to the literature, which I too will use in the next chapter), I might well find that certain policies—such as privatization—were seldom challenged. Yet this is clearly not the case: because the high court's jurisprudence regarding privatization was already well established by the early 1990s, use of high court instruments was not a viable tactical option for policy opponents. Adversaries of privatization therefore often used lower courts as a tactical alternative; according to Almeida (2004, 66), 460 legal suits were filed against privatization efforts between 1992 and 1997. Such critical details about court use should become more evident using a "vertical" approach that traces a single policy's multiple and often multidirectional paths into and throughout the judicial hierarchy.

Policy Type and the Use of Courts

Theodore Lowi's work famously inverted the common view of policy as an outcome of the political process. As McCool (1995, 175) notes,

> Until Lowi, policy was viewed as a product—an outcome—of government. In other words, politics determined policies. But Lowi reversed this relationship; his typology is based on the assumption that the perceived attributes of the policy determine the attributes of the political process that makes that policy.

The cases in this chapter were selected on the logic that just as "policy determines politics" (Lowi 1964, 1972), so too, policy may determine *judicial* politics. In thinking about how courts may be activated on policy issues,

TABLE 3.1

Policy types, as determined by the incidence of costs and benefits

	Concentrated Costs	Distributed Costs
Concentrated Benefits	*Type I* Concentrated benefits with concentrated costs *Case studies* Agrarian reform Judicial debt payments	*Type II* Concentrated benefits with distributed costs *Case studies* Automotive industry policy Education spending
Distributed Benefits	*Type III* Distributed benefits with concentrated costs *Case studies* Social security reform Privatization of CVRD	*Type IV* Distributed benefits with distributed costs *Case studies* Electricity rationing CPMF tax

then, it makes sense to consider court use as an extension of politics: legal tactics are often an extension of broader political strategies implemented across a variety of political institutions. As a result, the degree to which the judiciary is activated to contest policy will depend greatly on a policy's salience to potential plaintiffs, and the extent to which this salience is sufficient to trigger collective action, in the courts as elsewhere. Salience to a potential plaintiff, in turn, is determined by how the costs and benefits of public policies are spread.

This argument also relies heavily on the policy typology built by Wilson (1995), which characterizes policies according to the incidence of their costs and benefits (and in turn, builds on Lowi's original argument by classifying policy types according to the politics they are likely to incite).[4] The central insight is that focusing on the costs and benefits of policy, rather than solely on its substantive content, may reveal patterns of political contestation common to each possible distribution of costs and benefits. Four broad categories can be created according to the concentration or diffusion of these costs and benefits, as shown in Table 3.1. As a result, it is possible to aggregate substantively dissimilar issues, such as electricity rationing and the special "CPMF" tax, under the same category of distributed costs and distributed benefits (Type IV). The bottom of each of the four cells shows primary and secondary case studies that exemplify each policy type in the Brazilian case during the Cardoso administration. We now turn to each in order.

Agrarian Reform as a Type I Policy

BACKGROUND

During Fernando Henrique Cardoso's first term in office, the president included agrarian reform—the resettlement of the rural poor on unused or underutilized agricultural land—among his government's top priorities. At roughly the same time, two widely publicized mass killings in 1995 and 1996 further increased public attention to the issue of the landless and reinvigorated the Movement of Landless Rural Workers (MST), a group created in the 1980s to push for better distribution of agricultural property.[5]

Throughout the 1990s, the MST's principal tactic was to seize (or, in commonly used parlance, *invadir*) portions of large agricultural properties. The MST "invasions" originally targeted underutilized properties, but by the late 1990s, many of the land seizures were also aimed at political targets, such as farms owned by Cardoso's sons and key congressional leaders. In addition, the MST led or participated in many public protests against the Cardoso government.[6] The joint strategy of land seizures and public demonstrations was focused on keeping the issue of the landless in the press, and was conducted with the support of the Catholic Church's National Council of Bishops (CNBB) and Pastoral Land Commission (CPT), as well as the opposition Workers' Party (PT) and the CUT labor federation.[7]

Public sympathy for the MST made the issue of agrarian reform a particularly thorny one for Cardoso. Justifications for the land seizures came from a host of opinion makers; one former finance minister, associated with Cardoso's Real Plan, noted that the judiciary was so slow at judging expropriation cases that it practically forced the MST to seize land (Ricupero 1998). Others argued that the legislative process was biased by a congress that over-represented large landowners. A 1997 survey illustrated that inequality in the countryside was even greater than in the cities: 1 percent of the population owned 46 percent of the land while the 50 percent poorest owned only 2.7 percent, and the concentration of land has grown more unequal since the 1920s (Nassif 1998a). And violence in the countryside was significant, leading to the deaths of 349 victims between 1993 and 2002 (Pastoral Land Commission 2003), boosting sympathy for the movement.

POLICY DESCRIPTION

The federal government's reaction to the continued violence in the countryside was twofold. First, it unsuccessfully pressured state governments for rapid resolution of the massacres in state courts, especially after international human rights organizations condemned the violence and inaction in bringing the accused to justice (*Human Rights Watch World Report*, 1996–2002). Second, whether or not it was a direct result of the "massacres," the federal government engaged in an ambitious land-resettlement project, which claimed to have resettled nearly six hundred thousand families on new land between 1995 and 2001, a threefold increase on the number of total resettlements between 1964 and 1994 (Maschio and Scolese 2002).

These claims are disputed, both in terms of the quantity of families resettled and the effectiveness of the resettlement.[8] But agrarian reform remained a key political priority for the Cardoso government. In 1996 and 1997, arguing that the government needed to unify its efforts on agrarian reform, decentralize the issue to the states, and increase public support for agrarian reform (Cardoso 1997), the Cardoso administration pushed through a package of laws increasing taxes on unproductive agricultural land, transferring capital crimes committed by the police to civilian courts and rewriting the national Agrarian Law.

As the issue of agrarian reform continued to boil, the government in 1999 adopted a second policy initiative aimed at deepening its previous policy by depoliticizing the process of resettlement. It focused partially on landowners, aimed at ending what the Agrarian Reform Minister called the "industry of super-evaluations and resulting super-compensations" in expropriation cases (Jungmann 1997). But it also put strong checks on land seizures, prevented "invaded" properties from being audited for expropriation, and removed such lands from consideration for expropriation for two years. It also forbade those involved in "invasions" of agricultural land or public property from participating in resettlement programs. Agrarian reform, as represented in these two policy moments, fits neatly into Type I policy. It pit landowners against the landless, with concentrated costs and benefits limited primarily to these two groups.

JUDICIAL CHALLENGES

The use of the courts to bar, block, or alter the implementation of agrarian reform policies was relatively sparse in comparison with other policies. Both landowners and landless groups did indeed employ the courts, but sparingly. In the federal courts, the landowners, aside from a few unsuccessful "original civil actions" (ACOs) to prevent individual expropriations,[9] mostly shied away from broad challenges to these two waves of agrarian reform policy.[10] Landless groups also largely avoided the use of the courts, except to defend specific MST members from penal and civil suits. The MST did not directly engage in constitutional challenges to these policies, in part, no doubt, because it had no standing for direct challenges in the STF, but also perhaps

---

SECONDARY CASE STUDY: JUDICIAL DEBT PAYMENTS AS A TYPE I POLICY

A second example of the judicialization of Type I policy refers to the change in policy regarding judicial debt payments. A September 2000 constitutional amendment (No. 30) extended the period during which debts incurred in court decisions (known as *precatórios*) could be repaid, permitting debtor governments at the state and municipal level to parcel out these judicial debt payments over ten years.

This policy had concentrated costs among individuals who were owed money by government; the benefits were concentrated among incumbent governments that suddenly faced similar conditions to their debt-free counterparts. The largest debtors in these cases were frequently state governments with enormous debts: São Paulo state led the pack, for example, with outstanding debts of roughly R$5 billion in 2000 (Godinho 2000).

The extension of *precatório* payment terms led to a middle level of judicial challenges. Three constitutional challenges via ADIN were filed in the STF protesting the policy, one by the National Confederation of Industry and two by the Brazilian Bar Association. In lower-level courts, there were literally thousands of cases filed for nonpayment of *precatórios,* and requests for federal intervention in nineteen of Brazil's twenty-seven states to force payment. However, these cases largely contested the nonpayment of *precatórios,* rather than the new policy itself, which drew few judicial challenges.

---

because the MST may have had difficulty in resorting to legal avenues given the tenuous legality of its own tactics and its rejection of the existing power structure.[11] The MST's challenges to agrarian reform policy as a whole were thus limited to specific cases, rather than overarching policy challenges. That said, the MST leadership was vocal in its public criticism of the judicial process, forcing STF ministers to defend their record and even to take the unusual step of meeting with MST leaders to discuss their concerns.[12]

Broader constitutional challenges to the implementation of Cardoso's agrarian reform policy were instead the purview of leftist political parties and the Confederation of Agricultural Workers (CONTAG)—associated with the CUT labor union—which shared many objectives with the MST. The Workers' Party (PT) filed two *Ações Diretas de Inconstitucionalidade* (ADINs) to unsuccessfully challenge the right to use federal debt bonds (*títulos da dívida agrária* or TDAs) to finance land expropriation, as well as to challenge the provisional measure that excluded "invaded" lands from expropriation.[13] The

Confederation of Agricultural Workers also filed two ADINs: the first challenged the means by which land could be withdrawn from consideration for expropriation, arguing that this created ample opportunities for delay; the second argued that the method by which land reform was carried out was procedurally flawed.

The only direct constitutional challenge by ADIN that succeeded in thwarting agrarian policy implementation was filed by the Brazilian Bar Association (OAB), which obtained a partial injunction against a provisional measure that implemented the second stage of Cardoso's agrarian reform. Why would the bar association be interested in agrarian reform? The OAB contested several portions of the provisional measure, but was successful in its primary aim of winning an injunction against a section of the law that capped the honorarium payable to lawyers in expropriation hearings (at R$151,000). With its success, the OAB significantly undermined the government's goal of limiting the costs of compensation and succeeded in its goal of protecting lawyers' income in land expropriations.

IMPLICATIONS OF JUDICIAL INTERVENTION

In comparison with other policies explored in this chapter, the judiciary appears to have been used in a restricted fashion to challenge agrarian reform policy. While the costs of defending against individual landowners' suits brought to halt, delay, or reverse individual expropriation proceedings were not trivial (and certainly influenced the content of the second wave of agrarian reform policy), the effects of such suits on overall policy implementation appear to have been negligible. Meanwhile, constitutional challenges brought by opponents of the agrarian policy proved to be weak on the merit ascribed to them by the STF, with only one constitutional challenge—by a peripheral actor, the OAB—succeeding. This successful policy challenge was filed by the OAB against an element of policy that better fits the rubric for Type III policies, since it sought to limit lawyers' possible earnings in expropriation cases (concentrated costs) as a way of improving overall judicial efficiency and the general cost to taxpayers of land reform (diffuse benefits).

This raises the question of why actors such as the Contag or PT chose to bring constitutional challenges, if the chances of success were low. The costs of such a challenge may be one explanation; the costs of bringing an ADIN are virtually nil for established political parties or organized professional groups such as the OAB. A related explanation is that court use provides "voice" for the parties involved, even when it is unsuccessful. In arguing their case before the Supreme Court, the lawyers for the Confederation of

Agricultural Workers wrote that the use of the provisional measure has been abused, but that,

> [s]ince none of the occupants of the three branches seem preoccupied in bringing an end to this situation, it falls to the common citizen to resort to the old maxim of "complaining to the bishop," which may not resolve anything, but at least comforts (ADIN 2411; translation mine).

The logic of political expression will be further detailed in later chapters, but it is sufficient for now to note that Type I policies such as agrarian reform and judicial debt payments triggered a fairly moderate use of the courts to contest policy.

Automotive Policy as a Type II Policy

BACKGROUND

The Brazilian automotive industry was a powerful political player during the 1990s, claiming to account for nearly 12 percent of GDP and more than ninety thousand direct jobs in 1998 (O'Keefe and Haar 2001, 8). The top auto companies, cohesively organized in the National Association of Automotive Vehicle Manufacturers (ANFAVEA), thus had a vital role in domestic policy debates.[14] In the wake of economic opening by President Collor, and with the advent of the Real Plan, Brazil became an increasingly attractive base for international manufacturers. Between 1990 and 1997, the domestic auto market grew by more than 150 percent, to 1.6 million vehicles per year, and although it subsequently weakened in the wake of the Asian crisis, Brazil's auto industry closed the decade as one of the ten largest in the world.

President Cardoso came to office on the heels of the Real Plan, committed to continuing the trade opening begun by Collor, but within two constraints: building the Mercosul regional trade agreement inaugurated in 1994, and upholding the fixed exchange rate that anchored the Real. The explosive growth of the domestic automotive market in the wake of the Real Plan could not be fed by domestic production alone, however, and as a result, auto imports rose sharply from 4 percent of total consumption in 1993 to 18 percent in 1995 (Santos and Gonçalves 2001, 211). This explosion of imports raised two problems: (1) the increasing sectoral trade deficit contributed to severe pressure on the currency (especially in the wake of the Mexican peso crisis), and (2) given strong regional demand, it became clear that Brazil was in serious competition with Argentina as a site for new Southern Cone manufacturing capacity, undermining Brazil's recent commitment to Mercosul.

POLICY DESCRIPTION

These two potential problems led the Cardoso administration to adopt a substantively new policy toward the automotive industry early in 1995. The first of the three components of the policy package was a February increase in the industrial production tax (IPI) on small "popular" cars, from 0.1 percent to 8.0 percent, aimed at slowing the fastest growing area of consumption. The second component aimed at reducing imports, including through a sharp increase in import tariffs on assembled vehicles, from 20 percent in 1994 to 32 percent in February 1995, and then to 70 percent in March.[15] The restrictions also included limits on auto imports, which were temporarily restricted to half of the previous six months' imports, while manufacturers' imports were restricted to a share of their exports, and quotas were established for nonmanufacturing importers. The third component of the policy package created fiscal incentives to encourage the development of domestic production capacity, including accelerated depreciation for capital investment and tax benefits for auto exporting manufacturers.

SECONDARY CASE STUDY: PRIMARY EDUCATION FUNDING AS A TYPE II POLICY

A 1996 constitutional amendment (No. 14) aimed to improve education by setting lower boundaries on state and municipal primary education spending at 15 percent of local tax revenue; tying certain federal tax revenues directly to state and municipal education; and guaranteeing that federal funding to maintain primary education spending would be kept at R$300, at a minimum, per student per year.

The costs of this policy package were widely distributed across the tax base, while benefits accrued to a concentrated group of primary teachers and students, thus making it a typical Type II policy with diffuse costs and concentrated benefits.

Few legal challenges to this policy are apparent. No lower court cases against this policy package were found, and there were only two constitutional challenges filed. These contested the sacrifice of nursery school funding to primary school funding; the transfer of spending away from other priorities to education; and the loss of state and municipal autonomy in determining spending allocation. In other words, these complaints were elaborated largely on the basis of the trade-off between specific constituencies' concentrated costs and benefits; that is, against aspects of the policy that pertain more to Type I conflicts than to Type II policy conflicts.

The first element in the Cardoso automotive policy—the February increase in the IPI tax—clearly does not fall into the rubric of Type II policy, with diffuse costs and concentrated benefits. The IPI tax change proved to have Type III characteristics of costs concentrated among specific industrial, labor, and consumer groups, and diffuse benefits in terms of currency stability. So, too, did the increase in the import tariffs, the cost of which was borne by vehicle import firms and the transport business, with benefits limited to broader macroeconomic performance.

The second element in the policy package—import quotas—was, however, a clear example of Type II policy: quotas result in widely distributed losses among consumers, specific gains to producers, and quota rents, which accrued to the companies allowed to import under the new rules. The third component of the measures implemented between February and June 1995—incentives for domestic production—also clearly fit the Type II rubric. These incentives emerged from many forms of pressure on the government, including the very obvious trade deficit and threats that the auto industry might relocate to Argentina if it were not offered better conditions (Nassif 1996). The measures resulted in lower competition and rising domestic car prices (which increased nearly 50 percent between 1995 and 1997, according to Rosenberg 1997), in exchange for promises that the car industry would maintain industrial employment levels and increase investment.[16] In other words, concentrated gains were offered to automotive manufacturers that would ultimately be paid for by a wide base of consumers and taxpayers.[17]

JUDICIAL CHALLENGES

Opposition to the policy package could have come from two main groups: Brazil's trading partners, and auto parts manufacturers. But these opponents did little to contest policy in the Brazilian courts. Foreign trading partners made a great deal of public hay out of the policy, with Argentine president Menem threatening to boycott an important Mercosul meeting (Rossi 1995), and the United States, Japan, and South Korea threatening retaliation in the World Trade Organization. But for obvious reasons, these foreign governments were unable to challenge policy in the Brazilian courts. Meanwhile, the auto parts industry saw little advantage in legally challenging its customer base, and the auto parts federation Sindipeças largely avoided public conflict with the government or automakers, even as it undertook negotiations with the automakers to try to guarantee that a certain proportion of auto parts would be purchased from national manufacturers (Pereira Filho 1995).

IMPLICATIONS OF JUDICIAL INTERVENTION

Judicial challenges to the government's automotive policies were, on the face of it, few and far between. There were few judicial challenges to the policy as policy *per se,* and what challenges did come forth were aimed mainly at the import tariff, which, as noted earlier, had all the characteristics of a Type III policy. The import tariff was—perhaps as a result—the most contested element of the automotive industry measures, facing one ADIN, filed unsuccessfully by an association of vehicle importers; a smattering of lower court injunction requests, filed most notably by the public defender's office and the National Transport Confederation (CNT); and a number of lower court suits over the specifics of how to implement the tariff.[18] The other major aspects of the automotive policy—which more accurately fit the Type II rubric—faced no significant judicial challenges. Neither the IPI tax, nor the fiscal incentives and quotas, were contested as policy in the courts.[19]

In sum, in both the case of automotive industry policy and the secondary case of funding for primary education, the Type II policies analyzed here faced few policy challenges in the courts, and those challenges that were filed tended to question elements of policy that might better be labeled as having concentrated costs (either Type I or Type III policies).

Social Security Reform as a Type III policy[20]

BACKGROUND

Social security reform was a top policy priority for the Cardoso administration from early in its first term, prompted if nothing else by necessity. The social security budget, including both National Social Security Institute (INSS) payments to private sector retirees and the government's payments to public sector retirees, grew rapidly from 1988 through the 1990s due to the generous terms laid out in the new Constitution. Demographic factors, including a population that was growing to retirement age far faster than the working age population was increasing, added further pressure for change (Ministério da Previdência Social 2003).

The total social security deficit stood at US$14.2 billion in 1996 (equivalent to 1.9 percent of GDP). This was a major drain on the country's accounts, exceeding federal spending on primary and secondary education, as well as the inflow of foreign capital the government was struggling so hard to attract (Giannetti 1998). The system lived hand-to-mouth, running annual deficits because of generous benefit payouts untied to real contributions into the system (Velloso 2003).

The system was also patently unbalanced, with the public sector accounting for a large share of the spending. In 1996, 48 percent of social security spending went to 16.6 million private sector workers, while 52 percent was spent on 2.9 million public sector retirees. In other words, the average INSS private sector retiree earned 16 centavos for every Real earned by the average public sector retiree. Perhaps most damaging, public sector employees paid in contributions equivalent to only 17 percent of total public sector pension outlays in 1996, as compared to 94 percent in the INSS system (Godoy 1998; Ministério da Previdência Social 1997, 2003).

POLICY DESCRIPTION

Brazil's social security reform under Cardoso clearly falls into the Type III rubric of distributed benefits and concentrated costs. The benefits accrued to no specific group: they ranged from fiscal responsibility, essential to the Real Plan and the stability of the Real, to greater equality between public and private pensioners. The costs were, on the other hand, highly concentrated, and were to be borne primarily by the civil service.[21]

Pushed by the need to guarantee the fiscal anchor of the Real Plan, the Cardoso administration submitted a major social security reform to Congress in March 1995, two months after Cardoso's inauguration.

The proposal called for a minimum retirement age, with a sliding benefits scale depending on how long pension contributions were made by the employee; a ceiling on benefits for both private and public sector workers; a tax on pension benefits paid out to public sector retirees; and changes in the formula by which pension benefits were calculated.

This constitutional amendment proposal was to face a turbulent, nearly four-year uphill battle in Congress. The first report out of committee, a year after the proposal, was rejected by the Chamber of Deputies. A revised and diluted reform proposal was finally approved by the Chamber in July 1996, after significant judicial intervention (discussed in the next section), but was then altered by the Senate, requiring new hearings in the Chamber.

It was not until November 1998, under the gun of the Russian crisis, that the Chamber approved the final constitutional amendment on social security (Amendment No. 20). But this reform had been substantially diluted (*Folha de São Paulo* 1998c), and its troubles were not over. One component of the reform—a 30 percent tax on civil service retirees' pensions over R$1,200 monthly (the so-called *contribuição dos inativos*)—was narrowly rejected when heard by the full Chamber. The government then tried an end run around Congress, issuing a provisional measure that established a withholding tax on civil service pensions, a measure that was subsequently

SECONDARY CASE STUDY: CVRD PRIVATIZATION AS A TYPE III POLICY

The Cardoso government included sale of a majority stake in the Companhia Vale do Rio Doce (CVRD, a state-owned conglomerate valued at over R$10 billion), among the top priorities in its privatization program.

This being a Type III policy, with diffuse benefits and costs concentrated among the public sector workforce, we would expect a flurry of legal challenges to privatization. This is exactly what ensued, with a sequence of judicial action that one investor described as a "tragic comedy" (Rossi 1997).

The original auction of the federal government's voting shares in CVRD was set for April 29, 1997. A flurry of over 120 suits, of which more than 20 included injunction requests, flooded lower-level courts. Although most of the injunction requests were rejected, at least two were upheld in federal regional courts. Despite frantic government attempts to call a special court session, the auction was postponed indefinitely.

The government appealed to the STJ, where all twenty-seven pending injunction requests were thrown out, and a single court was named to centrally decide all cases related to the sale. Simultaneously, the government was defending itself against an ADIN filed in the STF by opposition parties. After a number of legal maneuvers, the sale was rescheduled for May 7. Seven minutes into the bidding, a new injunction arrived at the bourse, suspending the auction. This injunction was struck down five hours later, and the sale was quickly consummated, fetching R$3.2 billion for the government coffers.

But even when all this heart-stopping legal action was over, the auction was still not official. A handful of further injunction requests were upheld in the wake of the sale, questioning the legitimacy of the buyers, the right to call a shareholders meeting to officially hand over control of the company, and so forth. All have since been appealed, and CVRD is no longer in government hands, but the path to this end was an arduous one, and as of this printing, a handful of suits remain outstanding.

converted to law during the devaluation crisis of January 1999. This law was to be overturned by the STF nine months later, alongside an accompanying law setting rules for contributions by nongovernmental organizations. The final stage in the Cardoso government's social security saga was the approval of a further law in November 1999 that set the formula for how retirement benefits were to be calculated, the so-called "pension factor." This law, too, faced significant challenges in the courts, as the next section illustrates.

JUDICIAL CHALLENGES

The Cardoso administration's three successive legislative initiatives on social security reform—passage of the constitutional reform package, the civil service pension tax legislation, and the "pension factor" legislation—all led to major court action. Throughout the debate over policy, and then as implementation began, there was significant resort to the courts through constitutional challenges at the STF and via challenges in the lower courts.[22]

The courts joined in the fray early on. Responding to a request from the Communist Party of Brazil (PCdoB), STF minister Marco Aurélio de Mello issued an injunction (without hearings *en banc*) to suspend congressional hearings on the social security reform in April 1996.[23] Supporters of the decision, including the Brazilian Bar Association (OAB) and the Association of Brazilian Magistrates (AMB), argued that it was entirely appropriate, as the Chamber had already rejected the proposed report out of committee, and the Constitution makes clear that no rejected bill can be newly submitted during the same congressional session (Silva Martins 1996).[24]

Critics argued that the case for judicial suspension of congressional hearings was weak, given that there was no imminent risk (*periculum in mora*) of bypassing the legislative process. Others noted Minister Mello's past as the author of a controversial injunction that suspended the 1993 constitutional revision process, also in response to a request from an opposition party. Criticism of the courts was louder than approval, however, and the editorial page of one newspaper—no friend of the Cardoso administration—commented, "reforms face obstacles that come from where, *a priori*, one would least expect them" (*Folha de São Paulo* 1996b; translation mine). On May 9, one month after the injunction was released, the full STF voted 10 to 1 to suspend Minister Mello's injunction.[25]

With the final congressional approval of the reform package between November 1998 and January 1999, constitutional challenges by ADIN flew fast and furious, with an unprecedented thirty-three ADINs filed against the social security laws. Although the success rate of these ADINs was lower than the average overall ADIN success rate, this was partly because so many targeted the same laws, allowing the STF to bundle some of them together.[26] Two of the three ADINs that were approved or partly approved by the STF were very specific in their effects, with little significance in terms of reversing the broader implementation of the new reform.[27]

The third ADIN, however, was a bombshell. In September 1999, the STF approved an injunction requested in an ADIN by the OAB, suspending the tax on civil service pensioners and the increase in the pension contribution paid by active civil servants, a decision that the government estimated would cost R$2.4 billion annually. Minister Celso de Mello, rapporteur of the decision, argued that the law was unconstitutional because the amendment on which it was based clearly stated that no such contribution would be contemplated in law. Thus, any change would require a constitutional amendment.

More fuel was added to the fire at the end of October 1999, when STF president Carlos Velloso argued publicly that a new government proposal that would enact the tax on civil service pensions through a constitutional amendment was also likely to be unconstitutional. Top presidential aide Aloysio Nunes Ferreira responded testily, "Velloso reveals himself as a man of audacious innovation. He has invented a new attribution for the STF: the *prior* constitutional control of juridical norms. He resolved to do it through the press" (Freitas et al. 1999). Ultimately, though, the Cardoso government took the message to heart and refrained from proposing any further amendment.

Meanwhile, in the lower courts, the government faced fewer significant challenges to its reform. In part, this was because binding mechanisms of constitutional challenge are nonexistent in the lower courts. Despite the vociferous opposition of lower court judges to social security reform, most cases in the STJ and lower federal courts dealt with specific individual circumstances, such as failure to pay benefits or disputes over inappropriate claims to pensions. These offered little traction for major constitutional challenges to the reform package, which were instead advocated via ADIN by political parties, the OAB, and professional unions.

IMPLICATIONS OF JUDICIAL INTERVENTION

Recourse to the judiciary on social security reform was significant, especially in the upper reaches of the judiciary, where the breadth of constitutional challenges brought against the reform was unprecedented. Vociferous exchanges between the three branches of government added to the confusion and uncertainty surrounding the Cardoso government's fiscal anchor, and certainly contributed to the uneasiness that led up to the January 1999 devaluation of the Real. This strong enunciation of judicial interests continues today, with social security reforms by the Lula administration eliciting a similar tone of vociferous opposition from the STF president and lower court judges (for example, Leitão 2003). Meanwhile, however, the examples of social security reform and CVRD privatization suggest that Type III policies tend to produce significant activation of the courts, albeit with procedural differences related to plaintiffs' ability to claim standing to contest policy directly in the high court. Plaintiffs were able to use the STF to some effect in the case of social security reform, while prior jurisprudence severely limited the STF's utility in challenging privatizations. In both cases, however, Type III policies triggered significant judicial contestation.

Electricity Rationing as a Type IV Policy

BACKGROUND

The Brazilian government's inability to finance a much-needed expansion of its state-owned electric grid raised fears during the early 1990s about the possibility of nationwide blackouts. Partly as a result, the Cardoso administration undertook reforms it hoped would attract much-needed investment, estimated to be on the order of US$4 billion to US$10 billion annually.[28] In 1996, Cardoso pushed Congress to approve changes in the regulatory framework for electricity production, most notably by creating an autonomous National Electricity Agency (ANEEL). The government also divested itself of large state-owned firms, continuing efforts begun by the Collor administration, and netting privatization revenues of over US$31 billion from the sale of federal and state electric companies between 1991 and 2002 (BNDES 2002). As a result, the energy industry underwent significant changes, with privatization of the major electricity distributors, the break-up and sale of major generating companies, and a shift among state-owned companies from a major role in all areas of energy supply to smaller responsibilities as transmitters.

Yet despite the changes, generating capacity continued to lag behind Brazil's growing demand for electricity. The annual shortfall approached 10 percent of total generation capacity and could not be easily supplemented through rerouting on aging transmission lines either among Brazilian states or from neighboring countries. The privatization of electric companies was not accompanied by well-planned regulation: industry sources complained about informal, politically motivated caps on distributors' prices (Ogier 2001); new companies were encouraged to build natural gas-fired plants, but balked at the cost of the gas piped in from Bolivia (*The Economist* 2002, 33); and some generation capacity remained in state hands, subject to tough public spending constraints (*The Economist* 2001a, 36–38). Most critically, generation also remained overwhelmingly reliant on hydroelectric sources, which accounted for more than 95 percent of all electricity produced in Brazil (Economist Intelligence Unit 2001).

This acute reliance on hydroelectric power generation proved to be a risky gamble. After four years of unusually low rainfall, by March 2001 it became evident to federal policymakers that without heavy rains, there would be a collapse in electricity generation in the southeast, northeast, and central western regions. The government put off a response, praying that much-needed rain would allow it to avoid the political costs of acknowledging a crisis, as well as the economic and social consequences of a potential blackout. By April, a technical working group called together to work on the situation came to the tough conclusion that the weather was not cooperating: dams in the affected regions were not only below the 49 percent level considered safe, they had fallen to a third of capacity. The choice was clear: Brazil would either have to face temporary blackouts, or drastically diminish consumption (Catanhêde 2001).

POLICY DESCRIPTION

Between mid-April and mid-May 2001, the government developed its emergency solution to the problem. An initial provisional measure, issued May 15, created a special Chamber for the Administration of the Energy Crisis (GCE). The gravity of the crisis was revealed by the GCE's composition: it was headed by Cardoso's chief civilian advisor, Pedro Parente, and composed of the major cabinet members, as well as presidents of public sector companies and the heads of all the regulatory agencies associated with energy policy.[29] This first provisional measure included no concrete measures for reducing consumption, but laid out objectives for the GCE. It also took the unusual step of freeing public agencies and companies from the usual procurement rules for purchases of goods and services required to address the energy crunch. This initial statement of policy goals was further developed in subsequent drafts of the provisional measure (the first released only one week later) and other accompanying legislation.

The government began a US$10 million national publicity campaign (Ogier 2001) to announce the strict rules governing its rationing program and ask for citizens' cooperation. The new measures required domestic consumers nationwide to reduce their consumption by 20 percent from the previous year or else face a suspension of electric service.[30] The price of electricity remained unchanged for small consumers, but was boosted by 50 to 200 percent for larger consumers (those consuming over 200kWh a month). Industrial consumers were forced to cut consumption to 75–85 percent of the previous year's levels, with a few exceptions in specific industries. The public sector, meanwhile, was required to reduce its own consumption sharply, by 15 percent in May, 25 percent in June, and 35 percent in July. Public sector workers' days were decreed to end at 5 P.M., and ministers were allowed to authorize six-hour workdays.

The CPMF tax ("Provisional Contribution on Financial Movements"), a tax created by constitutional amendment No. 12 in 1996, was sold to Congress as a means of financing spending on the national health system. The costs were widely distributed across all bank customers, who were taxed a fixed percentage on the volume of their banking transactions. Although the government claimed the revenues would finance health care nationally, the tax permitted fungible government resources to be directed to other goals; in other words, the benefits were spread over a number of policy arenas (and policy beneficiaries) rather than being sector specific.

Three constitutionality challenges via ADIN were filed against the CPMF amendment and its accompanying legislation by industrial federations and labor groups. But a number of cases were also filed against the tax in lower-level courts, challenging either the allocation of CPMF revenues or the propriety of the tax. Doctors went to court to try to force the Cardoso administration to spend the money on the health care system, rather than more broadly. One *ação popular* in Rio complained that CPMF revenues were going to be used to pay health ministry debt, rather than for actual health care, a natural consequence of the fungibility of revenues. Bank workers in São Paulo were able to obtain an exemption from the CPMF tax from a lower federal court. A single taxpayer convinced a lower-level federal judge in São Paulo to rule the tax unconstitutional, for her alone, until higher courts could hear the case. Supermarkets, cereal makers, and a tax consultancy in Paraná state all obtained injunctions against the tax. In sum, the tax generated substantial legal action at all levels of the court system, albeit at a level that was not as voluminous as in the Type III cases.

In addition to preparing citizens, businesses, and the public sector to make sacrifices for energy conservation, the government tried to shield itself against major legal repercussions. While easing procurement laws to facilitate new investments in generation, the government also attempted to make it more difficult for opponents of the new measures to stall them in court. The provisional measure implementing the policy required that all legal challenges that "aim to block or impede" the plan name the federal government and the ANEEL electric regulator as *litisconsortes passivos* (or roughly, co-defendants), allowing the government to keep a closer watch on all potential suits. It also limited the incidence of consumer defense laws and required legal challengers to use the formal federal justice system, without access to the small claims courts (*juizados especiais*).

The announcement of the rationing measures was politically devastating for an already weak presidency. Cardoso's approval rating fell from 42 percent in March to 30 percent in June, with disapproval jumping from 48 percent to 62 percent (CEPAC 2002). Practically speaking, however, the rationing had a valuable effect, preventing the further depletion of dams until the summer rains began to fall, and providing a hiatus in demand while new energy supplies were brought online.[31] Although the government's targets were not met in every month, worst-case scenarios that had the crisis lasting until 2003 were not realized, and rationing ended in February 2002.

JUDICIAL CHALLENGES

Judicial challenges against the rationing policy took place via both constitutional challenges and lawsuits in lower court. The rules governing lawsuits against electricity rationing helped to move most suits directly into the federal court system, and eased the tracking process for government lawyers. But the scope of the challenges was quite broad, and defending the policy required a major expenditure of government resources. Challenges against the plan ranged widely in subject matter, but the largest number and the greatest threat came in two categories: those challenging the new higher tariffs on "excess consumption," and those challenging changes in the legal instruments available to litigants challenging the plan.

"Excess Consumption" Tariff Rates. The first judicial intervention, in mid-May, illustrated the importance of personality on the high court, as well as the importance of STF "signaling," even in the absence of any legal decision *per se.* Outgoing STF president Carlos Velloso had consistently argued that blackouts would be far more dangerous than the damage the rationing measures might cause to constitutional rights. But incoming STF president Marco Aurélio de Mello—whose opinions had frequently clashed with the Cardoso government's objectives in the past—argued publicly that the new, higher tariffs on "excess" consumption amounted to "confiscation" (Freitas and Silveira 2001).[32]

In the ensuing press frenzy, Minister de Mello forcefully argued this point, and received public backing from the OAB and some lower court judges (one TRF judge went further, arguing that Cardoso should be impeached for his responsibility in the energy crisis; Freitas 2001). However, there was as yet no legal action at the STF, and this proved to be only a signal from Minister de Mello to potential litigants. On May 24, hoping to quell judges' worries and present the government's case, Pedro Parente—the

GCE head—made a special visit to the high court in an effort to sway other STF ministers to the government's position.

A number of injunction requests began to arise in lower courts by May 22, most of which were local and quite specific, such as a suit by a billboard company that claimed to depend on the lighting for its business. More serious, even though their possible effect was only statewide, were a series of suits filed by consumer groups arguing that the higher tariffs were a "social injustice" (Monken 2001). More than six hundred government lawyers, coordinated by the Federal Attorney General (AGU), fanned out to defend against such cases, trying to move them as quickly as possible into federal courts, where the government could join the defense.

The federal lawyers had mixed success against these early injunctions, with 140 injunction requests filed nationwide by the end of June, of which 38 were granted (*Folha de São Paulo* 2001a). A few such injunctions were carried up to the regional federal courts (TRFs), where they were not infrequently upheld. The First Regional TRF in Brasília, headed by the same judge who had called for Cardoso's impeachment, repeatedly upheld injunctions granted against the higher tariffs on "excess consumption." The AGU's lawyers succeeded more than they failed, but the number of injunctions continued to grow, and in the absence of a binding decision, more injunctions were likely.

The legal uncertainty surrounding the rationing plan in early June encouraged government critics to challenge the plan politically, as well. Former president and Minas Gerais governor Itamar Franco suggested that he would not implement the new rationing plan in his state until the STF had ruled that the excess charges were constitutional. Rio governor Anthony Garotinho, gearing up his presidential campaign, called a public demonstration in Rio against the "blackout" and threatened to sue the federal government for the state's tax losses from the plan, which he estimated at R$250 million. Opposition political parties, joined by the OAB, filed two direct actions of unconstitutionality (ADINs) challenging the policy.

In light of the growing uncertainty surrounding the plan, the AGU took the highly unusual step of filing a Declaratory Action of Constitutionality (ADC) suit with the STF on June 11. This was only the ninth use of the ADC mechanism since its creation in 1993. Although the ADC has the unique benefit of creating a precedent that is binding throughout the judicial system, it is seldom used by governments because of the potential risk that the STF might find some portion of the questioned law unconstitutional. In this case, as the number of successful injunctions continued to rise, the government took a calculated risk and filed its ADC. In an 8 to 2 decision at the end of June, the STF declared the program constitutional, in the process quashing the fifty-eight injunctions that had been granted to date, as well as the injunction requests in two new ADINs filed against the plan by a metalworkers' union and an opposition party.

Limitations on Legal Recourse. The various iterations of the rationing plan approved by the government included a number of limitations on the normal use of the courts. Among these, resort to the Consumer Defense Code was restricted, and the government was required to be named as *litisconsorte passivo* in all cases that aimed "to block or impede" the laws and decisions governing the plan. The government hoped that restricting the use of the Consumer Defense Code would prevent a tide of suits against electric companies for damage to blenders, washing machines, TVs, and other home appliances in the event of a sudden blackout. As noted earlier, the decision to have itself named as a *litisconsorte* was aimed at centralizing the judicial process so that the government's lawyers would be aware of all challenges and able to defend against them rapidly. Both measures were to face significant challenges.

In an informal evaluation of the plan following Pedro Parente's visit, STF ministers publicly noted that "in theory," preventing citizens from resorting to the Consumer Defense Code was a usurpation of their fundamental rights. Over the course of the next week, prosecutors who worked on consumer protection in state *Ministérios Públicos,* meeting for an annual conference, argued vehemently against the measures. They noted the abusiveness of the measure, and threatened a nationwide "judicial attack" to overturn it (*Folha de São Paulo* 2001b). A day later, after a meeting between President Cardoso, the attorney general, Pedro Parente, and state prosecutors, the government beat a hasty political retreat, announcing that a new version of the provisional measure would be released that would not limit the use of the Consumer Defense Code by residential consumers.

The policy of forcing litigants to name the federal government as a co-defendant was also contentious, and was the subject of a broad ADIN filed by opposition parties (PT, PCdoB, and PDT). The STF granted an injunction in the ADIN, although the impact of this decision was relatively minor, as the STF only impugned this rule as it applied to CGE decrees. In other laws implemented by the government, litigants were still required to name the government as co-defendant. The broader policy challenges in the 126-page ADIN request were discarded, inasmuch as much of it overlapped with the findings in the ADC. The full merit of the ADIN has not been heard to date (meaning that it probably never will, given the end of the rationing system).

IMPLICATIONS OF JUDICIAL INTERVENTION

The use of the judiciary to affect the implementation of the electricity rationing policy was influenced to some degree by the government's efforts to change the rules on how the judiciary could be used, thus funneling cases up to the federal level, and instituting efficient mechanisms for government oversight of cases filed across the court system. In addition, the government's decision to take the rare step of filing an ADC allowed it to play the ace in its hand and simultaneously eliminate all of the injunctions and ADINs the policy faced. That said, the courts were heavily used at all levels to challenge the specific implementation of the policy as it affected individuals. The high courts were also brought in to address a number of issues of alleged constitutional merit. And the vocal opposition of some judges, joined by members of the *Ministério Público,* played a major role in the government's decisions on policy implementation. In sum, both the rationing policy and the CPMF tax led to significant policy contestation in the courts, although this was still less significant than in the Type III cases of social security reform and the privatization of CVRD.

Conclusion

This chapter has illustrated the significant degree to which federal courts at all levels—and not just the STF—have been used to contest public policy in the post-military period. Policy routinely finds its way into the court system, where it is challenged on a variety of grounds, with both legal and political objectives in mind.

Although the sample size is necessarily small, the case studies here suggest that policy salience and collective action dynamics, determined by the distribution of policy costs and benefits, play a role in the decision to use courts to contest policy. Table 3.2 shows these results graphically. Each cell depicts only those elements of the policy cases studied here that most closely conform to the ideal type the cell represents.[33] As the shading of Table 3.2 illustrates, there is a clear divide between the degree of recourse to the judiciary in Type II and Type III policies, with the other two types falling a bit less clearly somewhere in between. Type III policies such as social security reform and the sale of CVRD (concentrated costs and diffuse benefits) led to the highest degree of recourse to the courts. Automotive policy and the primary education policies described here, as Type II policies with diffuse costs and concentrated benefits, lay at the other end of the spectrum, generating very little legal activity. Type I and Type IV policies lay somewhere in between, generating significant legal opposition, but not on the scale seen, for example, with social security reform. Type IV policies in particular draw considerable public limelight, in part because they by nature affect broad swathes of the population (diffuse costs and diffuse benefits). But although they led to medium to high levels of legal contestation, they did not reach the extremes seen with Type III policies.

The strong legal response to Type III policies suggests that cases in which the onus of societywide policies is fairly concentrated are likely to lead to significant judicial action, independent of the policy subject, given their salience to potential plaintiffs and the strong incentives to collective action. This finding is reinforced by the fact that of the other policies studied here, the elements of policy that were most challenged in the courts were those

TABLE 3.2

Judicial contestation, by policy type

	Concentrated Costs	Distributed Costs
Concentrated Benefits	**TYPE I** *Agrarian Reform* Constitutional challenge: medium (4 ADINs*) Lower courts: low (individual-specific cases) *Judicial Debts* Constitutional challenge: medium (3 ADINs) Lower courts: low (individual-specific cases)	**TYPE II** *Automotive Policy* Constitutional challenge: low (1 marginally relevant ADIN**) Lower courts: low (policy-specific injunctions) *Education Spending* Constitutional challenge: low (2 ADINs, both contesting Type I elements of the policy) Lower courts: low (none found)
Distributed Benefits	**TYPE III** *Social Security Reform* Constitutional challenge: high (33 ADINs) Lower courts: high (individual-specific cases) *CVRD Privatization* Constitutional challenge: low (1 ADIN) Lower courts: high (100+ cases)	**TYPE IV** *Electricity Rationing* Constitutional challenge: medium (4 ADINs) Lower courts: high (policy-specific injunctions and Civil Public Actions-ACPs) *CPMF Tax* Constitutional challenge: medium (3 ADINs) Lower courts: high (policy-specific injunctions, ACPs, *Ações Populares*)

NOTES: (*)Excludes ADIN filed by OAB, which contests a Type III policy decision.

(**) There was only one topical ADIN filed, and it was a long shot, with a plaintiff who was not recognized as a legitimate plaintiff by the STF. A second ADIN was filed by the PT, but this was part of a broader protest about the use of provisional measures, having nothing to do with automotive policy *per se*.

most similar to Type III policies. The case study of Cardoso's automotive policy found that the element of policy that was most challenged in the high courts was in fact the element that was most like a Type III policy: the import tax increase. Other elements of automotive policy that were more clearly Type II policies led to no constitutional challenges. The same phenomenon was evident with agrarian reform legislation, when the successful OAB suit challenged a classic Type III component of policy: a reduction in lawsuit honoraria that would have hurt the OAB's narrow group interests.

Collective action dynamics influence the courts' role in Brazilian policy implementation in three ways. First, the strength of executive branch influence over the legislative process—described in greater detail in the coming chapter—means that courts not infrequently are one of only a few venues available to those shut out of policymaking, allowing the courts to fulfill the countermajoritarian role commonly ascribed to them. Second, it may be easier for narrow organized groups hurt by a policy decision to organize to use the courts than it would be for more diffuse groups; it may also make sense for a small group to pay the low relative costs of court action than to face major policy losses.

Finally, the interaction between policy salience and the judicial institutional environment is especially relevant: given the rules governing judicial review in Brazil, and in particular the privileged standing provided to select interest groups and political parties in filing constitutional review cases, policy contestation in the courts seems likely whenever the interests of these specific groups with direct standing in the STF are particularly affected. As the coming chapter will discuss, because not all burdened groups are given direct access to the high court under the 1988 Constitution, not all can bring constitutional challenges with the same ease. Without access to the ADIN mechanism, for example, the losers in automotive industrial policy had no standing to challenge policy in the STF. On the other hand, although it was seemingly a peripheral group in debates over agrarian reform, the OAB's access to the ADIN mechanism gave it an important veto over agrarian policies. Given that several such groups either may have no voice in developing policy (for example, the OAB in agrarian reform) or may be minorities in the process of approving policy (such as opposition political parties in social security reform), the relative ease of constitutional challenge in the Brazilian court system offers one further venue in which to contest policies whose costs may accrue to a small group. Chapter 4 now turns to an analysis of the relative success of various veto players in using constitutional challenges as a policy tool and what it may tell us about the courts' role in the broader political environment.

Chapter 4

The Supreme Federal Tribunal and Veto Players in Brazilian Politics

The extent to which courts have been activated in the Brazilian policy process, especially by groups who expected to bear the brunt of policy, should by now be evident. But it is not yet clear which groups are the most successful at contesting policy, or, alternatively, why the groups that did not do well in legal battles might still employ the courts. To begin answering these questions, this chapter analyzes the use of one constitutional review mechanism, the *Ação Direta de Inconstitucionalidade* (ADIN) in the Supreme Federal Tribunal (STF).

I begin by situating the judiciary within the literature on the broader Brazilian political system, with special attention to the judiciary's use as an alternative venue for policy contestation. The second section explores how the literature on veto players can be productively applied to courts. Finally, I analyze the use of ADINs over a fifteen-year period, showing how the rules governing judicial review may capacitate some political actors to act as veto players in the STF, and the significance of this legal enfranchisement for broader policy outcomes in the overall political system. Throughout, two questions guide my thinking. First, drawing on the literature on "veto players," which has been applied productively to presidents and assemblies worldwide but seldom to courts, what lessons can we draw about the policy impact of the judicial institutional environment? Second, do the rules governing judicial review in civil code systems privilege some actors over others, and if so, what sort of leverage does this provide them in the broader policy game?

The Judiciary in the Broader Political Environment

It is commonplace to argue that well-functioning courts offer an institutional locus for checking and balancing other branches of government, providing a guarantee of a separation of powers and protection for minorities (as per Madison et al. 1961; Montesquieu 1990). But as Chapter 1 noted, courts are inherently passive, and must be activated by external actors before they can have much effect. The degree to which the courts are called upon to serve as referees in the conflict between political forces or between other political institutions therefore depends not only on the courts themselves, but also on two factors that lead to their activation: the salience of individual policies and patterns of policy debate within the broader political system. The salience of policy—especially when it imposes costs on a small minority—plays some role in the degree to which courts are activated to debate policy in Brazil, as noted in Chapter 3. I begin here by exploring the second factor: how the political environment (including the effects of both contingent political conditions and more stable institutional rules) may contribute to the courts' importance as alternative venues for policy players marginalized in the legislative process.

Portrayals of Brazilian politics tend to range between two extremes.[1] One side sees the political system as so replete with potential veto players that decision making is intrinsically sclerotic, and only proposals with supermajoritarian support can be approved. In this atomized political system, a number of factors curb decision making: (1) the programmatically weak Congress, in which disproportional representation empowers smaller states, while loose lines of accountability resulting from open-list proportional representation favor special interests and facilitate constant party-switching; (2) the weak party system, which embraces an unusually high number of fragmented, unstable, and regionalized parties; (3) the fractiousness of presidential cabinets, which are used in part as an instrument to hold together congressional coalitions; (4) the self-serving nature of the state, and especially of civil servants within the state bureaucracy; (5) a Senate with unparalleled powers to interfere in most policy realms; and (6) the federal system, and in particular, its powerful governors and the contentious politics of fiscal decentralization (see, for example, Abrucio 1998, Ames 2001; Kinzo 1997; Mainwaring 1995; Stepan 2000). Institutional chokepoints on policy abound: as Kinzo notes, political representation in Brazil "reproduces to the nth power the system of checks and balances of the Madisonian model" (2001, 11; translation mine).

Political scientists on the other side of the debate suggest that decision making and policy change may not be as tough as the skeptics think. Facilitating factors include (1) the president's strong control over the policy agenda, aided by the concentration of budgetary powers in the executive branch and strong legislative powers wielded by the president; (2) muscular mechanisms for party control in the legislative (rather than electoral) arena; and (3) the strength of the congressional leadership (the *colégio de líderes*), its strong control over the legislative agenda, and its close ties with the Executive branch (for example, Figueiredo 2001; Figueiredo and Limongi 1999, 2002). As Figueiredo and Limongi (1999, 24) note, only 0.026 percent of executive proposals voted on by the full Chamber were rejected in the post-constitutional period. While the Congress may be less autonomous than desirable, this lack of autonomy boosts the incentives for congressional representatives to cooperate with the executive branch on policy.

These two opposing views are less dichotomous and mutually exclusive than the rigid straw men and one-dimensional portrayals often offered up as evidence. Indeed, there is considerable middle ground, if for no other reason than the fact that the post-military political experience has been marked by constant evolution—in the institutional rules, in the players involved, and in the policy process itself—suggesting that both camps may have been right at different times. Pereira and Mueller (2003), for example, argue that both camps are essentially correct. On the one hand, they note that decision making is decentralized by electoral rules (particularly open-list proportional representation), by the multiparty system, and by federalism. But on the other, they note that decision making is centralized by the internal decision-making rules within Congress and the strong legislative and budgetary powers of the presidency (737–738). The result is an "extremely dynamic" and delicate balance between centralized and decentralized decision making. Successful policymaking therefore relies to a great extent on the skill of the president and congressional leadership in providing electoral and financial benefits that attract potential supporters.

Under able leadership, it may be possible to create what Amorim Neto et al. (2003) label a "parliamentary agenda cartel," in which the legislative agenda is hammered out between the executive branch and leaders of allied political parties before any proposal actually goes to a vote. The benefit of such an arrangement is that it prevents individual veto players from gumming up policy deliberation, while also circumventing the loss of agenda control that may result from the quasi-parliamentary trading of votes for cabinet slots or pork. Considerable "recurrent bargaining" may be needed to move any policy agenda forward, but as Armijo et al. (2006, 781) note, this may be "understandably frustrating but *not necessarily dysfunctional* from the viewpoints of (a) consolidating democracy and (b) simultaneously accomplishing profound structural reforms of the national economic regulatory system." In sum, policy gets made, but the process relies heavily on skillful leadership and the construction of an agenda hammered out among members of the majority coalition. It is a process that works, in the sense that it produces some policy change, but is usually slower and less decisive than reformers might wish.

But where do the courts fit into this picture?

Brazil's courts add a seldom-mentioned layer of complexity to the picture just painted. Even under Cardoso, a president who was able to cobble together significant super-majoritarian coalitions in favor of reform, courts were called upon to contest all of the administration's major policy initiatives. Cardoso's government bullied, cajoled, persuaded, and bargained its way to legislative majorities that could overcome the tough procedural rules for constitutional amendments or complementary laws in the Senate and Chamber. But at the end of these herculean legislative efforts, the judicial contestation of reform was a recurring theme, with the most significant countervailing pressures against policy implementation emerging in the courts. As Taylor (2006a) illustrates, of the ten most prominent policy initiatives undertaken by the Cardoso government, all ten were contested in some fashion in the judicial branch, and seven of the ten were altered or delayed in some fashion in the STF.[2]

In light of this manifest role—and regardless of whether one accepts the centralized, decentralized, or mixed versions of decision making described earlier—it is clear that the judiciary begs to be included in our understanding of policy change in Brazil. Otherwise, policymaking processes will be incorrectly specified, and the policy influence of specific political actors may be overlooked. In particular, the role of the "losers" from the executive and legislative policymaking process—precisely the groups who are most likely to use the courts and least likely to appear in accounts of bargaining between the executive and legislative branches—will be neglected in our understanding of policy change.[3]

To what extent, though, do courts really influence the broader political environment by offering an alternative venue for policy contestation? To begin to answer this question, I turn to the concepts of veto players and veto points, which constitute the remainder of this chapter.

Veto Players and Veto Points in the Courts

Policy change in any given political system can be directly tied to the number of veto players in that system, as Tsebelis (1995, 2002) has noted, defining a veto player as "a political actor—an individual or collective—whose agreement is required to enact policy change."[4] The greater the number of veto players with discrete preferences, the more likely policy reform will fail and the policy status quo will prevail.

But not all opponents of reform are created equal. The toolkits available to each potential veto player are very different: bureaucrats have considerable control over resources, but no vote on legislation; a congressional representative may be able to vote on legislation, but not shape it significantly without a seat on the drafting committee; a member of the drafting committee will have less influence than the chair who controls the procedural rules; and so forth. Institutional opportunities to exercise a veto are therefore essential to the final shape of policy, and to the very identity of who can mold policy outcomes.

These "veto points"—institutional venues that permit political actors to exercise or threaten to exercise a veto over policy[5]—therefore matter as much as "veto players" in explaining policy change. Examples of veto points cited in the literature include plebiscites, representation on regulatory boards, referenda, and bicameral voting procedures.[6] They are relevant for several reasons: they permit political actors to exercise vetoes of policies that threaten their interests; given the implicit veto threat they possess, a political actor with access to such a veto point may have leverage over policy negotiations prior to implementation; and access to veto points may give veto players greater political weight, through their ability to represent other groups with similar interests who do not have access to the veto point. By contrast, the inability to use a given veto point will force opponents of policy to seek other venues from which to challenge policy. In the absence of such venues, they will have no institutional recourse for blocking policy change.[7]

Drawing a distinction between veto players and veto points provides at least three important insights. The first is that even relatively small or otherwise weak political groups may be able to behave as veto players and paralyze reform if they have access to institutional veto points. Immergut (1992), for example, concluded that the relative success of Swiss doctors in vetoing national health insurance was due in large part to their access to the referendum process. As she noted, the existence of veto points also allows potential veto players to be more intransigent in their defense of the status quo, even if they never resort to using their veto. A second insight is that not all potential veto players may have access to the same gamut of veto points, leading different political tactics to be employed by otherwise similar veto players. A third insight is that comparisons of otherwise similar political disputes may incorrectly identify the most relevant veto players, if they do not take into account the relevance of veto points to the identity of veto players. In the process, they may incorrectly specify the potential "winset" of policies that can replace the existing status quo.

Together, these three points serve as a warning about the possible consequences of failing to incorporate courts and other potential veto points into
our analysis of policy formation. Further, they suggest a potential shortcom-
ing of much veto analysis of courts: courts have generally been portrayed as
a veto player in their own right, rather than as a veto point that can be used
by other political actors.[8]

The Brazilian case provides an intriguing exception to the view of the
judiciary as a single veto player with uniform preferences. It is clear that
judges are not passive bystanders, and that policy opponents' use of legal tactics is often deeply influenced by signals from the courts, as in the cases of
social security reform and electricity rationing policy, when judges' signals
suggested that legal contestation might be welcomed by the courts. But for
a variety of institutional reasons already described in Chapter 2, the full federal judiciary seldom acts as a cohesive veto player. It does, however, offer
the institutional venues, or veto points, from which other policy actors may
exercise a veto.

This suggests that the judiciary may be more important than the relative
inattention to its role in the policy process suggests. By providing veto points
to select political actors, it gives them greater voice and leverage over policy,
in some cases enfranchising them as veto players even when they have little
influence elsewhere in the political system. Further, the evidence suggests
that Brazil's judicial institutional structure provides for the emergence of veto
players which are not immediately evident in otherwise masterful studies that
focus on policy change solely in the executive and legislative branches. The
ADIN constitutional review mechanism offers a particularly good example
of the effect of such judicial veto points, and the new groups and interests
they may introduce in the policy process.

The ADIN as a Veto Point

Earlier, I noted the paradox of the Brazilian federal judiciary. It is a strong institution: it is one of the best-funded court systems in the hemisphere, it is
highly independent, its decisions are adhered to, and its members are the elite
of the already elite legal profession. Yet this strength coexists with more prob-
lematic institutional characteristics, especially the extreme congestion and resulting sluggishness of the full court system. The effects of these contradictory
institutional characteristics are multiple, but have three important upshots for
policy. Because of the opportunity for highly disparate decisions and lengthy
delay, the judicial process tends to lead to particularistic rather than broadly
applicable decisions. Second, given the federal government's ability to delay
almost perpetually and to outlast other legal players, the judicial institutional

environment has tended to privilege the concerns of the executive branch in the medium term, no matter what decisions are taken by the lower courts.[9]

Perhaps the most important effect from a policy perspective, however, is that the judicial institutional environment motivates policy actors to access the high court in such a way as to obtain a binding, universally applicable, and definitive decision. The best and most efficient way of accomplishing this in Brazil is through the veto point of constitutional review cases, which allow plaintiffs to skip the lower courts and directly challenge federal government policy at the STF. The breadth of the standing granted for constitutional review in Brazil is without question broader than in European courts outside the strictly American model of diffuse constitutional review (for example, Stone 1992), and the STF's only real competitors in this regard within Latin America are the Colombian constitutional court (Cepeda Espinosa 2005; Rodriguez-Garavito et al. 2003; Uprimny 2004) and the constitutional chamber of the Costa Rican supreme court (Barker 2000; Rodríguez-Cordero 2002; Wilson and Rodríguez-Cordero 2006; Wilson et al. 2004). This broad standing to employ such review mechanisms boosts the potential for a wide—but nonetheless limited—range of veto players to influence policy more efficiently and effectively than individuals forced to start at the lowest rungs of the federal court system.

In redesigning the judiciary, the constituent assembly of 1988 created or strengthened several instruments aimed at facilitating constitutional review at the STF.[10] I focus here on the most widely used, the *Ação Direta de Inconstitucionalidade* (ADIN), specifically on the more than one thousand ADINs filed against laws passed by the three branches of federal government between 1988 and 2002.[11] The 1988 Constitution substantially broadened the list of those empowered to bring ADINs, from one player (the prosecutor-general), to nine categories of players, which include the president, the Federal Senate leadership, the Chamber of Deputies leadership, state governors, the head of the *Ministério Público* (the prosecutor-general), the national bar association (OAB), political parties with congressional representation, and unions or "class associations" with national representation.[12]

ADINs therefore allow a select group of political actors to challenge the constitutionality of a given federal or state law directly at the STF.[13] Given the direct access to the STF provided by the ADIN, it is in theory a powerful instrument for quickly pausing or reversing the implementation of policy, with no possibility of further appeal. ADINs challenge federal laws that have been passed by the executive branch (such as provisional measures), by Congress (such as constitutional amendments), and by the courts (such as court administrative decrees). Although ADINs have also been filed to cut off congressional deliberation, for the most part, STF jurisprudence suggests that ADINs cannot be successfully filed until the law in question has been approved.[14] This means that ADINs largely challenge policies at the moment of implementation: a policy must have been formulated and adopted by legislation before it can be challenged by an ADIN.

To reiterate, ADINs are of great interest because they are heard (relatively) rapidly, meaning that it is possible to analyze their effects on policy between 1988 and 2002, with few cases pending; because they may be brought by a wide but nonetheless restricted range of political actors; because their effects are universally binding and cannot be appealed; and because they are brought with the express intent of influencing policy. But to what extent is the ADIN an effective instrument for contesting policy? And is it equally effective for all plaintiffs with standing? The model that follows addresses both questions.

THE 'ADIN' INJUNCTION MODEL

Ruling on an ADIN offers two somewhat independent chances of thwarting a law: either through a temporary injunction, or through a decision on the merit. First, the plaintiff may file for a temporary injunction (*medida cautelar* or *liminar*), seeking to suspend a law or portion of a law until the full STF has a chance to discuss its constitutionality.[15] Second, in all cases, the plaintiff seeks a decision from the full STF that the "merit" of the ADIN is correct, that is, that the law (or portion of the law) in question is unconstitutional. A ruling in favor of the plaintiff on the injunction temporarily suspends the implementation of the law (or portion of the law); a ruling in the plaintiff's favor on the merit strikes the law (or portion of the law) from the books.[16]

The chances of the injunction or the merit of the ADIN being upheld by the STF are low: of the cases decided to date, 76 percent of injunction requests have been denied, and 89 percent of ADINs have been denied on merit grounds. But because most ADINs are brought requesting both decisions, the two decisions add up to a more-than-one-in-five chance of derailing a given federal law.[17]

Thinking in purely cost-benefit terms, these are not long odds for a political actor contemplating an ADIN. The legal costs are low, limited to legal fees and the risk of having a law's constitutionality upheld. While the latter may seem highly consequential, it is often not, as ADINs are often filed after all possible remedies in the executive and legislative branches have been exhausted. These relatively minimal potential costs are usually counterbalanced by the large potential rewards. In light of the possibility that the implementation of the policy may have high costs to a political actor's core constituency, these benefits include either the political benefits from thwarting policy implementation or, even when unsuccessful, being seen as taking the battle forward on another front. As Werneck Vianna et al. express this second benefit (as it applies to political parties), use of the judiciary permits policy players to stake a claim, "establishing a position against the majority and expressing to [the political party's] adherents and the public in general the [party's] disposition to exhaust, in the institutional environment, all the possibilities open for intervention" (1999, 127; translation mine).

Two possible models could be constructed to analyze the ADIN: one focusing on injunction decisions and one focusing on merit decisions. The model here focuses on the former because injunctions in ADIN cases frequently cause changes in the underlying legislation before the merit decision is reached, and are thus often more definitive in their effects than the merit decision itself. Second, partly as a result of the importance of injunctions, fewer merit decisions have been made over the course of time, and because of delays in hearings on the merit, the underlying legislation is oftentimes altered in such a way that the merit decision does not ultimately lead to major *post hoc* effects on policy. Finally, given my focus on political—rather than legal—effects, the injunction decision is often more important because of its effectiveness, which causes the immediate delay or the cancellation of policy implementation.

The model is a binary logistic regression, which predicts likelihoods for a dichotomous dependent variable, the yes-no decision on whether or not to grant an injunction. The independent variables are as follows:

Plaintiff. This variable tests whether the identity of the plaintiff affects the likelihood of a favorable decision. State actors—which include state governments and the *Ministério Público*—may be more likely than other plaintiffs to obtain a victory on an ADIN, given the great legal and administrative resources available to them. Political parties may be less likely to win, given the fact that they may use the courts not only for legal purposes, but also to highlight their displeasure or disagreement to constituents even when legal success seems a long shot. Figure 4.1 illustrates the distribution of plaintiffs in federal ADIN cases.

Topic. The descriptive data suggest that certain topics, such as social security reform, are more likely to engender constitutional review cases than are others, such as budget laws. This degree of contentiousness was measured by comparing the difference between the distribution of laws and the distribution of ADIN challenges, by topic.[18] If the proportion of ADINs filed in a certain issue area were equal to the proportion of laws in that issue area, this would suggest an amount of legal contestation roughly equivalent to the amount of legislating on this topic. The topic that comes closest to this point is taxation (−1 percent). A greater proportion of ADINs filed than

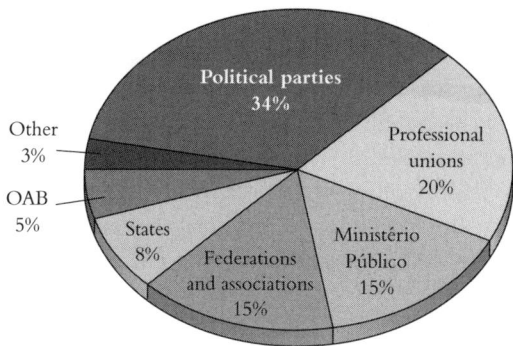

Figure 4.1. ADINs filed against federal laws, by plaintiff, 1988–2002
NOTES: The "States" category includes all three branches of government at the state level. The "Other" category includes individuals and municipal governments, neither of which has the legal standing to bring ADIN cases, but nonetheless attempted to do so in these cases.

laws passed in a certain issue area suggests a generally contentious subject, as was the case of social security (+48 percent) and economic regulatory laws (+119 percent). A smaller proportion of ADINs filed than laws passed in a certain issue area suggests a subject that is less legally contested via ADIN, as in the case of budget laws (−87 percent), privatization (−40 percent), and electoral and political rules (−17 percent).

Law Type. I hypothesize that the type of legislation affects the likelihood of a successful constitutional challenge. Legislation such as amendments to the Constitution, which require strong super-majorities, undergoes more significant deliberation than more easily approved legislation, such as ministerial decrees. The likelihood of constitutional challenges is expected to decrease as the requirement for deliberation increases; further, greater deliberation would presumably nip many constitutional issues in the bud (see Chapter 3, footnote 13 for greater detail on the procedures for approval of each type of legislation).

Legal Professional Group Dummy. This is a dichotomous variable that denotes whether the plaintiff is a legal professional organization or association, such as the Brazilian Bar Association (OAB), the Association of Brazilian Magistrates (AMB), or the National Association of Members of the *Ministério Público* (CONAMP). The legal professions accounted for 10.5 percent of all ADINs against federal laws.[19] I exclude the *Ministério Publico* itself from this variable, because the *Ministério Público* is often acting at the behest of outside actors, rather than in an attempt to advance its own corporatist interests (in which case its members might act through the CONAMP). My hypothesis, drawing on several prominent cases (including those described in earlier chapters), is that plaintiffs associated with the legal profession have a greater chance of successfully challenging the constitutionality of a law. They may not be any more familiar with the law than other plaintiffs (who have their own lawyers, after all), but given that their legal reputation is on the line, and that any challenge on constitutional grounds will require internal consensus, they may more thoroughly vet the questions they take to court.

Administration. This variable refers to the administration in office at the time the challenged law was passed. It broadly tests the role of court attitudes, questioning whether the identity of the presidential administration that passes the law being challenged has any effect on the willingness of the STF to uphold the constitutionality of the law. As noted in Chapter 2, individual judges' attitudes would seem on the face of it to explain little between 1988 and 2002. But perhaps the court had an especially touchy relationship with a particular incumbent: the most obvious potential example is that of political outsider President Collor, whose relation with the court was extremely contentious, and thus might lead to a greater likelihood of his administration's laws being overturned, other things equal.

SUMMARY OF MODEL FINDINGS

I briefly list here the key results for each of the independent variables, shown in Table 4.1, before turning to some broader conclusions.

Some *plaintiffs* are far more likely to obtain a favorable injunction decision than others, with state actors at the top of the pecking order. Professional unions are only 18.6 percent as likely as state actors to win an injunction; political parties only 25 percent as likely, other things equal. Commercial and industrial federations are slightly more successful, with approximately 58 percent the success rate of state actors.

The *topic* of the law being challenged affects the likelihood of obtaining a favorable injunction decision, with laws governing judicial benefits and structure far more likely to be successfully challenged than any others. The results suggest two groups of probabilities. Cases dealing with civil service, fiscal relations, taxation, other economic issues, and the "other" category are between a third and two-fifths as likely to result in a successful injunction request as judicial legislation. Cases dealing with social security and electoral and political rules are even less likely to result in an injunction, with chances of obtaining an injunction between one-sixth and one-quarter the likelihood of cases in the judicial group.

TABLE 4.1

Regression results for injunction decisions

	Odds[a]	Significance[b]
Plaintiff (Requerente)	—	(.0000)★★
State actors	—	—
Commercial, industrial federations	.5761	(.094)★
Political parties	.2543	(.0000)★★
Professional unions[c]	.1860	(.0000)★★
Topic	—	(.0025)★★
Judicial benefits/structure	—	—
Civil service	.3799	(.0039)★★
Fiscal relations	.3982	(.0247)★★
Taxation	.3333	(.0037)★★
Social security	.2227	(.0067)★★
Other economic	.3395	(.0026)★★
Electoral or political	.1667	(.0002)★★
Other	.3131	(.0006)★★
Law type	—	(.0103)★★
Executive decree	—	—
Constitutional amendment	.9232	(.8947)
Complementary law	1.6550	(.4215)
Ordinary law	**2.1387**	(.0371)★★
Provisional measure	1.1986	(.6410)
Nonexecutive	**2.8404**	(.0071)★★
Legal dummy	—	—
Not legal	—	—
Legal	**2.6096**	(.0014)★★
Administration	—	(.6805)
Sarney	—	—
Collor	1.3558	(.4939)
Franco	1.3250	(.5459)
Cardoso I	1.2422	(.6201)
Cardoso II	1.7881	(.2104)
Model Chi-Square	171.187	(.0000)
Hosmer Lemeshow Test	11.4057	(.1798)
	Constant:	B: −0.3723
		Sign: .4804
	K–S Z[d]	41.3% (.000)
	N	773

NOTES: ★Significant at the 10% level.

★★Significant at the 5% level.

[a] Odds are calculated as Exp (B), or e^B.

[b] Significance is the statistical significance for each category. The significance listed for each category is the variable significance.

[c] Includes OAB.

[d] Kolmogorov-Smirnov Z, most extreme differences reported.

Law type, or the means by which a law is implemented, has only a slight effect on the likelihood of a favorable decision. Although this initially seemed like the strongest hypothesis, the model suggests that *ceteris paribus,* law type as an indication of the amount of deliberation and the size of majorities does not offer a clear-cut explanation of decisions. Indeed, for the one statistically significant category of executive laws, the evidence runs counter to my hypothesis: ordinary laws, which require far more deliberation than executive measures, are roughly twice as likely to face successful injunction challenges as executive decrees. Decrees issued by either Congress or the judiciary are 1.8 times more likely to face successful injunction requests than decrees by the executive branch.

Plaintiffs associated with *legal professional groups* are 1.6 times as likely to obtain injunctions as other plaintiffs. The legal dummy variable is statistically significant and suggests that members of the legal community do better using the ADIN mechanism than do other plaintiffs.

Finally, there is no statistically significant result illustrating bias against particular *presidential administrations* in terms of the success of injunction challenges to their laws.

Equivalence across legal cases is impossible to establish here, and the results are backward-looking, detailing the results of legal tactics adopted under very specific political conditions. But a hypothetical example may provide readers a better intuitive grasp of the predicted probabilities in the model. If, other things equal, the National Industrial Confederation (CNI) were to challenge a federal tax on industry, it would be less than 60 percent as likely to succeed as a state institution such as the prosecutor-general, and it would have only one-third the chance of success in obtaining an injunction as it would if it were instead challenging a decree on judicial benefits. In contrast, a professional union challenging a tax on its professional activities would be only 20 percent as likely to succeed in obtaining an injunction as the state institution (or a third as likely to succeed as the national industrial confederation). But, if for some reason that professional union was representative of the legal professions, its chances of winning that injunction against the tax on its professional activities would almost double, all else equal.

A few broader findings and research questions emerge from the model and its results.

Majority-Minority Conflict. A first insight concerning the judicialization of politics at the federal level emerges from the descriptive data collected, rather than the regression itself. The executive branch is named as defendant or codefendant in four out of five cases, and is thus the main target of ADINs at the federal level. Plaintiffs are predominantly from outside the political majority, rather than from other branches of government. Political parties file more than one-third of all federal ADINs, and of these, 90 percent are filed by opposition parties. Professional associations file another one-fifth of ADINs: of these, 60 percent are filed by professional unions with public sector ties, who were frequently allied with opposition parties during the period analyzed (1988–2002).

Constitutional conflict at the federal level, then, is not between branches of government; it is largely between majority and minority coalitions in the legislative and executive branches. This is significant, especially in light of the effective marginalization of minorities in the exclusive process of executive-legislative deliberations, described by Amorim Neto et al. (2003) and others. The ADIN mechanism at the STF offered a venue for the opposition to voice its claims and attempt to thwart federal policies it disagreed with, especially when it was excluded earlier in the deliberative process. Although success rates varied considerably by plaintiff, even the worst performers achieved some important successes, driving continued use of the mechanism.

Importance of the Legal Profession. The regression results highlight the existence of a potential veto player that has received little attention in other works on Brazilian politics: legal professional groups (a category that includes the professional organizations of lawyers, judges, and prosecutors). As the models illustrate, *ceteris paribus,* legal professional associations are far better at using the courts than are other groups, with nearly twice the likelihood of winning an injunction. The ADIN offers a veto point to the legal professions that is not available to them in the executive branch, and is less accessible and more costly to them in the legislative branch. The legal profession emerges more clearly in this context as an influential veto player, capacitated by its legal enfranchisement to use the veto point generated by the ADIN injunction mechanism. Among the various legal interest groups, the OAB in particular has been an active filer of ADINs, accounting for a plurality (46 percent) of ADINs filed by the legal professions, and 5 percent of all ADINs against federal laws. It has been especially successful in using injunctions to delay (sometimes permanently) the implementation of policies that hurt lawyers' interests, whether it was in limits on lawyers' fees, rules that would have delayed the payment of judicial debts, or changes in judicial and legal regulations. Without its standing to use the ADIN, the OAB would have had no privileged forum from which to press such interests. And without the threat of the ADIN, it is likely that the OAB's opinions elsewhere in the policy process would not have been given so much prominence.

Deliberation, Voice, and Court Use.   Contrary to my initial hypothesis, there is little relationship between the amount of deliberation a law receives and the success of ADINs. This conclusion knocks down any suggestion that—other things equal—the STF views the use of provisional measures as inherently more arbitrary or less constitutional than the use of other forms of legislation, representing a usurpation of power by the executive branch. It also suggests that the degree of deliberation received by a law does not ensure immunity from constitutional challenge, with the courts used regardless to press the preferences of minorities that lose in executive and legislative branch deliberations.

A second form of deliberation may also be at work here. In analyzing specific ADINs, I found considerable anecdotal evidence (which is not explicitly substantiated by the model here but is further discussed in the coming chapter) that both political parties and lower court judges may use the ADIN mechanism as an instrument of voice. Political parties in the minority—largely shut out of the political process in the elected branches—used the STF as a site for further deliberation on the merits of policy. Legal remedies, in other words, were not political parties' sole objective when they used the courts. Judges, meanwhile, were frequent losers in ADIN cases filed by the *Ministério Público* to contest lower court judges' self-decreed wage increases. The model shows that court administrative decrees are the most successfully challenged of all laws, with the chances of being suspended by injunction always more than twice as high as the chance of a successful injunction request against an executive or legislative decree. Speculating beyond the model's results, one might question why it is that judges—who are no doubt highly cognizant of the judicial process and the success or failure of past judicial decrees—might continue to push through administrative decisions they know are likely to be overturned. Although the model provides no direct evidence, one possibility is that in the absence of other forms of expression (other than voicing their concerns to the media, a venue where they were quite active), judges used court administrative decrees as one step in the policy game, in the hopes of influencing future policy decisions on judicial benefits.

Court Attitudes.   Finally, I find that the STF does not appear to have a significant bias in its constitutionality rulings for or against any particular presidential administration. The model tested whether the laws passed by any presidential administration were more likely, other things equal, to be considered unconstitutional. No such relationship was found, suggesting the STF has not exhibited any overarching political preferences regarding the occupant of the executive branch. The lack of a clear bias in favor of a particular incumbent contrasts with experiences elsewhere in Latin America, where elected officials have made various attempts to pack high courts (such as Peru under Fujimori, Argentina under Menem, and Venezuela under Chavez) and judges can be more clearly linked to the interests and ideologies of the president appointing them.

Conclusion

This chapter has emphasized why standing to bring ADINs provides a privileged venue within the overall judicial system, and how access to the veto point offered by the ADIN may increase the leverage of specific policy actors who might otherwise have little voice in the policy process.

To reiterate briefly, despite its impressive institutional strength, the Brazilian federal judiciary operates in an institutional framework that tends to delay clear, universally binding policy decisions. The ADIN mechanism of constitutional review, however, enables a select group of specific policy actors to contest policies in an expedited and broadly applicable manner directly at Brazil's highest court, thus avoiding the delays facing ordinary citizens contesting policy. Once there, plaintiffs have a roughly one in five chance of altering policy, although as the model shows, some actors—especially state actors and legal actors—are better at it than others. The ADIN veto point provides these groups with greater potential leverage over federal policies than they would otherwise have; this leverage may be used either in the courts or earlier in the policy process via an implicit threat to exercise such a veto. The rules governing standing are therefore essential to determining the course of policymaking and policy outcomes. I conclude with a brief heuristic example, based on the case of agrarian reform discussed in the previous chapter, which may better illustrate the significance of the ADIN mechanism as a veto point.

During its second term, the Cardoso administration sought to find some middle ground between the interests of landowners and the landless movement, a process culminating in passage of an agrarian reform bill by provisional measure. The bill fought excessive compensation in expropriation proceedings but also set important restrictions on the ability of the landless movement to seize land. Simplifying for the sake of argument,[20] it is clear that by and large, landowners would have preferred more restrictions on land seizures and fewer restrictions on compensation for expropriation; the landless movement would have preferred the exact opposite; and the government would have preferred more restrictions on both seizures and on compensation, as shown in Figure 4.2. In other words, it should have been possible to shift policy anywhere within the shaded sliver SQ_1:SQ_2, and, especially, to move from SQ_1 to a position closer to the government's core preferences, at SQ_2. That was the essence of the government's proposal, implemented by provisional measure.

Missing in the process of policy formulation was acknowledgment of a fourth interested party, the OAB. When the provisional measure was decreed, the OAB immediately moved to contest various elements of the new policy via ADIN. It was successful on one point of supreme interest to lawyers: voiding caps on the honoraria payable to lawyers in expropriation hearings. As a result, the OAB was successfully able to shift the policy outcome from SQ_2 to SQ_3, moving the resulting policy away from the government's core preferences and closer to its own (shown in Figure 4.3). Without the veto point provided by the ADIN mechanism, such an outcome would not have been possible, and the OAB would not have been empowered as a veto player in this policy arena.

The notion that institutional rules may enable potential policy actors to exercise a veto or partial veto over policies in which they might otherwise have little or no leverage is very revealing, illustrating how veto points in the judiciary may influence both the policy process and the very identity of key policy players. In the process of discussing veto points and veto players, however, I hope that I have also illustrated why the judiciary needs to be more fully incorporated into studies of the broader course of policy deliberation in Brazil, both to explain actual policy outcomes and to illuminate our understanding of the full gamut of veto players involved in policy deliberations. Even if, as in the example here, the judiciary is assumed to have

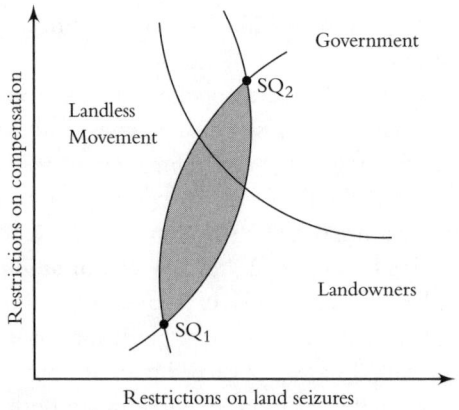

Figure 4.2.   Agrarian reform measure

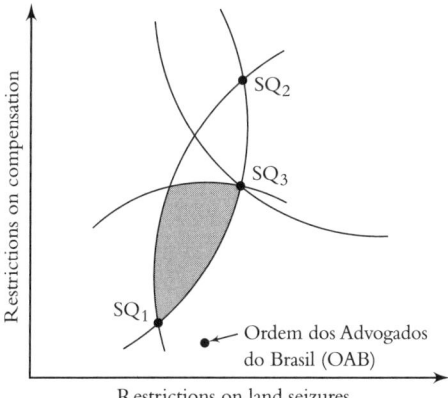

Figure 4.3.   Agrarian reform outcome

no preferences of its own, it may offer veto points that are particularly relevant to other policy actors who may in fact become veto players through their use of the court system.

The logic of this chapter can be applied far beyond the Brazilian case, to the potentially disparate effect of courts and other institutions on policy outcomes in various historical or geographical settings. By identifying significant veto points in the broader political system that provide an alternative venue for policy contestation, researchers may be able to identify political actors who, like the Brazilian legal profession, are not immediately apparent as important policy players in most analyses of policymaking, but whose absence would leave our analysis of policy choice incomplete. This insight will be further examined, with special emphasis on the role of courts in comparative perspective, in Chapter 7.

Before that, however, I turn back to the plaintiffs themselves, once again taking up the issue of how policy opponents' legal tactics fit into their broader political strategies. As the results of the model here show, political parties are among the worst of the players with standing to bring the ADIN, yet they are also its most frequent users, accounting for more than a third of all ADINs at the federal level. At the other extreme, the OAB is fairly economical in its use of the ADIN, but also far more successful. The next two chapters look more closely at the larger political strategies that motivate such different tactical use of the federal judiciary, both in constitutional review cases and in the lower courts.

Chapter 5

Judicial Contestation of Policy: Political Parties

It should by now be evident that the full federal court system—including, but not limited to the high court—is frequently used by a variety of actors to advance their policy and political objectives. This chapter and the next look at the use of the courts by two very different group plaintiffs with an interest in policy issues: opposition political parties, exemplified by the Workers' Party (PT) during the Cardoso administration and then by the PFL and PSDB during the Lula administration; and organized professional interest groups, exemplified by the *Ordem dos Advogados do Brasil* (OAB). The two chapters inquire into the motivations for court use by these plaintiffs, and in particular, how the tactical use of the full federal court system fits into their broader political strategies.

Courts, like other political institutions, are helpful in pursuing not only the goals of veto but also goals of voice. In pursuing a veto, political actors may use tactics that either attempt to delay policy implementation or seek to disable policy entirely. In pursuing voice, political actors may seek either to publicly declare their opposition to policy or to attempt to discredit policy on a variety of grounds. But the tactics that are used to achieve these objectives will vary considerably from group to group, and when the venue being used to pursue these tactics is the courts, much will depend on the specific opportunities afforded by the judicial institutional environment.

In keeping with the framework of legal tactical choice outlined in Chapter 2, I argue here that the salience of policy is essential to determining whether or not policy will be carried into the courts. But I seek in these two chapters to understand how organized political actors' determination of the salience of policy is shaped by these groups' own interests and ideas.

Second, these chapters look at how organized political actors' ideas and interests are mediated by institutional structure, and especially how institutional structure shapes the legal tactics they use in the service of broader political strategies. Two types of institutional structure are relevant here: the internal structure of the organized groups themselves and the structure of the court system. The first helps to determine both how strategic objectives are determined and how tactical choices are selected, while the second helps to determine which legal tactics are feasible alternatives. This chapter investigates the use of the courts by an eminently political actor, opposition political parties. Given the fact that the ideas and interests of political parties are publicly established through electoral competition, this chapter primarily addresses the influence of court structure on the tactical use of the courts. The next chapter reverses the emphasis, focusing on how internal structure mediates the amorphous interests and ideas that shape the OAB's policy and political preferences.

Together, both chapters illustrate that the activation of courts to policy ends is far more complex than commonly assumed. Legal tactics go far beyond the common focus on high courts alone. Judicial review in the high court is not always the best tactical option for policy opponents, nor are constitutional challenges the sole or even main legal instrument used by policy opponents. To reiterate an earlier point, obtaining a judicial veto of policy is not the only objective sought out by these actors: *courts can be effective political venues even when judicial review does not lead to legal victory.*

With that in mind, I turn now to a study of the tactical use of the courts by the PT while in opposition. The second section contrasts this with the PT's experience as an incumbent, and offers some speculative suggestions about which tactics of opposition may continue, and which may have been *sui generis* to the Workers' Party in opposition. Chapter 6 will explore the case of the OAB, concluding with a comparison of the two groups' choices of legal tactics.

The PT in Opposition

The Workers' Party was the largest and most vocal opposition party in Brazil from the early days of the New Republic until the inauguration of President Luis Inácio "Lula" da Silva in January 2003. The party was founded in 1980 (as the military regime loosened controls over political parties) from a broad "hodgepodge" of leftist groups espousing various shades of liberation theology, left-wing Catholic community activism, Marxism, and socialism. Its electoral constituencies were equally broad, including disparate groups such as academics, industrial workers, and members of the federal and state civil services. Yet despite the party's broad internal composition, it proved to be one of the most disciplined of Brazil's notoriously fragmented political parties: the party routinely adopted strong and largely unwavering party-line positions, after substantial internal debate on the major issues of the day. The PT unsuccessfully ran the popular São Paulo union leader "Lula" as its presidential candidate in three failed electoral bids before he won the presidency in 2002, after a substantive strategic shift by the PT toward more moderate, centrist policy stances (Samuels 2004). But in the intervening period, the PT consistently expanded its electoral representation and played a significant role as Brazil's leading voice of regime-loyal opposition.

Despite its prominence in the opposition, however, the PT remained a minority in Congress throughout the period, never electing more than 12 percent of the Chamber of Deputies. Although the party elected a steadily increasing number of deputies and senators (as well as mayors and governors) throughout the 1990s, the party and its allies never gained control of either house of Congress or the presidency before the election of 2002, nor did it join any of the pro-government legislative coalitions.[1] As a result, despite its vociferousness, the party was largely excluded from the development of the federal public policy agenda for the fifteen years following the writing of the 1988 Constitution. Use of the courts thus became an essential tactic in the PT's overall political strategy as an opposition party.

The *Partido dos Trabalhadores* and its members were active plaintiffs in the federal court system throughout the two-term Cardoso administration (1995–1998; 1999–2002). Although the party *per se* is only formally listed as a plaintiff in cases referred to the Supreme Federal Tribunal, my analysis of legal cases filed by key national leaders of the PT, lawyers associated with the PT, and PT members of the Chamber of Deputies and the Senate shows that the party also actively used the lower-level federal courts to contest policies during this period. Members of the party filed suit, for example, to challenge the Cardoso government's agreements with the IMF; to question supposed electoral use of the budget; and for seemingly less relevant issues, such as one PT congresswoman's suit against the finance minister, challenging a change in the methodology by which public deficit figures were aggregated. The Cardoso administration was cognizant of, and highly frustrated by, the opposition's use of the courts. Three hours before he was to be sworn in as a minister of the Supreme Federal Tribunal, Cardoso's former attorney general, Gilmar Mendes, publicly criticized the opposition's use of the courts as an outcome of a "spurious and antidemocratic culture originating from the totalitarian ideology of certain political currents . . . " (Freitas and Suwwan 2002; translation mine).

The PT's resort to the courts was often defended in purely countermajoritarian terms. The PT argued that its use of the courts was the typical recourse of a minority against the government's "tractor that overruns the opposition" in the Congress, and an expedient against the "fury of destruction of the Constitution" by the pro-government congressional alliance (Freitas 1997a). But the PT's use of the courts was also driven by a broader political strategy, grounded in firm opposition to the Cardoso coalition and its policy priorities of "neoliberal" reform.

In this broad strategy, courts became a tactical locus for further public debate, and their use was aimed at keeping policy choices in the public eye. After the Cardoso social security reform passed Congress in 1998, the chief PT leader in the Chamber noted, "The reform left the Chamber plenary, and will now cross the Plaza of the Three Powers [which divides the buildings housing the STF, the presidential offices, and the Congress] to be debated in the Supreme Court" (Madueño 1998, translation mine). A PT staff member told me that the party "used the courts in the way that best suited it," constrained only by the desire to make sure it did not get a bad reputation in legal circles that might jeopardize its continued resort to the judiciary. Otherwise the party did "anything [it could] to disable" policies it disagreed with (author interview).[2]

The tactical goals driving the PT's political use of the courts are best understood from the perspective of the party's overall strategic interest in halting policies it disagreed with; complicating the Cardoso administration's implementation of policy; and increasing its own political standing, both at a national and subnational level. In using the courts, the PT sought both veto and voice, through four tactical goals that aimed to do the following:

1. *Declare* the PT's opposition to policy and highlight the potential repercussions of policy to members of the public, as well as to the PT's members and constituents (in Portuguese, interviewees described these as *mostrar serviço* and *mostrar seriedade*)
2. *Delay* a policy's implementation through injunction or appeal
3. *Disable* policy through successful challenges that partially or totally rescinded the laws underpinning policy initiatives
4. *Discredit* policies through allegations of impropriety, as well as by sowing uncertainty about the possibility of implementation

The federal court system offered the Workers' Party many different institutional alternatives for achieving these goals. The four most widely used

are described in turn in the following text. It is worth noting, however, that
these are not the only instruments the PT used in the court system, and that
the various tactics were often employed in tandem, as part of a broader political strategy.

THE DIRECT ACTION OF UNCONSTITUTIONALITY (ADIN)

The most prominent legal instrument employed by the PT during the Cardoso presidency was the direct action of unconstitutionality (ADIN), which
offered political parties the possibility of delaying or permanently disabling
policy directly at the Supreme Federal Tribunal (STF).[3] Of the four approaches discussed here, the ADIN is the only one in which the PT party
leadership formally centralized the decision to resort to the courts. Most
ADINs were prepared by the PT congressional delegation's lawyers at the
request of leading party members, prior to being formally approved by the
PT's executive directorate and signed by the party president.

The PT was a plaintiff in 130 ADINs against the federal government during the Cardoso administration, bringing more than one ADIN a month, on
average, and accounting for nearly 1 in every 4 ADINs filed against the federal government during the period. As Figure 5.1 shows, the PT was also by

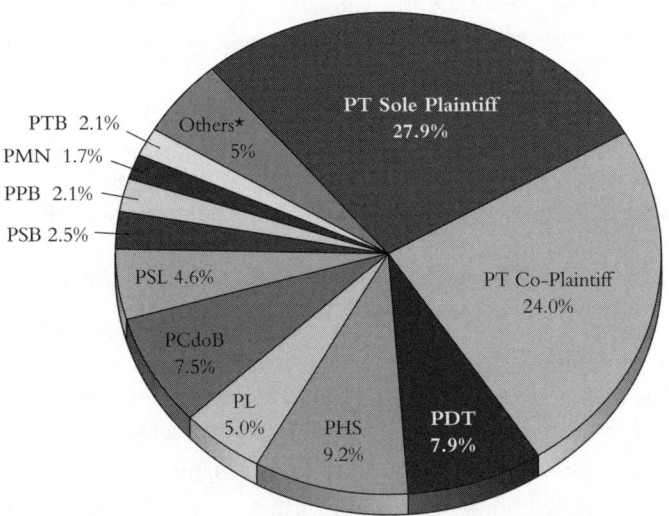

Figure 5.1. ADINs filed by political parties, 1995–2002
NOTE: The "Others" category includes the PMDB, PST, and PFL (two ADINs each),
as well as one ADIN filed by each of the following parties: PPS, PSTU, PPR, PSC,
PSDC, PTN, and PV.
SOURCE: Data are from the Supreme Federal Tribunal.

far the most active political party in bringing ADIN requests during the Cardoso presidency, appearing as a plaintiff or co-plaintiff in more than half of all constitutional challenges brought by political parties.[4]

The PT brought ADINs across a wide range of subject matter, but three subjects were responsible for 40 percent of its constitutional challenges during the Cardoso presidency: civil service matters, social security matters, and issues of denationalization and privatization. These topics were clearly ones in which a key PT constituency—often the civil service—was significantly affected. They blended contentious legal and political considerations over the justifiability and sustainability of rights granted in the 1988 Constitution, often described by advocates of the Cardoso administration as "unsustainable" while defended by the PT as "acquired rights" (*direitos adquiridos*). All of the laws in these contested topics had been passed in Congress or by executive provisional measures, despite significant PT opposition.

The PT's use of the ADIN was driven by a combination of the tactical objectives described at the outset. First, use of the ADIN was rapid, and widely reported in the press, generating considerable fanfare and drawing a line in the sand, making it clear that the PT had declared its opposition to the policy and was fighting it on all available fronts. Second, the ADIN offered not unreasonable chances to delay policy implementation. Although the party did less well than other plaintiffs in the ADIN game, it nonetheless obtained injunctions that delayed policy implementation in roughly one of seven injunctions it filed (as opposed to one in five injunctions in all ADINs against federal legislation filed during the same period).

The PT was successful in disabling policy by winning on the merit of the ADIN only three times during this period, making it less than a third as likely to win as other plaintiffs, on average. But the simple fact of filing an ADIN cast doubts on government policies, perhaps not discrediting them entirely but certainly generating doubts about implementation and keeping the topic in the public eye. Queried about why the PT had a much worse success rate on ADINs than the Brazilian Bar Association (OAB), one party staff member noted the importance of keeping policy under question: "[we] sought to create a political fact, generate an issue and a debate" (author interview).

The motivation for filing an ADIN, in other words, was not only legal contestation; the filing also aimed to get the issue—and the PT—into public debate. The relatively good chances of obtaining an injunction, and the doubts raised by a pending decision on an ADIN's merit, also helped to slow policy implementation in some cases. Meanwhile, despite lower-than-average success rates, members of the PT noted that the party was not the main watchdog of constitutionality. The party picked its fights, and allowed

(and sometimes encouraged) the *Ministério Público* and other plaintiffs to file
ADINs in cases of more obvious constitutional infringements. Together these
factors may explain the party's poor success rates on the more contentious
policy issues it took to court on its own, since there is no reason to believe
that the PT's lawyers would be less (or, for that matter, more) legally capable
than other plaintiff's lawyers.

THE AÇÃO POPULAR (AP)

A second popular instrument for political use of the courts was the *Ação
Popular* (AP), which party members used frequently—sometimes with some
national coordination by party lawyers and staffers, but most often not—to
challenge federal policies in lower courts. The AP originated in the 1934
Constitution, was written into law in 1965 by the military regime, but then
was broadened in the 1988 Constitution as a means of democratizing challenges to the government: under the current rules, "any citizen . . . can propose [an] *Ação Popular* which seeks to annul an act that is harmful to the
public patrimony . . . to administrative morality, to the environment and to
historical and cultural patrimony" (Brasil 1988; I, 5, LXXIII). Filing an AP
is free and can be proposed with virtually any evidence available; although
the Constitution includes a phrase prohibiting "bad-faith" litigation, in practice, APs have frequently been hastily assembled as a means of driving rapid
consideration of the laws or policies at hand.

The AP was widely used by members of political parties because unlike any
other legal instrument, it offered a chance for opponents to obtain an injunction against the president in lower court, with no special privileges of standing
for the president or his staff. Although members of the PT filed APs throughout the federal court system, in most cases in which the subject was federal
policy, the APs were filed in the first regional judicial district of Brasília.

Although the PT's lawyers accompanied the progress of key *Ações Popu-
lares* filed by party members around Brazil, the decision to file an AP is far
more individual or local than the decision to file an ADIN. There is no strict
constitutional rule requiring party acquiescence (unlike the ADIN, which
required the signature of the party president), and the PT itself had no formal rules governing the filing of APs by party members. The PT's use of
APs thus typically represented more specific individual interests and ideas,
but inasmuch as these conformed to the policy preferences of the party as a
whole, they were frequently representative of PT objectives, if not always of
centrally orchestrated or party-approved tactics.

Thus, for example, of a sample of twenty-two APs filed in Brasília by PT
members between 1995 and 2002, the topic matter conformed highly with

PT political goals and the subject matter of other PT legal challenges: nine of the APs sought to halt privatization proceedings; seven accused the Cardoso administration of administrative malfeasance (*improbidade administrativa*); four sought to reverse Cardoso civil service measures; and two challenged the government's alleged abuse of public coffers for allegedly electoral purposes (data provided by interviewees).

Although injunctions in APs were often rapidly forthcoming, the merit of APs was unlikely to be settled as quickly and definitively as it was in ADINs, and the decision on either the injunction or the merit in APs often resulted in repeated appeals. The result was that the primary political use of APs was as a means of reiterating policy preferences and policy opposition, as well as discrediting administration policies, rather than as a means of delaying or disabling policy implementation. Another downside to the AP was the fact that APs were sometimes "lost in the shuffle"; because they are filed in lower courts, unless an injunction against a prominent policy was granted, the AP had little news value and could easily and quickly fall from the public eye.

But the benefit of APs over constitutional challenges by ADIN was that they enabled party members to challenge the means by which policy was being implemented, without the need to contest specific legislation (as in the case of ADINs). They would be particularly useful in challenging privatization proceedings, which (once the legal framework behind the National Privatization Program, or PND, had been created) were undertaken more by administrative means than by national law, meaning that privatization was almost impossible to challenge in the high court. And, as the next section argues, the AP could be a useful tool when applied in combination with other instruments as part of a broader legal strategy, creating the impression of a significant wellspring of popular opposition when filed in tandem across the lower courts.

BROAD-BASED LOWER COURT EFFORTS

The PT leadership occasionally took advantage of the "atomized" nature of the lower courts (Arantes 1997) to file broad-based judicial challenges to key policies. In what one observer has termed *guerilha jurídica*, or juridical guerilla warfare (Sadek 1999a, 298), this tactic sought to generate a wave of legal challenges, employing a variety of case types, across the lower tier of the judiciary. The goal was threefold: first, to create a political "happening" that would draw attention to the policy being questioned and the breadth of opposition to it; second, to attempt to generate such broad-based court challenges that the government would find it hard to defend against all of the challenges in a timely fashion; and third, by "pulverizing [challenges] to the utmost," to increase the likelihood of drawing a sympathetic judge in at least one of the many cases filed (author interview).

These "pulverized" legal onslaughts, in other words, played a numbers game. Any case going before a lower court is randomly assigned to a judge who will decide whether to grant an injunction (if applicable) and whether or not the court should rule on the merit of the case.[5] Any number of factors might determine a lower court judge's decision to counteract a Cardoso government policy: agreement with the plaintiff's legal argument, sympathy with the plaintiff's political objectives, a desire to grandstand in the press, pique with Cardoso administration positions regarding judicial salaries and benefits, or some combination of all of the above. Further, an individual judge in the lower courts has considerable decision-making leeway, as Chapter 2 noted, because of the formal and informal norms governing the judiciary. The weakness of hierarchical administrative controls and the considerable room for differences across judges in different regions of the federal courts mean that different judges, acting under different circumstances, may well come to different interpretations of the same combination of case and law.[6] By spreading challenges across the various regions of the full federal judiciary, the PT increased the odds of hitting on a judge who might rule in the party's favor. Second, given that the average lower court judge was more likely than higher court judges to share at least some of the PT's programmatic views (and, perhaps, opposition to Cardoso policies), resort to the lower courts boosted the chances of obtaining at least a temporary legal victory.

A good example of the use of this tactic was the PT's challenge to the Cardoso administration's electricity rationing program, implemented by provisional measure in May 2001 (and described in Chapter 3). The PT was very active in opposing the provisional measure: party members spoke out against the rationing on the floor of Congress, criticized it on editorial pages, and also turned to legal action. The PT legal staff in Brasília drew up a draft suit against the provisional measure, which was distributed widely among supporters and allies throughout Brazil. The result was a groundswell of suits, numbering in the hundreds, many of which "mirrored" the PT's lawsuit. Within a month, there were nearly two hundred suits pending against the law, and more than a fifth resulted in an injunction.

In sum, just as it had during various privatization proceedings and would again when a new tax on electricity consumption was imposed in 2002, the PT attempted to use broad-ranging legal challenges to complicate the implementation of the rationing policy of 2001. By doing so, it simultaneously managed to declare its opposition and to delay and discredit a crucial Cardoso administration policy. While it did not fully disable the policy, it was able to use the broad challenges to raise public debate about the rationing, draw attention to its potentially unequal effects, and score a few points against its main political opponent.

Interestingly, the PT was forced into a new strategy regarding electricity rationing in June 2001, when the miniscule *Partido Social Liberal* (PSL, with one congressional representative) filed an ADIN against the government's measures. At this point, although PT staff members would have preferred to wait for the groundswell of broad court cases to grow, the party decided to file its own ADIN (author interview). If it had not filed an ADIN, the PT-inspired wave of favorable lower court decisions would probably have been abruptly undercut by a decision from the STF. Filing an ADIN allowed the party to at least challenge the rationing program in the high court on its own terms—rather than the PSL's—and in a way that would test the very legal issues that the PT found most disturbing. In this case, the PT was probably wise to file: the PSL's ADIN was rejected in its entirety, while the ADIN filed by the PT (alongside co-plaintiffs from the PCdoB, PSB, and PDT parties) led to a partial injunction.

SUITS AGAINST PUBLIC FIGURES

Finally, the PT membership was active in pressing suits against individual public figures, albeit often without clear central control from party leaders. In interviews with party members, one recurring claim was that filing suits against leading public figures was not a political strategy: it was a legitimate legal response to malfeasance on the part of leading government officials. Party members expressed a high degree of conviction on this point, and one staff member noted that leading policymakers knew what they were getting into when they took office (author interview).

That said, some anecdotal evidence suggests that the PT was in fact cognizant of the political uses of such suits. For example, late in the second-term Cardoso administration—with unusual legislative support from the recently victorious PT—the government was able to pass a law that would guarantee the president, his cabinet, governors, their cabinets, and mayors a special "forum" in the high courts. The Cardoso administration argued that this special standing was essential to protecting leading federal public servants, who because of their federal role might otherwise face the exorbitant costs of defending themselves from suits in any one of the hundreds of federal courts spread across the country. The PT's support for this bill, while not an admission of the political use of the courts, certainly highlighted the party's fear that such legal strategies might be used against the incoming

Lula administration. It may also have reflected the growing realization within the party that it, too, was facing a number of such suits in state and local government; leading PT members, especially those who had held executive posts at the municipal level, had been increasingly targeted by opponents in the courts.[7]

Newspaper accounts claimed that Cardoso was motivated by the experience of his neighbor, former Argentine president Carlos Menem, who was placed under house arrest shortly after leaving office (for example, Alencar 2002). Cardoso apparently feared that upon stepping down, detractors and opponents might hound him and his cabinet. Certainly the subject of the high personal legal costs of public service had seeped into the political mainstream: one supposed candidate for the Central Bank presidency refused an offer from the incoming Lula administration partly for this reason (author interview; Patú et al. 2002).[8]

Such concerns about the legal hounding of policymakers were not unfounded: two Central Bank presidents who had served during the Cardoso administration reportedly faced more than fifteen lawsuits apiece (many filed by members of the PT) at the end of Cardoso's second term (Barros 2002, referring to Arminio Fraga and Gustavo Loyola). Pedro Malan, who as Cardoso's finance minister for all eight years became a lightning rod for opposition to the administration's economic policies, faced over twenty suits in the federal regional court of Brasília, the STJ, and the STF, of which roughly a quarter were brought by plaintiffs identified directly with the PT.[9] Meanwhile, without assessing the validity of cases against any of the ministers, a compilation undertaken by the *Ministério Público* showed that as of the end of the Cardoso administration, there were thirty-nine pending cases alleging administrative malfeasance or other crimes against Cardoso's cabinet ministers in the federal court system.[10]

Lessons from the PT's Tactical Use of the Courts

The PT's use of the courts during the Cardoso presidency showed an interesting mix of tactical political maneuvering and genuine legal conviction. Together, the four tactics described here enabled the party to use the courts as a means of declaring its opposition to key policies of the Cardoso administration; to discredit policy and policymakers; and to delay or disable policy initiatives. Overall, the PT's use of the courts shows that the judiciary provides one more locus for the extension of policy debates: disputes that could not be resolved to the PT's satisfaction in the deliberative process in the executive and legislative branches were frequently carried over into the courts.

The goals of policy voice (declare and discredit) do not always overlap with the goals of policy opposition (delay and disable), and in some cases, they were directly inimical. For example, filing an ADIN is one of the best ways of delaying or disabling policy implementation. But as the electricity rationing story showed, the greater political noise was created not by an ADIN but by a groundswell of legal suits against the plan, initiated in part by the PT's *Ação Popular*. A high court challenge, whether filed by a member of the PT or another opposition party, may in fact undermine efforts to use political voice, by limiting legal opposition to a single, make-it-or-break-it case in the STF. In other words, if the goal is to voice opposition, the best tactical use of the courts may not coincide with the best political-legal strategy for delaying or disabling the policy.

A second consideration is what the PT's use of the courts says about the party's beliefs about Brazilian legal institutions. When questioned directly about the biases of the courts, PT members and staffers noted that the STF was stacked against them, because all the judges on the court during the Cardoso administration had been appointed by presidents the PT had opposed.[11] Party members complained that STF ministers occasionally delayed important cases by requesting additional time for review (through *pedidos de vistas*). And they noted how decisions often turned against the party, while simultaneously admitting that not all cases filed by the PT were aimed at winning outright, or were as legally sturdy as those filed by the bar association or the *Ministério Público*. On the other hand, PT members noted the importance of "sympathetic" lower court judges, and expressed a general agreement and willingness to work within the confines of the key institutions and tenets of the legal system. In other words, the system might very well be biased toward the government, but it did not necessarily shut out the PT entirely. Indeed, the PT's use of the court system in a tactical manner aimed at achieving its larger political strategic goals shows a willingness to work within the confines of the system, thereby implicitly ratifying its role.

Court Use Under the PT as Incumbent

The experience of the Lula administration suggests that courts continue to be used by political parties as an extension of executive and legislative politics. The major difference is the reversal of the parties in power: Lula, the PT, and their allies on the left and center now hold the presidency and a (somewhat unstable) majority in Congress, while Cardoso's *Partido da Social Democracia Brasileira* (PSDB) and its sometime ally the *Partido da Frente Liberal* (PFL) are in opposition.[12] This section briefly lays out the available evidence of court use by a new set of opposition parties during the first fifteen months of the Lula government.[13]

I begin with three general propositions. First, given the changes in the law regarding suits against public figures, cases filed against leading incumbents and ministers may have decreased, regardless of the strategic political considerations of the actors involved. Second, as parties with a grass-roots base that is substantially smaller and less mobilized than the PT's base, it is likely that the legal strategies of the PSDB and PFL will emphasize high court action via ADIN over the broad-based lower court challenges that were a common part of the *guerilha juridical* used by the opposition to Cardoso. Finally, given the different ideological focus of the two parties in comparison with that of the PT, the subject matter and focus of court action is also likely to have changed, with the types of policies salient to the opposition differing significantly.

SUITS AGAINST PUBLIC FIGURES

Working my way backward through the four types of legal strategies most often used by the PT, I begin with legal tactics focused on suing public figures, which are limited in part by the new law passed in 2002. In a search of cases filed against President Lula, Finance Minister Palocci, Central Bank President Meirelles, Planning Minister Mantega, and presidential chief of staff Dirceu at the upper three levels of the court system, prior to the scandal of 2005, I found only one suit filed by an individual who could clearly be tied to the opposition (he was from the PFL).[14] This suggests a marked decline in this tactic, but it is impossible to untangle the effects of this new law from the possible inclinations of the PFL and PSDB in the absence of such a change.

BROAD-BASED LEGAL CHALLENGES

Proceeding in reverse order, I find no evidence that the PSDB and PFL used broad-based lower court efforts of the sort that were so damaging, for example, against privatization or against Cardoso's measures for the electric sector. There are at least two potential explanations: (1) the Lula administration did not engage in policies that rankled the opposition as much as Cardoso's policies did, and therefore did not generate the same sort of widespread opposition needed to implement such a legal strategy; or (2) the PFL and PSDB did not adopt this strategy because they were either unable or unwilling to use it.

There may be some truth to both of these statements. The Lula administration by and large trod a conservative economic policy path, following and even improving on the Cardoso government's strict fiscal discipline; approving a controversial social security reform it most certainly would have fought if still in opposition; and keeping monetary policy tight. Its policy innovations during this period were limited largely to social welfare policies, such as *Zero Fome* (Zero Hunger), whose implementation generated some controversy, but whose ends were largely consensual. The PFL and PSDB largely supported the economic policies bequeathed by Cardoso, and broad use of the courts might have backfired in social policy, given the overall political environment and, especially, the lip-service all parties gave to such social welfare goals. In sum, it is unlikely that the PFL and PSDB would have been able to achieve the broad-based adhesion to a legal campaign along the lines of that mobilized in opposition to Cardoso's privatizations: the parties' allies in civil society were less mobilized; the issues under debate were less polarizing; the costs were less concentrated; and the opposition parties themselves, as a result, were less stridently opposed to the broad objectives of the Lula administration during this period.

THE AÇÃO POPULAR (AP)

Unlike broad-based court action, the decision to file an AP requires no central party control; unlike the ADIN, the AP is a legal instrument that does not require central party acquiescence. In sum, like suits against public figures, the decision to file an AP can be individual and thus formally isolated from the party's strategic objectives, even as it reflects ideas and interests common to party members. As we saw earlier, when the PT was in opposition, the APs filed by its membership largely conformed to the party's interests; although the party credibly claimed little control over these suits, it did keep track of ongoing cases.

The use of the AP by opposition parties declined significantly from the Cardoso administration to the Lula administration. Although APs continued to be used frequently in state and municipal politics, at the federal level only a handful of APs were filed against leading government figures. Among these the most prominent were an AP filed by a PSDB senator against Social Assistance Minister Benedita da Silva, whose trip to Argentina to attend a prayer breakfast at taxpayer expense generated a public uproar (and ultimately her resignation), and an AP filed by a PSDB congressman against government-paid advertisements about social security reform.

The decline in the number of APs and the change in their focus may reflect a number of different factors. To a small degree, it may reflect some opposition-incumbent consensus (or at least, not as wide a breach of opinions) on policy objectives. But it also may be an outcome of the opposition's own frustration with the use of APs, lingering from the PFL and PSDB's time as incumbents. Giving credence to this argument, in March 2004, Senator José Jorge, a leading member of the opposition PFL, suggested in his draft of a judicial reform bill that the process by which APs were filed against government officials should be further restricted (by requiring APs against government officials to be filed in Brasília, rather than nationwide).

THE DIRECT ACTION OF UNCONSTITUTIONALITY (ADIN)

The data suggest that the opposition to Lula was slightly less likely to use the ADIN at the outset of the Lula administration than the PT was in the comparable period in 1995–96. Analyzing the forty-eight ADINs filed by political parties against Cardoso between January 1995 and April 1, 1996, and the twenty-five filed against Lula between January 2003 and April 1, 2004, I find that the major differences are in the plaintiffs and the topics they address. As Figure 5.2 illustrates, the party distribution of ADINs is predictable: the more left-leaning the party, the more likely they would file an ADIN against Cardoso; the more right-leaning, the more likely they would file against Lula. Given the difficulty of classifying parties by ideology in Brazil, however, Figure 5.3 shows the same data in a different way, classified by parties that are either in or out of the governing coalition. There

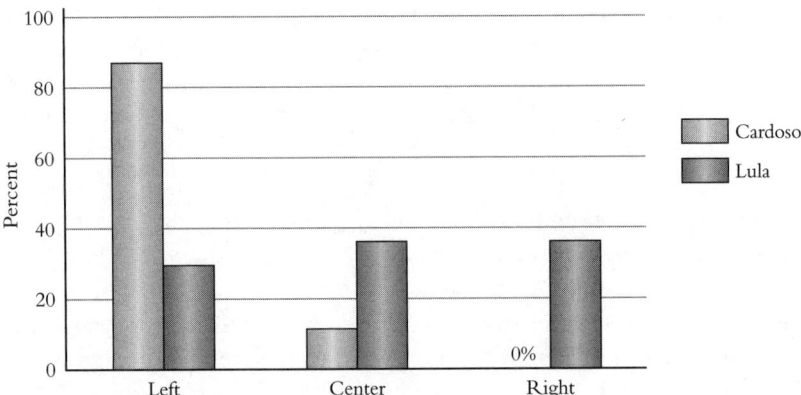

Figure 5.2. Distribution of ADINs by party
NOTE: Left parties in this sample are the PCdoB, PDT, PSC, PT, PTB, and PV (at the time, a PT ally); center parties are the PL, PMDB, PP, and PSDB; right parties are the PFL and PRONA.
SOURCE: Taylor 2004.

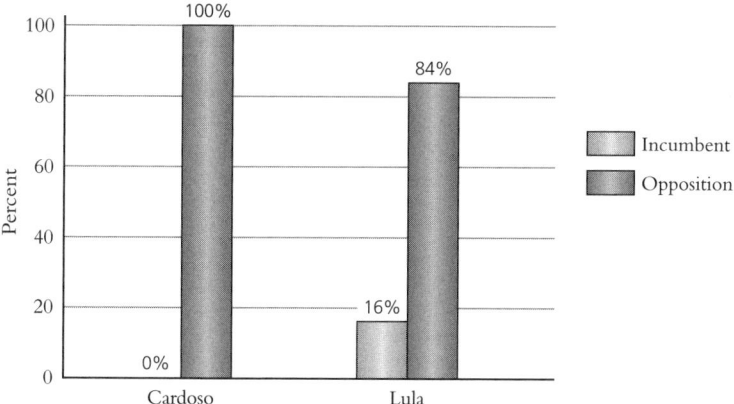

Figure 5.3. Distribution of ADINs by incumbency
SOURCE: Taylor 2004.

are none filed by Cardoso allies during his first fifteen months; four were
filed by Lula's erstwhile allies.[15]

As for topic matter, the key finding here is a major difference in focus.
ADINs filed by political parties against Cardoso policies focused primarily
on issues affecting the civil service. This corresponds roughly with the PT's
policy objectives, which over the course of the Cardoso presidency primarily focused on opposition to changes in the civil service and social security
systems, and issues of denationalization and privatization, associated with the
"neoliberal" thrust of the reforms surrounding the Real Plan.

The ADINs filed against the Lula administration centered on taxation,
agriculture, and the regulation of the electric sector. Tax law has been contentious, with the PSDB and PFL both objecting to the means by which
Lula's tax legislation was pushed through the Chamber, as well as the content, which increased the tax burden on service professions considerably and
ran counter to governors' wishes in states run by the two opposition parties.
The key issue in agriculture was the government's controversial decision to
allow the planting of genetically modified soybeans, which led to ADINs
being filed against the Lula government by one of its allies (the PTB), as
well as by the environmentalist PV and the conservative PFL. Regulation of
the electric sector was perhaps the topic that most approximated the policy
divide seen between incumbents and opposition under Cardoso: the Lula administration's more statist approach to the sector was criticized as undermining the autonomous regulatory agencies set up under Cardoso. Ironically, the
PFL and PSDB also objected vociferously to the fact that the changes were

implemented by provisional measure (a form of presidential decree legislation; see Chapter 3, footnote 13 for a description), echoing a complaint voiced frequently by the PT while in opposition.

It is too early to evaluate the results of these suits, as the STF has yet to rule on most of the ADINs filed during Lula's first term. Political parties have historically been by far the worst plaintiffs in the STF, obtaining injunctions or winning on the merit of the case less than any other plaintiff group. There is no reason to expect the opposition to Lula to fare any better: opposition political parties still use the STF to declare their opposition to, or to discredit, incumbent policies as much as they do to actually delay or disable them, and political parties continue to file suits only if they think they need to make their case, when they are certain other legal actors such as the *Ministério Público* will not make it for them.

Conclusion

A few ironies came to light in the course of the previous section, which suggest beyond a doubt that the use of the courts in Brazil is often driven by the broader strategic goals of plaintiffs, rather than strictly legal criteria, and that incumbency is inversely correlated with court use by political parties.

In a number of cases, the opposition to the Lula administration voiced the same criticisms the opposition to Cardoso used. For example, an ADIN filed by the opposition PSDB in 2003 criticizes the Lula administration for attempting to alter electric sector regulatory arrangements by provisional measure, citing as precedent—remarkably!—a successful ADIN filed jointly by the Communist Party of Brazil (PCdoB) and the Brazilian Socialist Party (PSB) in 1999. The two leading opposition parties today, the PFL and the PSDB, repeatedly complain in their court cases that the use of provisional measures is unconstitutional and abusive, echoing the equally strident complaints of the PT while in opposition. The current opposition also complained loudly of the fact that a Lula-appointed STF minister delayed hearings on the ADIN challenging the Lula administration's electric sector regulation, eerily echoing PT complaints about Cardoso appointees' delays in hearing cases (delays referred to as *engavetamento*, or roughly, "stashing in a drawer"). Although the underlying policies are different, opposition parties appear to have learned the tactical lesson that challenging the constitutionality of the use of provisional measures may be an effective means of, at the very least, discrediting policy, even if courts are not sympathetic to their legal arguments.

A second set of ironies comes from the PT's qualified adoption of policies it opposed during the Cardoso administration, a situation the PSDB and PFL find bitterly humorous. After the Lula administration awkwardly cut social security benefits to pensioners over ninety years old, as a means of updating the pension lists by seeing how many would in fact appear to request their pensions, former social security minister Roberto Brant remarked, "if that had been done by me or by anyone else in the past government, the PT would have already provided [us] with [an] *ação pública and the devil*" (*Folha de São Paulo* 2003; translation and emphasis mine).

There are clearly some differences between the two oppositions' use of the courts. The opposition to Lula appears to be more narrowly focused, perhaps in part because (1) the PSDB and PFL still have considerable leverage in Congress, where they have helped the Lula administration, for example, to approve its social security and judicial reforms; (2) the opposition to Lula may still be learning, and it may be some time before its legal-political tactics are as evolved as those the PT developed during its long period in opposition; (3) the Lula administration has adopted many of the old Cardoso policies, meaning that policy differences are less acute than they might otherwise be; (4) the Lula administration has a tenuous legislative majority, especially in the Senate, whose fragility prevents it from carrying out policy changes that are as profound and potentially divisive as those carried out under Cardoso's more ample coalition; and (5) as a result, the types of policy being implemented are far less costly to specific constituencies (Type III policies) than many of those undertaken by Cardoso's strong coalition.

Regardless of ideology, however, it is clear that political parties in Brazil frequently turn to the courts as a tactical extension of their strategies elsewhere in the political system. The judicial institutional environment plays a role in determining their choice of legal tactics, ranging from direct constitutional challenges in the STF to broad-based action in the lower courts. But Brazilian political parties are also constrained by their own internal characteristics, such as the broad-based roots of the PT, as compared with the more elite-based and less programmatic opposition to Lula. These internal institutional structures and the patterns of internal decision making they engender play a role in determining which of the panoply of available legal tactics will be used by a given party. The salience of policy will of course provide an incentive or disincentive to mount an organized challenge to policy, in the courts as elsewhere. Given the increasing salience of reform to its members during the 1990s, the PT found itself forced to adopt a central hierarchy and programmatic coherence unmatched by other contemporaneous political parties. The party's forceful opposition to Cardoso's reforms, combined with strong internal discipline and a professional legal staff working directly for the PT congressional delegation, permitted the party to undertake more elaborate legal tactics than those used by many other opposition political parties.

To further inquire into how group plaintiffs determine whether and how to contest policy in the courts, I now turn to the case of the OAB, analyzing this group's motivations for using the courts and the legal tactics it employed.

Chapter 6

Judicial Contestation of Policy: The OAB[1]

In 2001, the president of the *Ordem dos Advogados do Brasil* (OAB) gave a speech in the presence of Brazilian president Fernando Henrique Cardoso during which he condemned the Cardoso administration's "despotic manner of legislating" (Rodrigues 2001; translation mine). This was no small choice of words, in a very public forum, from the head of an association that prided itself on its contribution to bringing down the military regime and building Brazil's new democracy.

The OAB's combative opposition to the Cardoso administration on the judicial front paralleled these tough words. Previous chapters have noted the OAB's intense use of the STF, where it was responsible for filing 5 percent of all constitutional review cases brought against the federal government using the Direct Action of Unconstitutionality (ADIN) between 1988 and 2002. Furthermore, although it was far less active than political parties and other groups in filing ADINs, it was, as Chapter 4 illustrated, far better at it. The OAB succeeded in using the ADIN and other legal instruments to halt, alter, or delay several Cardoso policy initiatives, including agrarian reform, changes in judicial rules, civil service pension reforms, and various changes in electoral law.

But why was the bar association involved in these policy debates in the first place, and why did it go to such lengths to contest policy in the courts? In some cases, such as agrarian reform and proposed changes in judicial rules, the pecuniary and professional interests of lawyers were clearly at stake. But unlike the PT and its constituents, the OAB and its members were not directly affected by civil service pension reform, privatization, or several other Cardoso policy initiatives that the OAB fought in the courts. So why did the OAB play such a prominent role in contesting these policies, especially if it had so little apparently riding on the outcome and might actually stand to lose by getting involved?

Once again, I focus here on how plaintiffs' broader political strategies influence the overall patterns by which federal policies have been legally challenged, and how judicial structure has influenced the legal tactics adopted by the OAB in policy debates. But unlike the previous chapter, my approach here tries to better understand the complex internal motivations driving the OAB's use of the courts. I explore how the interplay between ideas, interests, and internal institutional structure shaped the bar association's role as a prominent opposition actor in the policy debates of the Cardoso administration.

I first discuss the overlapping concepts of ideas, interests, and institutions as motivations for, and constraints on, policy contestation in the courts. The second section studies how these influenced the OAB's role in three prominent public debates. On the basis of these cases, the third section reflects on the motivations behind the OAB's policy stances. I conclude with some final reflections on the use of the courts by the PT and the OAB.

Ideas, Interests, and Institutions

THE OAB'S IDEATIONAL CONSENSUS

In trying to understand why the OAB was so active in judicially contesting policy during the Cardoso administration, I focus here on a common set of ideas that has coalesced over the course of the OAB's history. Although it can be "very difficult to disentangle ideological or cultural factors from other kinds of variables" (Hall 1997, 185), it may only be possible to understand the OAB's policy role by making reference to the broader *weltanschauung* that unites its otherwise diverse membership. Ideas provide the "focal points" around which disparate groups coalesce, the "basic meaning systems" that permit collective action, and motivations for action, within broader formal institutional frameworks (for example, Arjomand 1992; Blyth 2003; Hall 1997).

In the case of the OAB, the ties between ideas, interests, and institutional rules clearly influenced the bar association's policy attitudes throughout the 1990s. The recent history of the OAB has been constitutive of its ideals and structured its preferences such that defense of the 1988 Constitution is a principal ideational motivator. At the same time, the complex institutional changes taking place in the political system since the transition to democracy—including the writing of a new constitution, the creation of a new statute governing lawyers, and "neoliberal" reforms—have forced the OAB to defend its professional interests in a climate of rapid change. The resulting institutional framework has also played a role in shaping shared OAB interests and ideas. Externally, the OAB was given a privileged place in the 1988 Constitution, historically unparalleled access to the high court, and as a result, an important voice in national policy decisions. Internally, the loose hierarchy of the OAB, the public prominence of its president, and the unrepresentativeness of the Federal Council of the OAB all structure how its policy stances—the concrete expression of its interests and ideas—are determined.

Four historical factors have been crucial in shaping the OAB's ideational consensus and hence its position in policy debates: its long history as a professional body, its prominent role in the transition to democracy, the extension of its role in the 1988 Constitution, and its continuing political prominence during the post-authoritarian period. Each is addressed in turn here.

Over the past two decades, the OAB has been an important architect of Brazilian democratic politics, assuming a dual role as constitutional watchdog and leading advocate for the national legal profession. But the OAB's history goes back much further: the OAB first emerged in 1930, at the outset of the highly corporatist Vargas era in Brazilian politics.[2] The OAB today remains clearly corporatist in the sense of being a "corporate unity," with compulsory membership, monopoly over its profession, and a role recognized by the state (Malloy 1977; Power and Doctor 2004; Schmitter 1971; and Wiarda 1973, 1981, 2004). This corporatist foundation has a continuing influence on the OAB's role in policy debates: the OAB's long-standing role as the leading legal professional group in Brazil imbues its members with a strong commitment to the OAB's anointed role as guardian of a particular form of democracy and constitutionalism. As Bonelli (2003, 1047) notes, "the defense of juridical order has been at the core of lawyers' collective identity, maintaining group cohesion and the public legitimacy of [the] OAB."

Which brings us to the second factor: the OAB's prominent role in the Brazilian transition to democracy. Between 1964 and the early 1970s, the OAB made a difficult transition from its previous support for the military regime to very public opposition, and from the mid-1970s through the 1980s, the OAB was a fundamental voice in structuring the military's exit from power and the democratic institution building that followed it. As a result, since the 1970s the "OAB has been civil society's spokesperson for the rule of law, human rights, and citizenship, which has made [the] career path of cause lawyers less peripheral" (Bonelli 2003, 1048–49).

The OAB had initially supported the 1964 overthrow of leftist President João Goulart, ironically by arguing that the military's intervention was needed to prevent the "dismantling of the democratic state" by subversive groups who sought "the destruction of the primacy of democracy and the implantation of a totalitarian regime"(Cavalcanti 1964; translation mine). But within months of the coup, the federal leadership of the OAB was publicly debating the legality of the new government, and the OAB acted forcefully to rebuff the military's requests for it to restrict the professional standing of lawyers whose political rights had been suspended by the military (Venâncio Filho 1982, 133, in Skidmore 1988, 27).

By the early 1970s, in light of increasing human rights violations and arbitrary legal maneuvers by the government, the OAB had coalesced in public opposition to the military regime. The 1974 OAB national convention vociferously advocated for the rights of political prisoners, launched a campaign for rights awareness, and questioned the legitimacy of the military government's 1967 Constitution (and the military's Institutional Acts). The military responded with threats (ultimately unfulfilled) to remove OAB privileges and subject it, like most other professional associations, to oversight by the Labor Ministry (Skidmore 1988, 185–87).

As an elite organization, the OAB was not subject to the same overt repression as other groups, yet the OAB's prominence was not without its costs. As the military slowly adopted a policy of gradual *abertura* in the late 1970s, the OAB did not ease up. It called with mixed success for investigations of disappearances and torture, as well as the revocation of the worst national security laws. These efforts resulted in a number of attempts at intimidation by hardliners within the regime, the worst of which came with the letter bombing of the OAB's offices in Rio de Janeiro on August 27, 1980, which killed the head of the secretarial staff as she opened it.[3]

The letter bomb had the opposite effect from that intended: the staffer's funeral turned into a major political event, and the very day of the bombing the OAB created a permanent Human Rights Committee on the Federal Council. By 1982, this committee had prepared a list of 333 dead and disappeared in the 1964–81 period, and was pressuring the government for its response to the abuses committed in its name. Meanwhile, the OAB was galvanized as never before in its opposition to the military regime.

With the military's decision to hold state elections in November 1982, the OAB prodded the government to permit true political contestation. By 1983, it was actively campaigning for a new constitutional convention, to replace the undemocratic military charter of 1967, as well as for the direct popular election of the president in 1984, under a campaign that became known as *Diretas Já!* (Direct [Elections] Now!). In the course of these campaigns, members of the OAB were exposed to further intimidation, including the October 1983 police "invasion" of the OAB's headquarters in Brasília and a mysterious fire in June 1984 at the same building. Ultimately, the campaign for a direct vote failed, but the OAB celebrated its primary goal of forcing the military from office. The OAB greeted the electoral college's selection of a new, nonmilitary president on January 15, 1985, with considerable satisfaction.

With the transition under way, the OAB's heroic phase of opposition came to an end. As in many other countries making transitions, Brazilian civil society faced a tough switch from fighting against the military regime to pushing for more specific and less consensual goals within the new democracy. Not all civil society groups are able to survive such transitions, in light of declining internal cohesion, and in the absence of a common enemy.

The OAB managed to avoid this trap, and indeed, the institutional privileges it was to gain in the 1988 Constitution—the third factor shaping the OAB's current ideational framework—may have helped the OAB to maintain the basic organizational consensus essential to its preservation. By virtue of its extensive participation in the Constituent Assembly, the OAB gained important influence over the rules under which it would operate in later years.

The OAB did not win everything it sought in the Assembly. Its initial bid to have the Constitution written by an independent body of illustrious experts (rather than incumbent politicians) failed, and a committee of notables that had drawn up a draft constitution had its report shelved by the Sarney administration. The Assembly, composed of elected members of Congress, ultimately blocked the OAB's draft judicial reform, its goal of creating a Constitutional Court along the European model, and its preferred reforms of the Labor Court system.

But as a result of its reservoir of public goodwill, its vaunted democratic credentials, and its strong presence in Brasília, the OAB was nonetheless a forceful presence during the Assembly, and was able to significantly influence the direction and scope of the 1988 Constitution. As Junqueira (2003, 71) notes, lawyers and the judiciary were among the most influential of the diverse groups lobbying the Constituent Assembly, and succeeded in "obtaining a constitutionally protected monopoly on judicial representation, creating a barrier to direct popular access to the courts." The OAB preserved its monopoly over membership in the legal profession, which has

114   CHAPTER 6

been essential to preserving its organizational strength in the years since. The OAB was influential in drafting sections of the 1988 Constitution on individual, social, and collective rights, and a number of its proposals for the constitutional text on the legal system were accepted. The OAB was also ascribed a major institutional role by the new Constitution. The word *lawyer* (*advogado*) appears no fewer than fourteen times in the main body of the Constitution. More important, the OAB is specifically mentioned—something no other professional association can claim—in three specific articles of the Constitution, giving it an important voice in the selection exams for judges and prosecutors, as well as allowing it to file ADINs (Brasil 1988, Articles 93, 103, 129).

The fourth factor contributing to the formation of a rough ideational consensus within the OAB arises out of its political prominence in the post-authoritarian period. Following the Constituent Assembly, the OAB played a leading role in two key events prior to the policy reforms discussed in the second section of the chapter. The first was its opposition to the Collor Plan, President Collor's attempt to control runaway inflation through a series of controversial price and wage freezes. After months of complaints about the Collor government's abuses of executive decree power and the resulting usurpation of legislative power, the OAB emerged as a principal opponent of the Collor Plan, arguing that it was written in a manner that belittled the role of the Congress. As this chapter will show, the use of provisional measures—democratic Brazil's version of executive decrees—continued to be a *bête noire* of the OAB for many years.

The second major post-Constituent event was the OAB's push for a thorough investigation of accusations of corruption in the Collor administration. Together with a slew of civil service organizations ranging from the National Conference of Bishops of Brazil (CNBB) to the Brazilian Institute of Social and Economic Analyses (IBASE), the OAB campaigned heavily for a congressional inquiry to investigate Collor's campaign finance director, Paulo Cesar ("P.C.") Farias, when allegations of serious high-level corruption surfaced. State-level OAB organizations lent considerable weight to the organization of popular protests against Collor, and the OAB national president at the time, Marcello Lavanère, breathlessly described the OAB's efforts as "the history of truth against lies, of truth against falsehood, of truth against all sorts of intrigues . . . (Ordem dos Advogados do Brasil 2005, translation mine; see also Netto Lôbo 1996). Once the evidence against Collor appeared irrefutable, Lavanère and his counterpart at the Brazilian Press Association (ABI) led a march from the OAB's headquarters to the Chamber of Deputies, where they presented their petition for impeachment, backed by twenty thousand signatures. The Chamber overwhelmingly voted for Collor's impeachment a few weeks later.

Through the rest of the 1990s, the OAB continued to hammer on these issues. Several interrelated ideas that gelled during this period would prove influential in guiding the OAB's policy positions. The OAB was watchful for signs of authoritarian regression; fearful of executive arrogation of power; and zealous in defending the rights laid out in the 1988 Constitution. It positioned itself as a watchdog of democracy, particularly against the perceived strength of the executive branch. Meanwhile, an emerging tendency within the OAB's federal leadership was opposition to so-called "neoliberal" reforms of the sort approved by Collor and eventually advocated by Cardoso (see, for example, *Folha de São Paulo* 1995). The reasons for opposition to these reforms were not necessarily interest-based or even consensual within the legal profession as a whole. But among the members of the federal council of the OAB, opposition to reform was driven by a growing distaste for the executive-centered methods by which some reforms were carried out; by the OAB's close ties to other civil society groups who opposed the reforms; and by the OAB's strong attachment to the letter of the 1988 Constitution.

THE INSTITUTIONAL STRUCTURE OF THE OAB

In addition to the broad ideational consensus at the heart of the OAB, a strong institutional framework influences the means by which the group has become involved in policy questions. Key among the institutional factors are its monopoly and oversight of the legal profession, its own internal decision-making structure, and an ample budget.

The OAB is structured by federal law and operates within an institutional framework it helped to draft. Although the OAB has existed since the 1930s, as a consequence of the 1988 Constitution and the general legislative overhaul that followed, the OAB has been governed since 1994 by the "Statute of Lawyers and the OAB" (Law 8.906). The Statute gives the OAB a central role in overseeing the legal profession; Article 3 of the law restricts the practice of law in Brazilian territory and the title of lawyer to members of the OAB. Unlike many national bar associations, the OAB thus exercises a national monopoly on the legal profession, while also serving as a government-recognized body for the defense of lawyers' rights and privileges.

The OAB's primary institutional purpose is thus to serve as a professional guild and advocate for the legal profession. In terms of guild-like responsibilities, the OAB sets the rules for payment of legal fees; establishes standards of behavior through its Code of Ethics; administers a rigorous bar exam required for law students who wish to practice law; and is responsible for investigating accusations of professional malfeasance against lawyers. As an advocate for the profession, the OAB is responsible for upholding the rights of lawyers as described in the Statute. Among these: lawyers cannot be imprisoned until convicted, and like other college graduates, have rights to a special jail cell; lawyers have access to a special room in courts to prepare their trial cases; and lawyers' rights to payment for representation cannot be infringed.[4]

The structure of the OAB is pyramidal: at the top sits a Federal Council made up of three councilors from each of the twenty-seven states (including the Federal District), headed by a president elected for a three-year term. Each state in turn has its own sectional council, headed by a president and made up of representatives from local districts.[5] Like the Brazilian Senate, which it resembles in size and geographic distribution, the OAB Federal Council suffers from a representative imbalance. Each of the three councilors from southeastern states such as Rio de Janeiro and São Paulo represents many thousands more lawyers than the three councilors from smaller, less developed states such as Tocantins or Acre, but their votes on the council are equal. As a result, the six southern states of Rio Grande do Sul, Santa Catarina, Paraná, Minas Gerais, São Paulo, and Rio de Janeiro account for roughly 70 percent of the lawyers nationwide, but they hold only 22 percent of the voting seats on the Federal Council (Ceneviva 2001). Meanwhile, the federal councilors' votes for Federal Council president are tallied en bloc by state and, ironically, given the OAB's prominent role in the campaign for direct presidential elections, thus play the role of an electoral college.[6]

Although the OAB is not publicly audited, it clearly oversees an ample (and tax exempt) budget. Every one of the roughly 450,000 members of the OAB is required to pay an annual subscription,[7] and although as many as 50 percent of the OAB members in recent years have failed to pay their dues (Lozano 1999), this nonetheless sums to millions of tax-free *reais*. The figure is boosted by mandatory contributions to state OAB pension funds from fees paid in some judicial cases.[8] The Federal Council reported an annual budget of R$89 million in 2003, and the sum total of the OAB's various sectional budgets likely tops this figure considerably: the São Paulo sectional budget alone showed assets of R$67 million in June 2003.[9]

As a professional oversight body, the OAB—and particularly the state OAB sectionals—have a great deal of control over the practice of law, overseeing the bar exams that lawyers are required to pass; advising the Ministry of Education on which law school programs should be authorized; and disciplining practicing lawyers. The most rigorous of these practices is the bar exam, which roughly three out of five candidates fail (for example, *Folha de*

São Paulo 1999a). At the state level, the state with the largest population of lawyers, São Paulo, routinely fails upward of 80 percent of aspiring lawyers.[10] The final oversight function of the OAB is its control over lawyers themselves, aimed at heightening the prestige of the profession. This role has not been the OAB's strong suit: in a study conducted for the São Paulo OAB, it was estimated that ethics complaints had been filed against 10 percent of lawyers (Nunes 1998); nationwide, the pace of ethics tribunals has been criticized, and a number of high profile cases have arisen in which questionable practices by lawyers had been overlooked by the OAB.[11] Over the past ten years, the OAB has implemented rules aimed at speeding up internal investigations, as well as other procedural changes to tighten internal oversight, but the criticism continues.

I have noted here the strength of the OAB as a guild, restricting and overseeing the practice of law and defending lawyers' professional interests with a large budget at its disposal. But how does institutional structure shape the OAB's policy stances and its participation in policy deliberations?

Although lawyers as a profession are well represented in Congress, by and large they do not act as a cohesive representational bloc.[12] Meanwhile, the OAB has even less direct influence in the executive branch. As a result, the key means by which the OAB directly influences public policy in Brazil are through its external public statements, most often expressed by the OAB president, or by turning to the courts.

Largely as a result of its internal decision rules, OAB preferences are often expressed only by a small leadership cadre, led by the president of the Federal Council. In expressing the opinions of the OAB publicly, once in office, the president is largely unconstrained, especially given that he (and it has always been a "he") is ineligible for reelection. In choosing whether to pursue legal recourse against federal policy, the OAB president is constrained by the need to build support in the federal council and by legal considerations concerning the legality and constitutionality of policy and policy challenges. However, given the weak representativeness of the federal council, the simultaneous electoral origin of its members, and the fact that the OAB president controls the OAB's purse strings, this constraint is not always significant.[13]

The external institutional structure that matters most to the OAB is the structure of the judiciary, and in particular, the OAB's access to the high court. As a result of its influence in the Constituent Assembly, and in recognition of its important role in re-democratization, the OAB was given standing to file ADINs. Over time, this privilege has been extended, and the OAB has been implicitly granted broader standing than most other professional groups; it is allowed to file ADINs across all policy areas, unlike commercial or industrial groups, who are limited to filing ADINs in their own specific policy realms. This, along with the high quality of the OAB's legal filings, may explain the OAB's relatively powerful policy influence, and hence, the prominence given to the OAB's policy-related pronouncements. In other words, the ADIN provides the OAB with a significant institutional veto point over policy (even when the ADIN goes unused), without which the OAB's policy role in the broader political system would be much less prominent.

THE TENSION BETWEEN OAB INTERESTS AND IDEAS

To summarize briefly, there are three major motivations that drive the OAB's involvement in Brazilian public policy debates at the federal level. The first is its role as a guardian of legal and constitutional rights, a role that is written into the 1988 Constitution and to which the OAB is passionately and historically committed. The second is achieving the consensual political goals of the OAB membership as a whole, inasmuch as these goals are enunciated and reflected by the OAB federal leadership.[14] The third is the goal of preserving the interests of lawyers as a professional group, including here both pecuniary interests and the preservation of lawyers' professional standing. All three motivations are overlapping and impossible to disentangle entirely, as they are founded on ideas and interests that are mutually constitutive. There is an inherent tension between the OAB's ideas and interests, however, which has led many to question the OAB's commitment to its ideals, and on occasion may have weakened the OAB's influence on public opinion. I explain this in the following text.

Given its history in the transition to democracy, the OAB has a reservoir of public goodwill for its role as a democratic watchdog. Examples of this ongoing watchdog role have included OAB calls for federal intervention in states where the rule of law was threatened;[15] OAB leadership of impeachment drives against corrupt local politicians (as in the case of São Paulo mayor Celso Pitta); OAB monitoring of military and police forces for human rights abuses; and OAB charges of conflicts of interest in federal and state courts.

These watchdog efforts have not been costless: during the 1990s, one member of the OAB Federal Council was killed after denouncing political wrongdoing in Roraima, the Espírito Santo state OAB headquarters was bombed, and several state OAB presidents had to flee threats to themselves and their families. Despite (or because of) their high human costs, these efforts have boosted the OAB's currency as a democratic voice, leading it to be called on to mediate in important conflicts, such as the tense standoffs between President Cardoso and Minas governor Itamar Franco over state debt payments, or between the Cardoso administration and the MST landless movement. The OAB also is frequently asked to name members to investigatory commissions studying police brutality and other abuses of state power.

That said, critics of the OAB argue that the bar association also has another, more corporativist side. As Sadek diplomatically notes, the OAB's "power and influence are recognized, and can be measured by the privileges it has conquered over time" (1999b, 17; translation mine). Sometimes, however, these privileges have been less than subtly defended. In one 1995 case, the OAB-SP began investigating a prominent and highly respected consumer rights group (IDEC) for offering legal services "irregularly," prompting a renowned legal scholar, law school professor, and former OAB federal *conselheira* to complain publicly to the OAB that its position left her, "indignant and appalled, not only for the unjust and arbitrary censure, but for the evidence of blind corporativism . . . (Ada Pellegrini Grinover, cited in Nassif 1995; translation mine). Another law professor complained in an unrelated editorial that

> by attempting to ignore and disqualify the criticisms of corporativism, [by creating] an unpopular monopoly, and [through] a habit of defending the Judiciary's interests, the former president of the OAB has won immediate internal applause, but created an external credibility crisis. . . . The institutional vocation of the OAB has always been the defense of the people, of liberties, of democracy. How can this vocation be reconciled with the defense of lawyers' labor, market and pecuniary interests? (Falcão 1995; translation mine).

As these examples illustrate, the OAB's "institutional vocation" of constitutional defense and its "pecuniary interests" as a legal professional association have often collided. The OAB's decision to fight the creation of lawyerless small claims courts, for example, while largely unsuccessful, generated a great deal of resentment across the political spectrum. More recently, the OAB has come under significant criticism from judges for favoring an external control body to oversee the judiciary while firmly rejecting any external audit of its own accounts.[16]

Less charitable critics from outside the legal profession have condemned the OAB's efforts to preserve and broaden its dominance of the legal market, at the expense of the broader public good. The late Roberto Campos, a conservative former minister of the military regime, complained in 1996 that the OAB was driven to oppose judicial reform by the fear that some measures, such as binding precedent, would limit the market for lawyers (Campos 1996). A prominent editorialist noted in 1998 that while in the 1970s and 1980s the OAB was an important instrument in the fight for re-democratization, when this was accomplished, it "was dominated by a smaller politics, of attachment to ideological groups and corporatist interests" (Nassif 1998b; translation mine).

The dramatic public posturing of OAB presidents has become somewhat of a tradition, but one that often also leads to criticism. Following in the steps of his predecessor's criticism of Cardoso's despotic manner of legislating, in 2004 OAB president Roberto Busato, in the presence of President Lula, called Brazil an "unconstitutional country," criticized Lula's minimum wage policies, and attacked the economic policies of the Lula government. As one national news magazine wrote, this speech was more fitting for student politics than for national politics. Furthermore, "[t]he OAB had an important role in the re-democratization of Brazil. Busato shows that it has lost its way now that [democratic] institutions are working again" (*Veja* 2004, translation mine).

When criticized, OAB leaders have reminded the public of their ties to the democratization movement, while downplaying the OAB's role as a professional interest group. For example, while arguing against a proposal that would require the *Tribunal de Contas da União*[17] to audit the OAB's books, the OAB president in 2001 noted,

> It is strange that they want to silence the OAB at a time when [it] is active and critical. They tried that in the era of the military regime. But now we live in a democratic rule of law. The voice of liberty comes out of the voice of lawyers (*Folha de São Paulo* 2001a; translation mine).

Despite these occasionally histrionic appeals to its history, however, it is quite apparent that the OAB is a professional guild, dedicated to defending its members' interests, like many other such professional groups in Brazil and with a corporatist bent that may not be all that unusual for bar associations anywhere. Many lawyers I spoke with noted that of course the OAB was corporatist: if it weren't, who would protect the rights of the legal profession?

Having unraveled some of the diverse and occasionally conflictual interests and ideas that may drive the OAB to oppose policy, I now turn in the second section to three policy challenges by the OAB during the Cardoso administration. My focus is on the OAB's choices of policy tools: its recourse to public opinion, and the legal tactics it turned to when pressed.

OAB Policy Stances During the Cardoso Administration

President Cardoso, like the OAB, was a major actor in the transition to democracy, as well as in the Constituent Assembly. Ironically, though, while lawyers as a profession would on the face of it be no more indisposed toward the Cardoso administration than other interest groups in society, the OAB at the federal level had an increasingly contentious relationship with Cardoso during the eight years he was president. This culminated in the extraordinary 2001 incident cited at the beginning of this chapter, in which the newly elected OAB president criticized the government's "despotic manner of legislating," no small choice of words from the leader of an organization that prided itself on defending democracy. The fact that relations reached this venomous breaking point suggests major differences had emerged between the OAB and the government.

The battle lines in the OAB-Cardoso conflict were drawn early. Two months into the Cardoso government, at his March 1995 inauguration as president of the OAB Federal Council, Uchoa Lima said that the OAB would be attentive to "the nefarious influence of unpatriotic minority groups who seek to denationalize [privatize] the country and destroy the constitutional rights and guarantees conquered by the people." Days earlier, the OAB Federal Council had held a seminar on constitutional reform, which concluded that the new government's reform proposals handed over "control of the Brazilian economy to foreign capital" (Trevisan 1995; translation mine).

The OAB-Cardoso conflict was in many ways a struggle over what the next steps in the consolidation of democracy would look like. For Cardoso and his allies, the first priority was economic stabilization and liberalization, which it was hoped would lead to social development. In this view, the 1988 Constitution was crafted in the service of a minority, and was an impediment to achieving the development necessary for improving the lot of the majority. For the OAB, the key priorities were preventing authoritarian regression and protecting lawyers' rights, without which they would not be able to perform their function as a guardian of societal rights. In this view, the 1988 Constitution had a primordial role as a document laying out the essential rights of individuals, regardless of its broader implications for governability and development, questioned by Cardoso and his allies.

In short, from the opening days of the Cardoso government, the Federal Council of the OAB was clearly on the side of defending the status quo against most reforms, whether this defense was driven by its interests, ideas, or a mix of both. The conflict was partly due to the intangible professional differences between economists' priorities in reforming the state and lawyers' interests in loftier constitutional goals. As one OAB president would later argue, the "acquired rights" (*direitos adquiridos*) of Brazilian citizens are "seen by some technocrats and economists as a mere accounting obstacle . . . (Castro 1999; translation mine). But the OAB also had profound professional interests in many of the battles it chose to fight with the Cardoso administration, as exemplified in its involvement in the agrarian reform fight (described in Chapters 3 and 4), where it successfully battled to defeat limits on lawyers' earnings. In the following, I examine three other contentious policy debates in which the OAB played a prominent role, to evaluate the motivations and tactics employed by the OAB to alter policy in areas salient to its leaders and membership.

PROVISIONAL MEASURES

As a legal organization, could the OAB legitimately object to the process of reform, if it was carried out in a constitutional manner? From this perspective, the most contestable portion of the Cardoso reform program was its use of provisional measures (Brazil's form of executive decree power; see Chapter 3, fn. 13 for more details). There was some question over the extent to which provisional measures could be reissued if Congress did not vote on them: the Cardoso government, like its predecessors, argued they could be reissued indefinitely unless they were rejected; opponents criticized the practice as a usurpation of legislative power. The OAB seized on the banner of provisional measures as one of its rallying cries, complaining of the "perturbing effect [they had] on the principle of separation of powers" (*Folha de São Paulo* 1998c) and calling for limits on their use. At its 1999 annual conference, the OAB published a "Letter of Rio de Janeiro," which saw "in the systematic disrespect for the Constitution and in the abuse of provisional measures factors which lead to ungovernability and institutional chaos." According to the letter, provisional measures were being used undemocratically: "The IMF's [interests] are superimposed over the legitimate interests of the Brazilian people" (*Folha de São Paulo* 1999b; translation mine).

So far, however, the OAB had used only the traditional tools available to it: public voicing of its opposition and support for those who joined with it in its campaign against provisional measures. By 2000, however, the continual tension between OAB presidents and the Cardoso government led the OAB to new tactics.[18] The final straw was a provisional measure (No. 1984) that had a direct impact on lawyers' professional standing, allowing the federal government to directly appeal to the STJ and STF any injunction against it in the lower federal courts, in addition to changing the rules by which government debt cases were addressed in the courts. The OAB declared legal and political war.

In November 2000, the OAB announced a professional ethics investigation into the federal attorney general, Gilmar Ferreira Mendes. As a lawyer, Mendes was potentially subject to the OAB's Ethics Tribunal, and as a key Cardoso subordinate, he was a convenient political target. The OAB considered the abuse of the provisional measure sufficient to warrant such an investigation, arguing that "without juridical security, there is no democracy" (Castro 2000; translation mine). OAB president Reginaldo de Castro noted that the provisional measure on injunctions and debt payments was a major blow against democracy, and a year later, the OAB filed an (as yet unresolved) ADIN against the provisional measure. Perhaps more important, the ethics investigation was staged as a means of derailing Mendes's probable nomination to the Supreme Federal Tribunal (STF), which had not been announced but was a distinct possibility given the impending retirement of an STF minister in late October. As a result, the widely anticipated nomination of Mendes to the STF did not take place in 2000. When Mendes was nominated in 2002, OAB president Reginaldo de Castro formally requested that the Senate investigate his ethical reputation before holding confirmation hearings. Although Mendes was ultimately approved for the STF minister's seat, his Senate hearings were embarrassingly postponed by the maneuver.

The results of the OAB's battle against provisional measures are hard to measure. The courts, although clearly concerned by the government's use of provisional measures, never acted to constrain the government's use of them. The OAB's constant harping on the subject may have contributed to the generation of congressional support for reform, especially in conjunction with Congress's increasing weariness with the measures. The outgoing administration, perhaps eager to constrain its successors, passed a constitutional amendment altering the rules for provisional measures in 2001. As for Mendes, if he was not already, he became a hardened opponent of the OAB, publicly accusing lawyers of fighting provisional measures because some of them hurt their pecuniary interests (for example, *Folha de São Paulo* 2001b).

PRIVATIZATION: THE CASE OF CVRD

From the outset of the Cardoso administration, it was clear that the government would push to privatize major state-owned companies, and it was equally clear that the OAB would oppose this effort on principle. The 1997 sale of Companhia Vale do Rio Doce (CVRD), a major mining concern, proved to be a bellwether for opponents of privatization, who saw it as a test of the government's commitment to privatization on a large scale, and, potentially, as a means of halting the pipeline of other planned privatizations. The OAB's Federal Council was to play a major role in this effort.

Passions within the legal profession ran high. As one former STF minister said while participating in an OAB-organized protest, the CVRD sale would be a "disaster" and a "true crime," leading to the loss of Brazil's "richest and most promising part"(Evandro Lins e Silva, cited in Freitas 1997a). The OAB joined with former president Itamar Franco, the Brazilian Press Association (ABI), the National Union of Students (UNE), the National Conference of Brazilian Bishops (CNBB), and opposition parties to voice its opposition publicly. The OAB president noted, "the patriotic campaign that was articulated against the sale of the state-owned company has nothing, could not have anything, to do with politics or partisanship. It is, above all else, a cause of nationality" (*Folha de São Paulo* 1997a; translation mine).

But given that privatization required little or no legislative approval (the legal framework had already been largely established under Collor) there was little the OAB could do in the political realm to influence the sale except publicly voice its opposition. So the OAB turned to its competitive advantage, judicial challenges. At the local level, lawyers associated with the OAB were involved in filing suit against the sale of CVRD in lower courts. But they did so without any institutional coordination with the Federal Council, or central control from it. The OAB at the federal level instead turned to its institutional strength in the STF and filed an ADIN questioning the legal instrument by which CVRD had been included in the national privatization program. To celebrate the filing, and presumably to play up its opposition, the OAB held a demonstration against the sale, then led a march from the OAB headquarters to the STF to deliver the suit (harking back to the famous march preceding Collor's impeachment). Ultimately, the ADIN failed, but the OAB had pushed its cause as far as it could in both the political and legal realms.

Why was the OAB opposed to privatization? On the face of it, there is no direct interest involved—lawyers were highly placed on both sides of the privatization debate. The OAB's ideals, however, had repeatedly shown through as constitutionalist, nationalist, and statist, allying them to an epistemic community that included numerous anti-privatization and anti-reform groups whose cause they backed here, as they would again in social security reform, even when lawyers' professional interests were not clearly in play.

SOCIAL SECURITY

The OAB's Federal Council was heavily involved in the debate over social security reform. Although no pecuniary interests of lawyers were directly at stake, the OAB seemed determined—partly as a result of its own dislike of Cardoso's reforms, partly because of its reluctance to see changes to the 1988 Constitution, and partly through its resulting ties to other opponents of the reform—to challenge the Cardoso administration's plans head-on, using both political and legal means. The social security reform was not passed until almost the fourth year of Cardoso's first term, in November 1998, but the Federal Council of the OAB was an active opponent during most of this period.

The first challenge to the social security reform came before it had even been voted on by the full Congress, with the April 1996 decision by maverick STF minister Marco Aurélio de Mello to suspend congressional hearings on the reform (at the request of the Communist Party of Brazil, PCdoB). The OAB, together with the Association of Brazilian Magistrates (AMB), publicly voiced its agreement with Minister Mello's legal reasoning about purported procedural problems in congressional deliberations of the amendment, although this injunction was overwhelmingly voided a month later in a ten to one decision by the full STF.

The OAB's opposition appears to have had less to do with interests than with ideas. The OAB defended the so-called unalterable clauses (*cláusulas pétreas*) of the Constitution assiduously, arguing that these could not be altered without grievously undermining "acquired rights" and the constitutional order. The OAB repeatedly joined with other groups in protesting reforms in Congress, participated in major protest marches on Brasília, and actively pushed its case in the press, illustrating great commitment to its espoused cause.

Institutionally, regardless of his motivations, the fact was that the OAB president—in all but the most unusual circumstances—needed the approval of the full Federal Council before he could file lawsuits that might further his cause.[19] This, indeed, was one of the reasons lawyers gave when I asked them to explain why the OAB was comparatively so much better at winning injunctions in ADIN cases than were other groups: the OAB thoroughly deliberated over most of the lawsuits it filed, with the result that they had far more rigorous and carefully vetted legal content. But the OAB president also often had great public voice and thus could drive internal OAB consensus to file suit.

By way of example, in another major challenge to Cardoso's social security policy in January 1999, the OAB president argued that a withholding tax on civil service pensions being debated in Congress was illegal, and threatened a suit if it should be approved. The threat was reported in major newspapers as "OAB threatens suit" (for example, *Folha de São Paulo* 1999c), neglecting to mention that only the president was threatening the suit, and that the entire council would need to deliberate before it could file an ADIN against such a law. Once the tax was approved, the OAB president once again was in the press, although this time pointedly making the observation that he would only be able to file suit after debate in the Federal Council. Perhaps as a result, he was able to bring the Federal Council on board, and the injunction requested by the OAB was granted in September 1999, in a major fiscal and political setback for the Cardoso government. A canny leader of the OAB could thus use the press and public opinion to stimulate debate within the OAB on matters he opposed, then build consensus within the Federal Council around his position.

To summarize briefly, the three policy areas just discussed show very different patterns and outcomes. The OAB never won an outright political or legal victory against the use of provisional measures, although alongside criticism from other actors its vociferousness probably succeeded in constraining the Cardoso administration's issuance of new provisional measures, and certainly helped in building congressional support for limits imposed on their use in 2001. Side efforts to embarrass Cardoso administration officials probably did little to help the OAB's cause, except to make a political point that had some resonance among opponents of "neoliberal" reforms.

The OAB failed completely in its opposition to the CVRD sale. On the legal front, there were simply very few options available to the bar association: unlike opposition political parties, it was not very good at posing broad, lower court challenges, and its constitutional challenge was undermined by the fact that there was no major legislative foundation that could be challenged by ADIN. The OAB thus relied primarily on public expression of its opposition, often in tandem with other opposing groups.

On social security, the OAB had a mixed record, but ultimately scored a major coup in its defeat of the withholding tax on civil service pensions. Once again, the OAB's direct interests in this measure were unclear, but its defense of the "acquired rights" offered by the Constitution, and its access to constitutional review mechanisms in the STF, meant that it scored an enormous victory by reversing a major Cardoso policy in the STF.

The OAB's Motivations

The OAB's motivations for contesting policy are driven by both interests and ideas, which are in many cases mutually constitutive, and whose practical consequences are always constrained by institutional frameworks. Indeed, without reference to these overlapping motivations and the resulting group ties to a broader community of reform opponents, the OAB's opposition to many Cardoso policies such as social security reform can seem irrational and perhaps even ill-conceived.

As for the institutional framework, the 1988 Constitution is in many ways beset by its origins in the prevailing worldview of the historical moment of 1987–88, during which the overriding objectives were to prevent a return to authoritarianism and to guarantee a wide-ranging list of political and economic rights. To achieve these ends, the institutional structure provided special judicial access to many of the groups best represented in the constitutional convention. Most striking for this discussion, lawyers and their bar association are better represented than any other single professional group in the 1988 Constitution, an advantage that has been repeatedly confirmed and extended by the courts. The OAB has been particularly good at using the ADIN mechanism to challenge policies it disagrees with, and its privileges of standing in the STF have expanded over time to give it better and broader rights than peer groups such as business and labor organizations. Meanwhile, the prominence of the OAB as a civil society organization gives it broad influence across many areas of policy in a way that is unparalleled by other professional organizations.

Sometimes, however, the same institutional framework has prevented OAB action. For example, in the run-up to the 1998 election, the OAB's ethics committee publicly protested mass mailings sent by Cardoso's social security minister, complaining that this was abuse of the government "machine" for electoral purposes. But although this was a complaint with clear merit, and an alleged abuse of power that may very well have shocked lawyers nationwide, there was no legal recourse the OAB as an institution could undertake, because under Brazilian law and the Constitution, the OAB does not have standing to file protests in the electoral court system (only the *Ministério Público* and political parties are legally enfranchised in this way). In other words, in this case there was no institutional venue or veto point available that would have permitted the OAB to act as a veto player.

Second, the mix of personal and political interests in a corporate body such as the OAB is shaped by its own internal institutional rules. Corporatism is not a system of interest representation: it is a system of interest intermediation. Corporations do not always transmit the preferences of their members; rather, they structure them (Wilson 1983). By way of example, although lawyers may share defense of the constitution as a key ideational goal, not all lawyers were likely to agree on the Federal Council's decision to contest the privatization of CVRD via ADIN. Driving the point a bit further, even among those who supported the decision to file an ADIN, not all lawyers were likely to support the decision to march the lawsuit by foot to the STF in a widely publicized OAB protest. In other words, the institutional structure of the OAB, with a very autonomous national president and a Federal Council floating largely uninhibited above the state sectionals and the great mass of lawyers, suggests that some ideas and interests will be privileged over others in the policy arena, and provides considerable tactical leeway to dynamic leaders.

Which brings us to a final point, the relation between the OAB and corporatism. Power and Doctor's 2004 analysis of the inertial elements at work in Brazilian corporatism is particularly relevant here. In their view, the obstacles to change in Brazilian corporatist structures include the entrenchment of networks of vested interests; the fragmentation of business and labor, which weakens collective action by business and labor groups; and the embedding of corporatism in the "legal framework, formal structure, and informal practices of the state's relations with civil society." All three are pertinent to the case of the OAB. The Brazilian bar association is heavily entrenched in the current constitutional framework, drawing a reserve of political power from the constitutional arrangements it helped to create. Largely as a result, the OAB was far better consolidated as an interest group opposing reform than the fractured and institutionally less-privileged labor and business coalitions.

The OAB's role in the new Brazilian corporatist system that emerged from the 1988 Constitution does show signs of evolution, albeit largely in the direction of even greater embeddedness. The OAB's efforts in the 1970s and its strength in the post–military period suggest that it has shed many vestiges of the cooptation, weakness, and dependency that mark corporatism as a political structure (Schmitter 1971). The OAB has virtually no subservient ties to the state; it is not constrained, but largely enabled, by the institutional framework it operates within; and it has employed the institutional access to the courts it obtained in the Constituent Assembly to block policies it opposes on ideational or interest-based grounds.

The larger normative question is whether the balance between defense of its interests and its ideas gives the OAB a valid claim on the institutional prerogatives it gained in the 1988 Constitution. The institutional structure of the judiciary created in the 1988 Constitution provides the OAB with leverage in the courts that is unrivaled among its peers in industry, commerce, and labor, and much stronger than that of individual citizens. The OAB defends these institutional prerogatives, arguing they are necessary if lawyers are to fulfill their constitutional responsibility of defending democracy and the democratic legal framework. From a political science perspective, however, the manner by which the OAB garnered and has performed its roles as constitutional guardian and professional interest group raises the complicated question of the extent to which corporatist forms of political representation displace political voice permanently into nests of organized interests, and the limits such interest groups place on the gradual opening of these institutions to new political actors.

Conclusion

Returning to the contrast between the use of the courts by political parties and by the bar association, it is clear that both have used very different legal tactics, driven by very different overall objectives, even though the two occasionally contested the very same policies. The model of legal tactical choice described earlier in this book suggests that policy actors' tactical choices are determined in part by the judicial institutional environment, and in part by the political environment. But both of these remained constant over the period analyzed. The broader lesson of these chapters, then, is that for organized policy actors choosing to use the courts, the group's internal institutional structure is very important to determining which policies will be considered salient enough to merit legal contestation by the potential plaintiffs, and secondarily, which legal tactics will be used in pursuit of what strategic political objectives.

Political parties, by nature, tend to publicly announce their interests and ideas, both as a means of attracting members and as a means of building electoral support. Although there is room for some mystery about parties' ultimate intentions and the tactics they will use to achieve them, parties' publicly announced interests and ideas can be confirmed against public actions, such as congressional votes, public demonstrations, or the legal suits filed by party members. As a result, political parties' legal tactics are generally more easily deciphered in terms of their overall political objectives than those of interest groups, who have little obligation to announce the interests and ideas underlying their political actions to any but their members. In sum, while the underlying strategic interest of political parties in attaining power may occasionally be trumped by immutable policy preferences, parties' ideas and interests are generally quite transparent and easily tested against actual behaviors.

By contrast, the ideas and interests of interest groups are oftentimes less manifest, and as a result may be harder to disentangle. Further, as this chapter has shown, institutions may well be constitutive of interests and ideas, which in turn will be closely linked to the institutions out of which they arose. This helps to explain the OAB's willingness to go to significant lengths to protect the Constitution from change. As Shapiro (2005, 288) notes, the law constitutes interests as much as interests constitute law: the close links between the institutional framework created by the 1988 Constitution, the interests of lawyers, and the ideational commitment to the Constitution led the OAB to use the courts to protect its own interests, often by defending the Constitution itself against change. It also has led the OAB to join forces with other groups which on the face of it share few interests with the Bar—trade unions, opposition political parties, and the Catholic Church, for example— but that formed part of the common epistemic community opposed to Cardoso's reforms.

A second contrast lies in these groups' internal institutional structure. The decision to challenge policy was much more broad-based in many cases within the PT than within the OAB. Although the party's legal staff played a key role in disseminating legal know-how, and in ADIN cases the party leadership needed to sign off on legal decisions, in many cases the party was extraordinarily effective in mobilizing organized but diffuse legal action throughout both the federal and state courts. By contrast, the OAB was much more centralized in its adoption of legal tactics: nothing prevented individual lawyers from challenging policy on their own, but when undertaking a legal case on behalf of the profession, the OAB usually decided to challenge policy after a far more centralized decision by the Federal Council, oftentimes driven to action by the president.

Once the PT or the OAB determined that policy was salient enough to merit opposition, and that the courts were the appropriate venue to contest policy, this internal institutional difference also played a role. The PT's most effective legal tactics were much more grassroots, in what could be called the "swarming" of the lower courts by PT members and sympathizers, whereas the OAB's tactics predominantly focused on constitutional review via ADIN. Partly as a result, the OAB more actively vetted the content of its suits, privileging the tactical objective of obtaining a veto, but only inasmuch as it could do so within the perceived constraints of the law. Differences in constituency groups make a large difference: lawyers are far less inclined than PT party members to head to the streets. But the OAB's differing tactics also reflected the institutional framework available to the OAB's federal council: it could file suit in a number of venues, but the most effective means for the OAB to do so, when consensus within the council existed, was via ADIN. Furthermore, within the OAB, the loose control the federal OAB exerted over the state OABs meant that broad-based lower court action of the sort the political parties frequently used against privatization was impractical and potentially divisive.

The PT was much less concerned with strict legality itself, and was willing to risk a legal defeat if use of the courts enabled the party to voice its opposition to policy in yet another forum. By contrast, while the OAB frequently voiced its opinion outside the courts, when the federal OAB filed suit, it seldom sought to use the courts as an instrument of voice. Except in cases of urgency, the full OAB Federal Council had to agree to file an ADIN, approved by the president, and there would be a natural professional anathema to filing suits with little legal content. The upside was that the OAB was more successful on ADIN cases proportionally than most other groups, perhaps because its decisions to file suit were more thoroughly vetted. The downside, of course, was that the OAB often became a strident opponent in political venues before reaching the internal consensus in favor of legal action. And if the OAB leadership failed to obtain such consensus, in the absence of a battalion of foot soldiers such as the PT's, all the OAB had was its public stridence. It is perhaps no surprise, then, that the presidents of the OAB became known as such discordant opponents of Cardoso and his policies, and more recently, of Lula and his policies.

Chapter 7

Courts in the Policy Process: Pension Reform in Cross-National Perspective

So far, this book has made two interrelated arguments about how courts are drawn into the policy process. First, that the type of policy—and more concretely, the distribution of a policy's costs and benefits—may influence the degree to which courts are drawn into policy debates. This is a subjective process, however, and potential plaintiffs' ideas and interests help determine how these costs and benefits are perceived, while in the case of group plaintiffs, internal institutional structure also helps to mediate the political tactics they choose to utilize, including in the courts. If plaintiffs decide that policy should be contested, the second argument is that the judicial institutional environment shapes the range of legal tactics that can be used to contest policy in the courts.

This chapter addresses this second point more directly, using cross-national comparison to illustrate how institutional structures shape opposition tactics in the courts. My aims are, first, to illustrate that the logic of institutional choice is as relevant to courts as it is to other governmental structures, and second, to emphasize the importance of better incorporating courts and judicial structure into our models of policy choice.

Institutions are important because they "mold the prior probabilities of outcomes" (Przeworski 1988, 79) and because "policy implications flow from such [institutional] choices" (Koelble 1995, 238). By analyzing the distinct experiences of four Latin American nations in the common policy arena of pension reform, this chapter illustrates how differences in the overall institutional environment influenced the comparative success of similar interest groups attempting to impose their policy preferences on a similarly salient policy reform.[1] In keeping with the overall emphasis of this book, I focus especially on the role of courts, highlighting the importance of studying heretofore neglected veto points outside the legislative and executive branches that have had a significant effect on policy outcomes.

Revamping pension systems has been a top policy objective for Latin American reformers over the past twenty years. During this period, much of the region has undertaken some degree of pension reform, following in the footsteps of Chile's path-breaking 1981 pension privatization, and goaded on by the more recent examples of their neighbors, as well as pressure and advice from international financial institutions. Reform was spurred on by ideas about increasing domestic savings, reducing capital dependency, and improving capital markets (Madrid 2005),[2] as well as fiscal necessity, especially among the countries with the oldest pension systems (Mesa-Lago 1997, 502).

Yet the outcomes of these reforms vary enormously, from full privatization (Chile, Mexico, Bolivia, El Salvador) to parallel systems that complement but do not replace public systems (Peru, Colombia) and mixed systems that allow contributions to, and benefits from, both public and private pension systems (Argentina and Uruguay) (Madrid 2002). There are also countries that are relative laggards in this field, such as Brazil and Costa Rica, which have had different degrees of success implementing far more modest "parametric reforms" that revise existing benefits without substantially altering the public pay-as-you-go system (Mesa-Lago and Müller 2002, 688; Huber and Stephens 2000).

Among the countries that decided on the need for some degree of pension reform over the past two decades—and here the greater part of Latin America fits the picture—two explanations have been given for the differing pace and direction of policy change. The first explains policy change in a largely pluralist fashion, as an outcome of the bargaining between diverse interest groups of varying strength (Mesa-Lago 1978). In this view, differing levels of labor or business mobilization and the resulting bargaining strength of each interest group are used to explain differing cross-national experiences. The second approach is critical of such accounts, arguing that there is "no clear correlation between interest group strength and policy outcome." Instead, institutions are seen as a crucial intervening variable, which "shape (but do not determine) political conflict by providing interest groups with varying opportunities to veto policy" (Kay 1999, 406, 412). As any reader who has come this far will recognize, I am clearly sympathetic to the logic of this second argument.

Yet which are the key institutions, do their effects vary across countries, and do they offer special advantages to specific political groups or policy actors? Using the logic of veto players and veto points developed earlier, and drawing on Immergut's insight (1992, 231) that "institutions alter the constellation of groups that are pertinent to a given policy decision, as well as the relative importance of these groups," this chapter addresses these questions with regard to pension reforms undertaken in Argentina, Brazil, Mexico, and Uruguay during the 1990s. The primary focus is on the degree to which differing institutional arrangements, both within and outside the executive and legislative branches, provided or failed to provide significant leverage to opponents of reform. Second, I illustrate how and why courts did not play as important a role in the pension reforms of Brazil's peers, and speculate about what possible changes in the institutional setting of the region's courts might mean for the judicial contestation of policy further down the road.

The Politics of Pension Reform in Mexico, Argentina, Uruguay, and Brazil

Seldom is it possible to compare reforms with similar distributions of costs and benefits, much less reforms that address the same topical issue in a similar time frame and economic and political setting, across four Latin American countries. Yet pension reform provides just such an opportunity, in light of the fact that most such reforms in Latin America began to be undertaken under similar transitional politics during the 1990s. This coincidence permits the use of a comparative framework that holds policy type constant, while allowing institutions to vary across country, complementing one-country studies that have investigated the politics surrounding different policies in the same institutional environment (for example, Melo [2002, 2003, 2004] on the Brazilian case). It also echoes the important cross-national single-policy analysis conducted by Immergut (1992) on the politics of health care reform in Switzerland, France, and Sweden, seeking in a similar fashion to understand how the existence of veto points enabled or constrained changes in the status quo across a number of countries facing similar budgetary and actuarial constraints, but extending this reasoning beyond Immergut's focus on primarily electoral and legislative veto points to the courts themselves.

Inevitably, even though the policy topic remains constant, there are important differences between the various reforms undertaken: the four countries analyzed here began the 1990s with pension systems in varying degrees of disarray, and pressure for reform and the urgency of reform thus varied considerably, leading to important differences in both scope and ambition. Nonetheless, the case study of pension reform is an intriguing one, in large part because the interest groups involved are quite similar—including pensioners' associations, labor unions, and opposition political parties—while the de facto outcomes, and the distance between objectives and outcomes, varies considerably. For brevity's sake, I provide only a skeletal outline of the politics of the reform process in each country, focusing on the first round of reforms in Mexico (1991–97); Argentina (1989–94); Uruguay (1990–95); and Brazil (1995–2000).

MEXICO

The most dramatic change in pension systems in these four countries occurred in the first wave of pension reform in Mexico between 1991 and 1997. The governing Institutional Revolutionary Party (PRI) was able to guide through two major reforms during this period. In 1992 the government introduced a mandatory supplementary, private sector administered, individual savings scheme funded by a 2 percent payroll tax. This was followed by the full privatization of the old pension system in 1995, with the new system beginning to operate in 1997 and a full transition from the old system completed by 2001.[3] The new system created a group of private corporations (*Afores*) to supplant the pension functions of the Mexican Institute of Social Security (IMSS), and future pensioners were mandatorily subscribed in the new private sector system.

The radical change that these initial Mexican reforms entailed—a full swing, in less than a decade, from a public pay-as-you-go to a privatized system—was only possible because of a nearly complete absence of veto points and of independent veto players under one-party *presidencialista* rule by the PRI. Reform might have occurred more rapidly were it not for the "PRI's need to recoup support after the highly tarnished 1988 elections" (Huber and Stephens 2000, 10). But otherwise, and especially in the wake of the 1995 peso crisis, all pressures were in favor of reform. Within the Congress, the absence of any serious legislative constraints enabled the government to achieve all of its initial objectives. Meanwhile, labor groups were weakened by economic reform, and even when they did express their opposition to privatization, they were successfully coopted by the government, as so often was the case under the PRI.

ARGENTINA

In Argentina, the decaying pension system became a major concern in the late 1980s, reaching crisis levels as pensioners successfully used the courts to force the government to pay cost-of-living readjustments it had failed to provide.[4] These successive court defeats resulted in "staggering public debt within the pension system" (Huber and Stephens 2000, 13), and pension reform thus rose to the top of the policy agenda early in Menem's first term (1989–94). Yet full privatization was not proposed by the Menem administration, partly because the government recognized the potentially enormous transition costs of privatization, but also as a result of agenda setters' recognition of the strength of the opposition that might ensue from unions and pensioners' associations (Huber and Stephens 2000, 13).

Instead, Menem's original 1992 proposal aimed for a more modest move to parallel public and private systems. Under pressure from his allies in Peronist labor unions, this was diluted to the even more modest goal of a mixed system in which individuals would belong to a reformed public system, but with the additional option of joining supplementary private accounts as part of the second-tier of pension provision. Menem was able to approve this reform in large part because he controlled labor unions and had broad popular support, while opposition from pensioner associations was muted in part because their rights were basically guaranteed by the reform and they had gained considerably from the 1991 cost-of-living readjustments. Even so, despite bargaining and significant concessions made to the unions, and in particular to the pro-Menemist CGT union, pension reform was approved in Congress only by using "parliamentary maneuvering of rather questionable legality" (Huber and Stephens 2000, 13; Madrid 1999). Legislative approval was obtained in this unorthodox fashion in 1993, with the reform going into effect in mid-1994.

URUGUAY

Uruguay's pension reformers faced vociferous opposition from a population that is significantly older on average than that of other Latin American nations, and in which a quarter of the population received pensions. Pension benefits had fallen calamitously even prior to the end of the military regime, and after the transition democratic leaders agreed to boost benefits. Ultimately, though, these increases were insufficient to staunch significant public protest, which culminated in the calling of a plebiscite on pension benefits in 1989. The plebiscite, approved by an overwhelming 82 percent of voters, had catastrophic results, leading to an increase in social security expenditures from 9.6 percent of GDP in 1986 to 16.1 percent in 1992 (Papadopulos 1998, cited in Huber and Stephens 2000, 14). Despite the impending crisis that rising pension outlays threatened through higher deficits and inflation, however, reform was to face a troubled future.

The Lacalle administration (1990–95) was the first to push for reform, submitting a rather tepid proposal to Congress in September 1990 to increase the retirement age and alter the benefits calculation. This was rejected outright, leading the government to establish working groups to study reform and draft a new bill, proposed in April 1992. This second proposal, which once again maintained pay-as-you-go while altering benefits rules, was also rejected by Congress, which was cowed by the strength and influence of the pensioners' association. Forced back to the drafting board, the government introduced minor changes to the system, setting a new maximum pension level and establishing anti-evasion rules. These were introduced rather controversially as part of an unrelated budget law in November 1992, but were overwhelmingly defeated by 72 percent of voters in a 1994 plebiscite that ruled the law's passage unconstitutional (Castiglioni 2000).

In light of the Lacalle administration's striking string of failures, before taking office, the coalition government under Sanguinetti (1995–2000) worked to build support among the Colorado and Blanco parties, as well as—briefly—members of the leftist opposition. The resulting reform proposal, approved in September 1995, went significantly further than its predecessors, instituting a mixed system under which the public pay-as-you-go system remained but workers under forty were given the choice of contributing to a supplemental private system. Although leftist opposition parties, unions, and the pensioners' association ultimately opposed the bill, the coalition was strong enough—and the government wily enough[5]—to guarantee congressional approval. Four years later, in 1999, a commission made up of trade unions, the powerful pensioners' association (ONAJPU), and the leftist *Frente Amplio* presented a petition for a plebiscite, but this was overturned by the Electoral Court on the grounds that forty thousand of the required signatures were invalid. As a result, the new mixed system was effectively preserved from further challenge.

BRAZIL

Brazil sought the least radical reform of the four countries analyzed here. This is not to say, however, that attempts at reform during the 1990s were unambitious: indeed, in light of the rigidity of the 1988 Constitution, even minimal reform required substantial executive leadership and energetic congressional mobilization to achieve the 60 percent super-majorities needed for constitutional amendment. Partly as a result of these difficulties, pension reform has remained a top agenda item throughout the past decade, from the outset of the Cardoso administration and through the Lula presidency, even though the proposals have emphasized the gradual, parametric reform of the system rather than a more ambitious move to a mixed or parallel private-public arrangement.

Cardoso sent a major reform proposal to Congress two months after his 1995 inauguration. This set a minimum retirement age, created a defined contribution plan, established caps on benefits, and altered the benefits formula. As Chapter 3 noted in greater detail, after being held up temporarily by an injunction granted by a high court judge in April 1996, the proposal was significantly altered in the Chamber of Deputies, then rejected on the Chamber floor when it went to a vote. A revised and diluted reform proposal was finally approved by the Chamber in July 1996, but was then altered by the Senate, requiring new hearings in the Chamber. It was not until November 1998, under the gun of the Russian crisis, that the Chamber approved the final constitutional amendment on social security. But this reform had also been substantially diluted, and a section of the amendment proposal taxing civil service pensions was narrowly rejected in a subsequent floor vote.

The government then tried an end-run around Congress, issuing a provisional measure that established a withholding tax on civil service pensions, which was converted to law during the devaluation crisis of January 1999. But this law was to be overturned by the Supreme Federal Tribunal (STF) nine months later, alongside an accompanying law setting rules for contributions by nongovernmental organizations.

The final stage in the Cardoso government's social security saga was the approval of a further law in November 1999 that set the formula for calculating retirement benefits, the so-called "pension factor." This law extended the time of service required for retirement, increased fines for late payment, and established the possibility of annual changes in the contribution formula. With final congressional approval of the reform package between November 1998 and January 1999, constitutional review challenges against the reform flew fast and furious, with an unprecedented thirty-three direct actions of unconstitutionality (ADINs) filed against social security laws in the STF. Three of these ADINs were upheld in whole or part, with one in particular—suspending the tax on civil service pensioners and the increase in the pension contribution by active civil servants—leading to significant alterations to the government's proposed reform.

The three successful ADINs had been filed by policy players that were seemingly peripheral actors in the pluralist account of pension reform, and were otherwise not a significant part of the executive and legislative deliberations over the reform: one small political party, the PSB, won a minor benefit by excluding maternity leave from a cap on pension benefits, and a relatively low-profile national health confederation (the *Confederação Nacional da Saude, Hospitais, Establecimentos e Serviços*) won another partial victory with an exemption from pension contributions for charitable organizations. The most significant victory, however, belonged to the national bar association (OAB), which won the September 1999 decision suspending the tax on civil service pensioners and the increase in the pension contribution by active civil servants, a decision that the government estimated would cost R$2.4 billion annually and which completely voided a significant component of the overall pension reform.

Veto Players and Veto Points in Pension Reform

There are four key conclusions that emerge from this brief overview of the four countries' experiences, relating to veto players' cooptation, internal unanimity, and shared preferences. The first is that some potential veto players were reined in by powerful governments. In all four countries, the most prominent interest groups involved in deliberations over reform were labor unions, pensioners' groups, and their political representatives (Kay 1998; 1999). These three groups also were sometimes able to draw support from other orbiting veto players, such as the bar association, religious groups, or military officers' associations, in part because of shared goals of opposition to other policy reforms undertaken during this same period. The relative importance of these veto players and their orbiting allies would be determined largely by their access to veto points. As depicted by the shading of the cells in Table 7.1 (darker shading illustrates more vigorous opposition), however, the coalition that might have been expected to oppose pension reform in both Argentina and Mexico during first round reforms was weakened by its alliance, cooptation, or sidelining by reformist governments, essentially negating its members' effective performance as veto players. Although there was some negotiation of the Argentine reform proposal to obtain union acquiescence, the degree and style of union opposition, especially from the CGT, was considerably restrained; the Argentine unions "had become dependent on the state" (Kay 1999, 411).

A second point is that the degree of unanimity on policy preferences *within* interest groups clearly plays a role in the effectiveness of their opposition as veto players. This is most obvious with regard to political parties, but it also is significant as it relates to unions and pensioners' associations. For example, the unified front presented by the ONAJPU (*Organización Nacional de Asociaciones de Jubilados y Pensionistas del Uruguay*) stands in sharp contrast to the divided retiree groups in Argentina, who were "fragmented along party,

TABLE 7.1

Key veto players in pension reform

	Labor Unions	Pensioners	Political Representatives
Argentina	Diverse unions; opposition came primarily from the smaller CTA union (rather than CGT or MTA) opposed, but weakly	Fragmented retiree groups	Radical Party Greater threat was from disaffected Peronists, who were "bought off"
Brazil	CUT and public sector workers' groups	Diverse pensioners' groups; none nationally organized	PT; PDT; PCdoB, and other small leftist parties
Mexico	Allied to or coopted by the state	Some protest, but largely coopted by the state	PRI-run Congress
Uruguay	PIT-CNT	Single unified pensioners' group (ONAJPU)	Leftist parties (especially *Frente Amplio*)

NOTE: The intensity of opposition is illustrated by the shading of the cells, with darker cells reflecting more intense opposition.

SOURCE: This table draws on my own research on Brazil and Mexico, as well as the framework and country data for Argentina and Uruguay in Kay 1998; 1999.

union and ideological lines" (Kay 1999, 410). Similarly, pensioners' groups in Brazil were weak and fragmented. As a result the strongest public opposition to Brazil's pension reform came from the CUT union and a diverse range of civil service associations representing both active and retired workers. Political parties—probably as a consequence of Brazil's system of open-list proportional representation—were largely fragmented and inefficient as collective veto players, although the resulting absence of party discipline led to what effectively became a plethora of individual veto players, with individual congressional representatives bargaining support for reform.[6]

Third, the unanimity of policy preferences *between* the veto players presented here is also crucial to the likelihood of successful veto playing, especially in Congress. The strongest veto player coalition against reform was found in Uruguay, where not coincidentally the electoral interests of the *Frente Amplio* and the strong monopoly of representation that the PIT-CNT and the ONAJPU enjoyed among their respective constituencies enabled a powerful anti-reform coalition to emerge as early as the 1989 plebiscite (Kay 1999, 411). In Brazil, a similar anti-reform coalition made up of civil servants' groups, unions, and leftist parties (which were unique among Brazilian political parties during this period because of their intense internal party discipline) coalesced rather predictably in opposition to major policy reforms undertaken by the federal government until 2002, when PT candidate Lula won the presidency. Nothing similar was seen in Mexico or Argentina during these first-stage pension reforms, due to the strength of the executive and the fragmentation and cooptation of the various interest groups that might otherwise have been expected to oppose reform. Yet although it may have significant effects on legislative outcomes through its effect on elected officials' stated policy preferences, the simple numeric strength of potential veto players cannot single-handedly explain the results of reform in these four countries.

The fourth major factor at work in the various reforms arises from the availability of veto points, of which several seem especially relevant in comparative perspective. As earlier chapters have emphasized, veto players are often unable to exercise a veto if they do not have access to veto points: the institutional opportunity to exercise a veto is thus often a primary, constitutive factor in the identity of veto players, providing them with a significant role in policy deliberations (or not).

Figure 7.1 illustrates the significant differences in the paths of pension reform in the four countries, ranging from Mexico and Argentina, where reform was relatively simple, to Uruguay and Brazil, where the path to reform

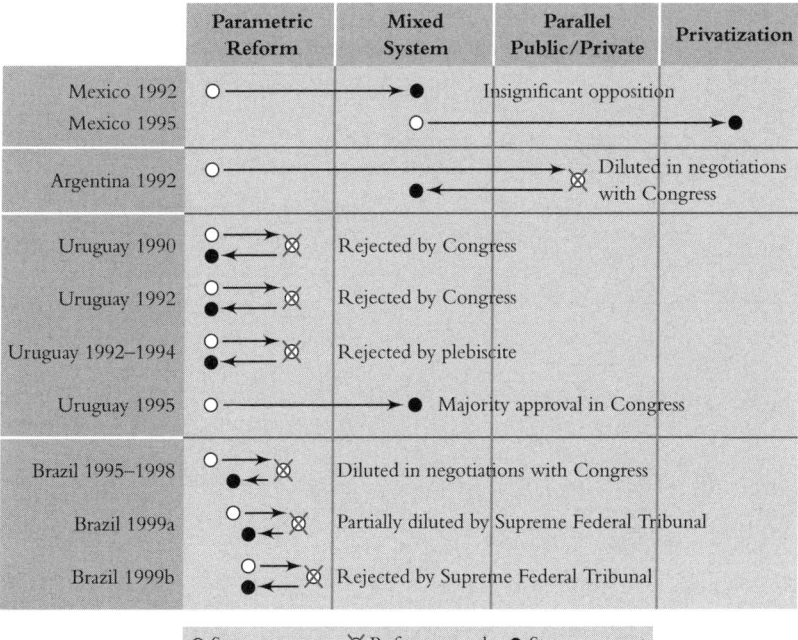

Figure 7.1. Paths of pension reform proposals

was arduous and required repeated efforts to achieve even modest gains. In comparative perspective, two veto points outside the executive and legislative branches are strikingly apparent in the latter countries: the plebiscite in Uruguay, and the courts—and in particular, the instruments of high court judicial review—in Brazil.

Were it not for the plebiscite rule, pension reform might have been approved as early as 1989, six years earlier than it actually occurred in Uruguay. As Kay (1999, 415) notes, if we compare Uruguay's experience with that of its western neighbor, the relevance of this veto point is quite apparent: in only three months during 1993, 1.3 million Argentines signed on to a 1993 petition against pension reform. Under Uruguayan referenda rules, only 400,000 more signatures would have been required to reach the 10 percent threshold of registered voters that would permit a referendum to be called. Absent such a rule in Argentina, this significant public protest against reform could not have been channeled into an institutional veto point even if the target of 1.7 million had been met, and thus Argentine pension reform proceeded without further ado. Likewise, courts in Brazil offered a significant veto point that was not available in the other countries during this same time period, as the next section shows.

Courts as Veto Points in Different Institutional Environments

The role of the Brazilian courts as a veto point on pension reform is illustrative of how institutional rules can affect policy outcomes. The judicial institutional environment, and particularly the rules governing standing, enabled certain veto players who were not particularly active in bargaining over reforms in the Congress to exercise a veto over policy *ex post,* after congressional deliberation and approval of reform.[7] That is, after all the negotiations between parties, congressional representatives, and the government were complete, and reform was in the implementation stage, courts were brought into the debate with a significant chance of altering or voiding the agreed-upon policy changes.

The question that arises in the context of pension reform is, why were courts not similarly influential in Mexico, Argentina, or Uruguay? The framework of legal tactical choice outlined in Chapter 2 notes the importance of structures of judicial independence and judicial review, as well as of the resulting judicial administrative performance. Together these may influence the likelihood that policy will be contested in the courts, and the tactics used to do so. This framework does not attempt to explain the likelihood that policy will be effectively overturned or diluted, but these factors help to explain the chances of a policy's being taken to court in a fashion that could credibly influence policy.

Although the judicial contestation of policy alone obviously does not imply a final veto forthcoming from the courts, it does have two important implications within the context of this book. First, other things equal, the higher the number of court challenges, the greater the risk that policy will be overturned by a judge or group of judges at some point in the court system. Second, the relative ability of some groups to use specific courts or legal instruments to challenge policy more than other groups—especially if it has proven effective in other cases—may enable them to threaten to use the courts as a veto point, establishing themselves as veto players and giving them some leverage in policy negotiations both *ex ante* and *ex post*.

Chapter 2 detailed the structures of judicial independence and judicial review. For purposes of rapid comparison here, then, it is sufficient to note the variables that were of most importance in the cases of pension reform described here. The first key variable that helps to explain the absence of significant court influence in the Argentine and Mexican pension reforms during the 1990s is rather obvious: judicial independence, and, particularly, its subcomponents of judicial autonomy and the "external independence" of judges. Judicial autonomy relates to the courts' institutional capacity to take decisions, and is affected both by structure and budgetary considerations; "external independence" relates to the ability of judges to take their decisions freely, without fear of reprisal from other branches of government. Certainly the judiciary in Mexico prior to the mid-1990s was weak on both counts and as a result was frequently subservient to PRI interests; while legality was an important component of PRI legitimacy, all too often it was subsumed by political necessity (Domingo 1999, 2000). Even if policy reform had been contested, which was unlikely in light of the perceived subordination of courts, it is also unlikely that before the mid-1990s such contestation would have led to significant policy reversals.

Meanwhile, in Argentina in the early 1990s, all the institutional checks negotiated between Menem and the Radicals proved too weak to counter the organized offensive carried out in favor of Menem's accumulation of power, including in the courts. This experience contrasts sharply with the Brazilian example since the 1980s: the Argentine judiciary was increasingly reduced to submission under Menem. Although there was still room for influential judicial decisions so long as they backed the executive branch (Larkins 1998),[8] actual legal challenges to the executive were undermined by a long history of short and involuntarily foreshortened judicial tenures (Scribner 2003), as well as Menem's packing of the Supreme Court, his efforts to slow passage of the regulatory framework creating a Council of Magistrates, and his unwillingness to reapportion the Supreme Court as he had agreed with the opposition in 1994. Further, the executive branch's compliance with challenges from the judiciary was uneven at best (Kapiszewski 2007).

Uruguay's courts, on the other hand, are marked by a high degree of judicial independence. As Bergara et al. (2004, 29–30) note, the appointments procedure for the Supreme Court "isolates the judiciary from major political discretion and manipulation" (even though the court is budgetarily less autonomous than its Brazilian peer). They also note that the courts *did* have an important influence on pension reform, as when the Supreme Court clearly signaled that, in its opinion, the 1992 pension reform was unconstitutionally approved, since it had been approved surreptitiously within the budget bill. That decision set the stage for the successful plebiscite overturning the reform in 1994. Yet the court did not have the power to overturn the reform itself, and as a result, at no time was it a credible veto point for groups seeking to reverse pension reform.

Why was the Uruguayan court not a significant veto point on pension reform, then? This brings us to the second relevant variable: the bindingness of judicial review. Many individuals sought to contest the Uruguayan pension reform law in the courts, and particularly in the Supreme Court. But the absence of abstract review and *erga omnes* effects meant that the reach of the courts' decisions, even when contrary to reform, was limited to specific individuals, rather than reversing the reform bill's effects on society at large. Courts of course have a political role to play even in the absence of broadly binding decisions, as the earlier example of the legal battle against electricity rationing in Brazil illustrated. But the point is that a broader and more widely applicable decision was not possible, and thus not a reasonable tactical objective. Uruguayan courts are therefore largely ineffectual veto points, even though they offer an alternative venue in which to voice opposition.[9]

In sum, the only court system that provided a veto point on pension reform in the four countries analyzed here was Brazil's judiciary. The policy relevance of Brazil's judiciary comes not only from the independence of judges from other branches of government but also from the structure of judicial review. The structure and rules governing Uruguay's courts are not likely to be reformed in the near term. Argentina's courts have undergone some reform, but as Larkins (1998) notes, the greater problem with the scope of judicial authority in Argentina had less to do with institutional rules governing judicial review than with a lack of insulation from political pressures (in other words, from the informal aspects of "external independence"). The

new century's turmoil in Argentine politics suggests that it is too early to analyze the emerging degree of independence of the courts and its impact on
policy under the Kirchner administration. This leaves us with one country
with which to illustrate the effects of changing institutional structure on
courts' role in the policy process: Mexico in the wake of one-party rule.

Mexico is slowly building a more independent judiciary, with significant
reforms under way since the mid-1990s. But how will changing institutional
rules influence the Mexican judiciary's role as a veto point in policy deliberations? Changes in Mexican institutional structure are still so young as to be
hard to stack up against the inertial effects of seventy-odd years of one-party
rule, in which the advancement of constitutional rights was all too often sub-
jugated to short-term political interests. But there have been hopeful changes
in administrative and financial autonomy, recruitment, and tenure procedures,
and in judicial institutional culture, that bode well for greater judicial independence. A 1994 judicial reform severely restricted politicization and increased the external independence of the high court by requiring two-thirds
congressional majorities for appointment to the Supreme Court. Together
with increased political competition, this has contributed to a radical increase
(almost a tripling) in rulings against the PRI in politically sensitive matters
between 1995 and 2003 (Tapia Palacios 2003; Ríos-Figueroa 2003; 2007).

There are two major differences between Mexican and Brazilian courts
that will continue to influence their likely participation in policy debates
as long as there is inter-party competition and judicial independence in
both countries: the degree of bindingness and the degree of standing (Ríos-
Figueroa and Taylor 2006).

In terms of bindingness, Mexico's Supreme Court serves less as a final
court of appeal or cassation than does its Brazilian counterpart. In large part
this is due to the fact that there are more binding mechanisms in Mexico:
despite the absence of *stare decisis* (an absence common to civil code systems, including Brazil's), both the Mexican Supreme Court and circuit courts
may establish *jurisprudencia* with binding effects by publishing five consecu-
tive and consistent decisions on a given point of law. The Supreme Court
also can issue *tesis sobresalientes* of jurisprudence, which are guidelines for interpretation that, while not binding, can be highly influential. These are
stronger in both form and function than even the most consistent string of
decisions from the Brazilian STF in terms of establishing permissible interpretations of statute. *Amparo* cases, in which the courts address individual
rights against the government as a defendant, meanwhile, can be heard or
not at the court's discretion. The result is that the Mexican Supreme Court

hears far fewer cases per year than its counterpart in Brazil (roughly eight thousand cases, as compared to over one hundred thousand in Brazil).

In terms of standing, aside from appeals up the ladder, the only individuals with standing in the two countries' high courts are those permitted to file *habeas corpus* or *amparo* suits, but because the effects of such suits are strictly individual, their broader policy impact is very limited (unless, in the Mexican case, *jurisprudencia* is created). As Navia and Ríos-Figueroa (2005, 210) note, this severely limits individual impacts on policy; individuals "can only question the constitutionality of laws but cannot aspire to produce *erga omnes* effects in case the judiciary positively hears their cases."

The most significant differences in standing, therefore, lie in the degree to which veto players, whose standing in the high courts provides them with a veto point with which to more directly influence policy, are able to effectively contest policy in the courts. Mexico's Supreme Court hears far fewer cases that come straight to its doors under its original jurisdiction than does Brazil's STF: the Mexican Supreme Court has original jurisdiction in only two types of constitutional challenges, with the result that cases heard under the high court's original jurisdiction total only 1.7 percent of the high court's caseload in Mexico, as compared to 7.7 percent in Brazil. Furthermore, Mexico's constitution is far narrower than Brazil's, which suggests that the high court may be less activated on policy issues; if rights as diffuse as a right to health care or civil servants' rights to a certain salary are embedded in the constitutional text, this makes it more plausible that high courts can be triggered to investigate policies that threaten such rights. Finally, the groups given standing—that is the groups that can become veto players through the use of the judicial veto point provided by the high court—are far more limited in Mexico than in Brazil, as shown in Table 7.2.

The importance of standing to policy change can be illustrated by two speculative thought experiments drawn from Brazil's policy debates during the 1990s. One group that Brazil excludes from standing in constitutional review cases is municipal governments, with interesting policy ramifications. If one were to imagine that Brazil's instruments of review had instead followed the Mexican constitutional text and granted municipal governments the right to challenge federal government policies via ADIN, a number of major policy decisions would likely have been heavily contested since the 1988 Constitution went into effect. Formal standing for mayors to file ADINs in the STF might have substantially altered the political negotiation of a number of bills in Congress, as well as the subsequent likelihood of implementation.

Perhaps most emblematically, the Fiscal Stabilization Fund—which was at the heart of the Cardoso government's strategy for combating inflation—

TABLE 7.2

Standing in Brazil's and Mexico's high courts

Brazil	Mexico
In ADIN and ADC	1. In *Acciones de Inconstitucionalidad*, federal laws may be contested by
President	
Senate	1/3 of either house of Congress
Chamber of Deputies	Prosecutor-general
Legislative Assembly	State law may be contested by
State governors	1/3 of state legislators
Prosecutor-general (*Ministério Público*)	Electoral law may be contested by
OAB	political parties
Political parties represented in Congress	2. In constitutional controversies
Unions or "class entities" with	All three levels of the federation
national scope	All three branches of government

SOURCE: Compiled from Ríos-Figueroa and Taylor 2006.

would have been practically impossible to approve as it was written, given its "temporary" suspension of constitutionally mandated revenue transfers from the federal to state and municipal governments. If the municipalities had been given a judicial veto point from which to wield their own potential veto of legislation, the policy picture would no doubt likely look far different than it does today, either because of the effect of such a threat on the negotiation of the Fund in Congress *ex ante,* or because of suits against the law actually filed by mayors in the high court *ex post.*

On the flip side, it is possible also to imagine how different policy outcomes might have been had certain groups not had the institutional veto point provided by the formal standing they were granted in the STF. If corporatist interest groups had been excluded from access to the Brazilian STF, as they are in Mexico, a number of successful challenges that resulted in major policy implications might never have been filed. These include a number of industrial and commercial federations' challenges to the Collor Plan's price freezes;[10] the bar association's suit against Collor's plan to restrict court challenges against his stabilization plan;[11] the bar association's challenge to Cardoso's agrarian reform;[12] judges' and prosecutors' associations' challenges to the broad privileges given to the bar association in the statute law governing lawyers;[13] the national industrial federation's challenge to social security reform[14] and a host of tax programs;[15] and labor unions' challenges to various labor policies.[16]

The growing independence of the Mexican courts from the executive branch has already led to significant changes in the degree to which policy is contested in that country's courts. Although the veto points provided by the courts in Mexico permit far fewer opportunities to policy opponents than they do in Brazil, opponents have nonetheless increasingly turned to the courts to contest the recent extension of pension reform to civil servants working for the IMSS state social security system (for greater details of this case, see Ríos-Figueroa and Taylor 2006, 759–61). The likelihood that the courts will offer a successful veto point for these civil servants, however, appears small. Not only is there no way for the civil service union to file a constitutional challenge directly in the Supreme Court contesting reform—in contrast to the multitude of actors who could have done so under similar circumstances in Brazil—but it also could not turn to a political party such as the center-left PRD (which opposed the reform) to file a suit on its behalf, as it might have been able to in Brazil. The last resort available to IMSS workers in the current reforms under way in Mexico is to file suit via *amparo*, without any chance of overturning this particular pension reform in its entirety.

Conclusion

The conclusions of this chapter are threefold, addressing (1) the methodological importance of distinguishing between veto players and veto points; (2) the contributions of such an approach to pluralist and institutionalist understandings of interest group representation; and (3) the determinants of courts' roles as potential veto points in policy reform. All three conclusions are relevant to understanding the paths of policy reform, both in the pension reforms of the 1990s and in current reform efforts under way across the region, as well as to understanding the increasing but variable degree to which courts have become involved in policy matters across the region.

IMPLICATIONS OF VETO POINTS FOR POLICY REFORM

Overall, the key lesson of the veto player and veto point framework is twofold. First, the more veto points that exist, the wider the variety of veto players (with differing preferences) that may be able to actively and credibly contest policy, increasing the costs of altering the status quo. Second, the fewer veto points that exist, the more concentrated government decision making will be. While this may facilitate and speed up decision making, two potential pitfalls have been identified with concentrated decision making. Concentrated policymaking makes politicians more accountable for policy outcomes, increasing the potential political costs of reform to decision makers (Pierson 1996, 152–3) and thus potentially slowing the adoption of costly but necessary policy reforms. Furthermore, and far more important, the more concentrated decision making is, the more likely policy will be volatile and possibly of weaker quality over the long haul, given the relative ease with which successive governments can reverse policy course over time (Spiller and Tommasi 2003). Decisiveness, in other words, may not be a desirable attribute of political systems if policy is not resolute over the long haul (Cox and McCubbins 2001).

The crisis in each of the four countries' pension systems was great enough in the 1990s that Pierson's concerns regarding accountability appear to have been overshadowed by the urgency of reform. Pierson does note, though, that in such situations, the politics of welfare-state policy retrenchment often leads policymakers to seek consensus to spread the blame (1996, 146–8). The presence of veto points in Uruguay and Brazil, especially, allowed potential veto players to declare their opposition to reform, and, in effect, to place the blame squarely on reformers, complicating their efforts in this regard. But the active opposition also led reformers to try to better spread the responsibility for reform, by seeking large majorities and negotiating some elements as broadly as possible. The process thus contributed to a more democratic reform process in these countries, founded in broader public evaluation of the costs and benefits of reform alternatives.

The cases analyzed here illustrate that reform was much more far-reaching in countries with a strong concentration of power in the executive branch and few veto points, such as Mexico and Argentina during the 1990s. Whether this will lead to good long-term policy outcomes is in question; as Huber and Stephens note in the Chilean case, not all of the results of radical pension reform have always been highly beneficial. That said, an absence of veto points may not necessarily lead to high policy volatility in the case of pension reform. Even in political systems with highly concentrated decision making (that is, fewer veto points and veto players), reversing pension reform entails extraordinarily high transaction costs, including the bureaucratic costs of shifting pensioners between systems, changing contributions and benefits, and so forth.

A final point extends beyond any single policy reform in its own right. The greater the number of veto points and veto players, the more likely that the overall reform agenda will be congested. This point is worth highlighting: the greater the dispersal of political power, the higher the likely congestion in all of the veto points in the political process. While on the face of it this is a rather banal finding, it may explain reformers' differing strategies toward pension reform across the four countries studied here: the very gradual approach to reform in Uruguay and Brazil made sense because pension reform was not the only policy change on the table. It was far better to move incrementally toward an end goal on pension reform than to gum up the works for all the other reforms—fiscal, tax, civil service, and so on—that were also under consideration at the same time. To make the same point in a different way, a high number of veto players may make policy less decisive and more resolute, but it does so both directly—by making any given policy more difficult to approve—and indirectly—by making the overall policy process slower and more deliberative. Under these conditions, it makes strategic good sense to seek only incremental, or parametric, reforms rather than wholesale change.

INTEREST GROUP CONFLICT

In terms of the conflict between pluralist and institutionalist accounts of interest group participation in reform, first raised in regard to pension reform by Kay (1998), this chapter has sought to find some middle ground. As repeatedly noted, veto players do not become veto players if they do not have access to some way of exercising their veto, which is where institutional rules come in. But on the other hand, as the previous two chapters noted, there is a great deal of strategic choice involved in how interest groups choose their battles and tactically employ the veto points available to them.

As we saw in Argentina during the 1990s, and have seen in the case of the pension reform undertaken by Lula during his first term, labor groups and leftist parties that have traditionally defended a large welfare state may see gains from supporting reforms they might otherwise oppose, especially if these are undertaken by a president who shares their longer-term goals and interests. In these cases, no matter how strong they are, such interest groups may simply drop out of the picture as veto players, seeking only minor concessions, or none at all. In effect these groups trade their policy preferences on pension reform for their long-term political preferences.

That said, when interest groups actively oppose reform, their strategies will be highly influenced by the existence of various types of veto points. Two concrete examples of the effective use of veto points have been described here, and both go beyond the usual focus in the veto point and veto player literature on the "relationship between the executive and legislative branches of government and on the rules of the electoral system . . . " (Immergut 1992, 228). The first, similar to the Swiss veto point Immergut highlights in her comparative study of health care reform, was the veto point provided by the plebiscite in Uruguay, which permitted the pensioners' association to influence policy debates *ex ante* and—when their back was against the wall—to trigger a plebiscite after policy reform had been approved in the executive and legislative branches. The second example of the successful use of a veto point to thwart pension reform outside the traditional legislative and executive focus comes from the highly effective contestation of pension reform in the Brazilian high court. Access to the ADIN constitutional review mechanism provided a small political party, a health organization, and, most effectively, the national bar association the institutional wherewithal to influence the size of the "winset" of the status quo (that is, the potential for effective policy change), including in the period *after* legislation had been approved.

Two examples have also been laid out in this chapter of how opposition may be entirely ineffective if veto points are lacking. The first was the experience of pensioners' groups in Argentina, whose enormously successful signature drive could not be converted into a significant veto of policy through a plebiscite, as it likely would have been in Uruguay. The drive therefore became simply a significant expression of political discontent, rather than a veto point. The second example referred to the opposition of Mexican IMSS workers to President Vicente Fox's reform of their pension system. Despite a rapid increase in judicial independence in Mexico since 1994, the IMSS workers and others like them have been unable to effectively contest pension reform in the courts, largely because of the absence of rules of standing that might provide an effective veto point.

Institutional rules, in other words, play a role in determining not just how policy is contested, but the very identity of those who can effectively challenge policy, regardless of their size and reputed political strength. Said another way, institutional rules determine where the veto points on policy change are found, and as a result, which interest groups are best able to achieve their policy preferences.

COURTS AS VETO POINTS

Finally, by zeroing in on the courts as potential veto points, this chapter has sought to illustrate how veto points outside our conventional view of the policy process, with its focus on executive-legislative relations, may influence policy change. Despite the policy relevance of courts in countries as diverse as Brazil, Colombia, Costa Rica, and increasingly Mexico, courts have too long been left outside mainstream accounts of policy change in Latin America, in large part because of the perception that they were insufficiently independent to impose constraints on executive branch decision making or insufficiently powerful to alter decisions made by large majoritarian coalitions within the executive and legislative branches.

Courts are of course limited in what policy issues they can hear by the form by which policies are contested. Because courts do not pick and choose policy engagements the way presidents or assemblies may be able to, they are strongly influenced by the "raw material" that arrives on their doorsteps: the specific policy dimensions that are challenged and the judicial instruments used to challenge policy are determined by plaintiffs. But the institutional rules governing policy debates are as influential in the judiciary as voting rules or agenda-setting in the executive and legislative branches. By analyzing these institutional differences more carefully, it may be possible to better understand the role courts play (or fail to play) as veto points in the policy process.

Chapter 8

Conclusion

Under uncertain transitional conditions, federal courts have played a significant role in shaping governance in Brazil. The judiciary has had a demonstrable policy impact that complements that of more widely and comprehensively studied institutions such as the executive and legislative branches. In sum, the judiciary's policy influence at the federal level over the past two decades has contributed to shaping the overall path of policy formulation during Brazil's democratic consolidation.[1]

The research here has largely focused on the 1988–2004 period in contemporary Brazilian history, but it is worth emphasizing that the policy role of the courts has changed little under the incumbent administration of Luis Inácio "Lula" da Silva. Keeping with past practice, during Lula's first presidential term, federal courts have remained an important decision point in public policy choices regarding past economic plans;[2] fiscal, tax, and social security policies;[3] the balance of power between members of the federation;[4] the relationship between branches of government;[5] the role and power of Brazil's decade-old regulatory agencies;[6] and even policies related to the judiciary itself.[7]

In this final chapter, I summarize this book's contributions to our understanding of how Brazilian courts have been brought in to the policy process. My first goal is to draw out the broader lessons that extend beyond Brazil, especially regarding the implications of institutional design for the role of the courts in the policy process. The second is to consider the implications of this role for the deepening of democratic processes in new democracies.

Courts and Policy

Over the past decade and a half, the judiciary has become the focus of a flurry of attention by political scientists studying Latin American democracies, following decades of neglect during which it was the poor and often unwanted cousin of presidencies and assemblies. But although the judiciary has begun to be better incorporated as an important political player into mainstream political science research on Latin America, all too often the judiciary is depicted as a veto player in its own right. Given the tendency of researchers to focus largely on supreme courts as the voice of judicial preferences, the judiciary is also often equated with the executive branch as a willful and nearly single-minded strategic political actor, from which judicial policy preferences mysteriously emerge to do battle with the preferences expressed by the executive or legislative branches.

The quotidian operations of a living, breathing judiciary, however, are extraordinarily complex. The politicization of the judicial function is seldom overt or judge-driven, with the judiciary vying for power and support in a division-of-spoils game. Rather, it frequently takes place despite, or even against, the wishes of many of the judiciary's own members. Nor is the judiciary ever truly "The Judiciary," a single entity akin to "The President"; rather, it is usually an internally divided institution, incorporating a plethora of interest groups, harboring an abundance of conflicting motivations, and permitting a wide range of actors to use its institutional framework to diverse tactical ends. Moreover, the process by which most cases rise through the court system means that even supreme courts are not always able to pick and choose the political battles they fight, or the means by which these battles are waged.

This book has tried to dig a bit deeper into the paradoxical dual nature of the judiciary's policy effects in Brazil: the courts' "high impact but low functionality." Early in the book, I speculated whether Brazilian federal courts might act more as "veto players," whose agreement is necessary for policy to be approved, or as "veto points," an institutional locus from which other, noncourt, policy actors could exercise a veto of policies they opposed. The evidence demonstrates that the Brazilian federal judiciary rarely acts as a uniform veto player in its own right. Except in issues of direct relevance to judges (such as very specific elements of judicial reform), the expressed policy divisions between judges are such that a range of opinions on almost any policy can be found within the federal courts. More important, the expression of these legal differences in judicial decisions also varies considerably across the various regions of the court system. This very absence of uniformity provides a number of hospitable tactical venues for external policy actors seeking to veto policy or voice their opposition to it.

Given the complexity of the courts, then, the contribution of this book to the broader study of comparative politics lies in its effort to explain how the judiciary as an institution helps to frame policy choice. My focus has been on the institutional factors that determine the "what," the "who," and the "where" of politics and policy debate (Lasswell 1936) within the judiciary, and how these factors shape the policy issues that emerge in the courts, just as electoral and party systems influence the policies debated in legislatures, or rules governing decree power or bureaucratic organization shape the content of the policy priorities expressed by the executive branch.

I have not made the claim that the judiciary is necessarily as influential in structuring national policy choices as are the executive or legislative branches. In fact, it is highly unlikely that courts could ever be as relevant as the executive branch, especially in the roles of policy formulation or policy implementation: neither task is in courts' overall job description, nor do courts have the resources to do a good job of either. Further, judges "seldom have either the first word . . . or the last word" in policy decisions (Melnick 2005, 33), since they rarely are involved in policy deliberations before being asked to interpret or review legislation, and legislators and administrators can often amend, refine, and even overturn court decisions once they are handed down. But this should not discourage us from extending our understanding of courts' effects on policy choice. Even if courts have a much smaller effect than the executive branch in explaining policy choice, this book has shown that in the Brazilian case, that influence on policy at the margin tallies up to a long list of costs, including many frustrated policymakers, a slower and more complicated reform agenda, and the occasional budgetary surprise for the executive branch. But this influence also provides many potential benefits, including greater consideration of policy changes, the incorporation of opposition parties and other minorities into the political process, and perhaps an increase in what Cox and McCubbins (2001) term the "resoluteness" of policy choices over the long haul.[8]

Formal institutional rules are not the only factors at work here: although courts, by the very nature of their law-centered process, are far more rule-governed than the executive branch, past research has shown that the attitudes and strategic considerations of judges as well as policy opponents also are clearly relevant. But institutional features govern how (or even whether) policy issues are brought into the judiciary, mold the tactics political actors use to get them there, and shape the normative filters by which the judiciary mediates these issues.

More than other branches of government, courts are limited in what policy issues they can hear by the "raw material" that arrives on their doorstep. A judge only rules on a public policy after it has passed through a number of filters that determine what policy choices or policy decisions reach the court at all. Policy salience, the overall political environment, and the judicial institutional environment play key roles in exercising a form of "birth control"— to make use of an artful term from Schattschneider (1957: 935)—over the types of policy conflicts that reach any given judge. In sum, long before any judge, much less a high court judge, makes any decision, other factors play a key role in filtering out certain policies and policy actors.

In keeping with this logic, two important arguments on the role of courts in the policy process have been highlighted here. First, some types of policy may be more likely to lead to political contestation than others. Policies with concentrated costs among a given group, other things equal, seem most likely to lead to political contestation, including legal contestation. "Type III" policies such as privatization and pension reform, described in Chapter 3, have consistently been the most incendiary of policies within Brazilian political life over the past two decades, generating an unparalleled degree of public interest and dominating the policy agenda in the elected branches, as well as the courts.

An important caveat in this regard, though, is that while broad patterns of political contestation may be explained by policies' location within this typology, ultimately the salience of policy to any given policy group may be influenced by the broader political environment, such as the party in power and the internal decision-making structure of policy groups. Incumbency makes a difference in terms of the degree of opposition expressed in policy debates; for example, pension reform by Menem benefited from his ability to coopt unions and Peronists, just as pension reform by Lula has benefited from subdued opposition from his political base.

Second, once a policy actor has determined that a policy is worth contesting in the courts, the judicial institutional environment is crucial to determining which tactical options will be available to that actor. While this argument is hardly profound, especially to anyone trained in the law, two corollaries with significant implications for comparative political inquiry emerge here.

1. Different institutional frameworks may lead to markedly dissimilar patterns of public debate in otherwise similarly salient policy questions. These

frameworks may vary across temporal lines (for example, differences between standing in Brazilian ADIN cases in 1964 and 1988, or differences in judicial independence in Mexico between 1993 and the present) or spatially (for example, varying across national boundaries, as in last chapter's comparisons between Argentina, Brazil, Mexico, and Uruguay). The framework of legal tactical choice, then, helps to explain the different ways by which courts are activated in policy debates, as well as variance in the patterns of court use and policy deliberation in otherwise similar policy questions analyzed in comparative cross-national research.

2. The judicial institutional environment, including the structures of judicial independence and judicial review as well as overall judicial administrative performance, may provide certain policy players (and not others) with a veto point in the court system. Such veto points are an important source of potential political power: the threat of a veto provides leverage over policy when it is being deliberated, while the actual use of these veto points may provide leverage after policy has been approved. As a consequence, the judicial institutional environment has effects that extend beyond the courts: in addition to providing alternative institutional venues that specific policy actors can use to influence policy, it shapes the membership and comparative strength of policy actors in the political system as a whole.

In thinking about courts as veto points, I have emphasized the important distinction between veto players' intentions to intervene in the policy process and their effective opportunities for doing so. The extensive use of a major constitutional review mechanism by those groups privileged with standing in Brazil suggested that although they were not always successful, the existence of the ADIN mechanism and the standing to resort to it provided select groups with important opportunities for challenging and on occasion overturning policies they disagreed with. Further, as the cross-national comparisons here illustrated, the policy environment in Brazil would likely be very different, for example, in the absence of the veto point provided by specific constitutional review mechanisms at the STF. If direct standing in the STF had not been available to political parties, corporatist "class" organizations, and the *Ministério Público* during the 1990s (or, alternatively, had mayors and other groups been given such standing), the policies effectively implemented by Brazil's new democracy would undoubtedly look very different today.

Together, these points suggest a readily apparent implication for both public policy and comparative political science. The institutional structure of the judiciary has clear consequences in terms of the legal tactics that policy actors use to contest policy, as well as in terms of the likelihood that public policy will be contested in the courts at all. While this finding does not necessarily lead to consistent conclusions on the likelihood of particular judicial *decisions* about particular policies, the filtering process described here certainly influences the crop of cases from which decisions are harvested, helping us to understand the general direction in which the judiciary is activated on policy questions. It also augments (without supplanting) alternative attitudinal, strategic, or traditionally legalistic analyses of judicial action, by suggesting that because judges are not always able to choose the policy issues that come their way or the plaintiffs they hear, patterns of policy deliberation in the courts are much broader than judges' attitudes or strategic interests alone would predict. Further, the potential for courts to be activated at many levels, and using a number of tactics that are not limited to supreme courts, allows for a variety of policy players to use the courts to strategic advantage in democratic politics. But what are the broader implications of this political use of an unelected institution in terms of the deepening of democratic practices?

Courts and the Deepening of Democratic Practices

Broadly speaking, the judiciary's contribution to Brazil's new democracy has been neither ideal nor abysmal: on the one hand, courts lent important procedural legitimacy to the debates over a number of controversial policy changes; on the other, as in most countries, patterns of judicial intervention in public policy debates have been unequal both in terms of the participants involved and the treatment they receive. As the previous section noted, the impact of courts on public policy cannot be easily disentangled from the institutional structure of the judiciary. The implications for democracy, however, are somewhat more ambiguous. Five points of ambiguity are worthy of final consideration here: the role of the judiciary as a deliberative as well as political venue; the impact of the judicial institutional structure on political actors' ideas and interests; the effects of an unequal judicial franchise; the relationship between inequality and institutional continuity; and the possibility of conflict with the elected branches.

The first point concerns the importance of the courts as a deliberative site in the policy process. There is clear evidence that the federal courts have been used in Brazil to advance broader political strategies. Political parties, in particular, use the courts in a manner that could not be explained by solely legal reasoning or legal objectives; the courts became an outlet for voicing opposition to policy when no further institutional venues were available to the minority. But in using the courts to voice their opposition, political actors also sought to impose costs on their opponents, by exposing the pitfalls of policy, highlighting their opposition, or delaying and calling into question the final implementation of policy. It is important to emphasize this last point: voicing opposition in the courts may be deliberation-enhancing, but it may sometimes seek only to increase the costs of policy implementation, without contributing one whit to reasoned deliberation.

A second consideration is how the judicial institutional environment influences and shapes group interests and ideas. Although the institutional structure influences the tactics group plaintiffs employ in the courts, the judicial structure also shapes these groups' own interests and ideas. In the case of the OAB, for example, it is clear that the judicial institutional environment has ensured this policy player's relative strength in the courts, as well as its continued prominence in the political system. Partly as a result, the OAB has maintained a strong commitment to the preservation of the 1988 Constitution and the favorable judicial institutional environment it created, and has been a powerful voice in favor of maintaining the status quo.

The third point of ambiguity is related: the judiciary's role in democracy cannot be easily separated from the question of who is best able to use the courts to influence policy, and the manner by which they can do so. Legal systems are innately unequal, privileging some groups or individuals more than others as a result of either institutional rules or their hierarchical status in society (determined, among other things, by class, wealth, and race). The courts' effects on public policy are also unequal: as the work of Dahl, Epp, Galanter, and others has suggested, some groups are inevitably given priority in the policy debate as it is carried through the courts. The structure of the court system plays a major role in determining the identity of such groups in the Brazilian case: the availability of privileged standing to present constitutional challenges, especially when combined with delay-ridden lower courts, provides veto points to policy actors in issues on which they might not otherwise have a means of expressing opposition as powerfully or influentially. The government's ability to appeal repeatedly, clog the system with many similar cases, and otherwise delay decisions that it will almost inevitably lose is an even more pernicious form of unequal judicial power. Legal enfranchisement, or the degree to which citizens are able to effectively express their beliefs and protect their rights in the courts, is weak among most individual Brazilian citizens, and thus potentially erosive of the concept of a universal rule of law for all members of this democratic society.[9]

The influence of specific policy actors in the courts—what is in essence an unequal judicial franchise—undermines the judiciary's democratic *raison d'etre* and poses complicated questions for the deepening of democracy. By shaping the distinct legal power of given groups, institutional rules influence the degree to which the "public of citizens" finds contested interpretations of the law convincing, and the degree to which an equality of "legal capacity" that meets expectations of justice will in fact exist (Habermas 1998: 395, 402). Competition between factions seeking their private gain is essential to most Madisonian-inspired conceptions of democracy, which argue that in jockeying for advantage, the factions' attempts at gain will cancel out and provide for the public good (Richardson 2002, 13). But if the factions represented are limited by the rules of the game, the jockeying will be restricted to a select group, and the corresponding representation of interests may be stilted. As Rousseau (1957 [1762], 27) noted influentially with regard to the electoral representation of such factions or associations: "the will of each such association, though *general* with regard to its members, is *private* with regard to the State. . . . By this means the differences being less numerous, they produce a result less general." Although such associations appeal to their work on behalf of the common weal to justify their privileges, this seldom if ever leads to the voluntary renunciation of the group's self-interest.

Certainly, access to privileged forms of legal standing is much broader in Brazil than in many other civil law nations, and the inclusion of political parties in this grant of standing has significantly amplified its use as a political instrument, in often positive ways. But legal enfranchisement at both the high court and among lower courts remains highly unequal. This comparative inequality becomes even starker in light of the overall administrative performance of the lower courts, which means that large sections of the population are condemned to a lengthy appeals process. Of course, individuals can push for redress through representative organizations that have standing in the high court. But such efforts will be mediated by these organizations in ways that may not faithfully represent the sum of individual grievances against policy. This is not to say that individuals are worse represented or more excluded in the courts than elsewhere in the political realm. Indeed, it is clear that Brazil's courts have been quite effective at expanding the number of participants in policy debate as well as shifting the deliberative justifications that go into choosing between policy alternatives (Ferejohn 2002, 45; Ríos-Figueroa and Taylor 2006, 765). But the promise of the courts in terms of the deepening of democratic practices has not been uniformly met, nor does the current judicial institutional environment offer much promise of an effective increase or broadening of citizen representation. Worldwide, few courts meet this promise, of course. But given the demonstrated effect of Brazil's judiciary on policy deliberations, the stilted nature of the judiciary's effects is all the more apparent, and its self-perpetuation a significant concern, as Brazil seeks to deepen its democracy.

This brings us to the fourth point. Brazil's recent history has had an important effect on patterns of legal enfranchisement: although the 1985 regime change and the 1988 Constitution brought a major overhaul of the political structure, a few groups had special influence in that process and were able to garner significant power in the post-1988 political structure. As North (1990, 16) has noted, institutions "are not necessarily or even usually created to be socially efficient; rather they, or at least the formal rules, are created to serve the interests of those with the bargaining power to devise new rules." Once created, these rules are often relatively easy to defend; as Moe (2005, 221) notes, "while a strong coalition may have been necessary to create [the institution], protecting it from formal change is much easier and can be carried out by a weaker coalition, a different coalition, or by ad hoc voting partners."

Brazilian judges, prosecutors, and lawyers all had a noteworthy role in the negotiation of the new Constitution, especially with regard to the judiciary. Judges were able to use the previous lack of judicial autonomy as a wedge to lobby for significant budgetary and administrative independence, as well as to veto discretion-reducing proposals such as a purely constitutional court. Prosecutors were equally active, gaining unparalleled autonomy as what would become a "fourth" branch of government. Despite its initial support of the 1964 military coup, the courageous subsequent opposition of the OAB to the military regime gave it particular influence: its members were guaranteed special protections, and the OAB was given special standing in the STF, which has gradually expanded over time. These same groups have also had a strong influence on attempts at judicial reform, shaping the content of the 2004 constitutional amendment on the judiciary and, perhaps more important, its implementation. It will come as no surprise that, although the 2004 constitutional reform approved the creation of a *súmula vinculante*, the only groups given the right to propose the creation or revision of such a statement of precedent are exactly the same select groups currently granted standing in constitutional review cases via ADIN.[10]

In sum, institutional change is slow and accretive, and often carries with it residues of the past. Changes that would radically alter the balance of judicial power or legal enfranchisement seem unlikely in the near future. This suggests both positive and negative normative conclusions for democracy: there will be no ruptures, but shifts in judicial structure are likely to be slow, ongoing, and inauspicious in terms of providing first-best solutions. Perhaps more important, because courts are usually pulled into the policy game by external policy actors, often in regard to the most contentious policy issues of the day, there is an ongoing hazard to democratic comity. Courts—and especially but not only high courts—are placed in a complicated position because they must rely on the very legislative majorities they may eventually rule against to "abide by, and sometimes even to carry out, their decisions" (Vanberg 2005, 170).

A final question in the case of Brazilian democracy is thus: up to what point can courts rule not just against legislative majorities, but against the powerful combined executive and legislative coalitions that are such a defining feature of the post-1988 political arrangement? Courts do not always act in counter-majoritarian fashion, of course, and it is evident that high court judges' origins within majority coalitions may further temper any such counter-majoritarian tendencies (for example, Dahl 1957; Rosenberg 1991). Counter-majoritarian effects are further limited by judges' ability to take narrow decisions, delay controversial decisions, and otherwise avoid decisions that might invite reprisal, or perhaps even more damaging to the integrity of the judiciary, decisions that might prompt the elected branches to fail to comply with court orders.

Having said all this, by the nature of the overall Brazilian political system, a significant degree of conflict between courts and the elected branches has been almost inevitable. On the one side, the elected institutions tend to express the prevailing beliefs of a highly dominant "*agenda cartel*" (Amorim Neto et al. 2003), which reflects the consensus interests of the super-majorities needed to approve many reforms, often without any incorporation or even consideration of minority viewpoints. Further, the highly contentious policy agenda of the post-transition period has contributed to the perceived salience of policy change, especially on the economic front, where the costs of reform were highly concentrated among civil servants, who were able to draw on a broader epistemic community of policy opponents in unions, the Catholic church, the landless movement, and often the OAB for assistance in fighting policy change. Into this volatile mix stepped a judiciary that was not very effective in controlling its own agenda, and could be activated in a number of tactical ways by a large number of policy opponents.

Certainly there is no great harm in further deliberation of policy and the inclusion of new actors in policy decisions, which may increase the overall staying power of policymaking. Further, judges are not defenseless, and even as they are increasingly pushed into the policy vortex, have used discretionary solutions such as delay, narrow legal opinions, and strict technical criteria to sidestep the most threatening situations (Kapiszewski 2007), in keeping with the practice of their judicial counterparts in Europe and North America (for example, Shapiro 1981, 2004; Vanberg 2005). But in light of the courts' activation by minorities excluded from policymaking in the elected branches, and the manifest effect of Brazil's judicial institutional environment on policy outcomes, it is clear that the insertion of courts in the policymaking process will be the source of ongoing tensions in Brazilian democracy.

Conclusion

The federal judiciary has clearly played a foundational role in deepening Brazil's nascent democratic regime. Despite enormous congestion and other administrative problems, Brazilian federal courts have had a degree of influence over policy decisions taken by the executive and legislative branches that is rarely paralleled in Latin America. By providing another arena for debate during a period of significant and contentious policy reforms, the Brazilian judiciary encouraged a democratic buy-in by members of society shut out of the governing majority. Furthermore, the courts laid down a thick bed of legal decisions, thus reconstructing a body of democratic jurisprudence lost during the military regime. In the process, the courts gained greater legitimacy for themselves and for the democratic regime as a whole.

That said, the balance has been skewed: although courts have been an important force in legitimating policy and encouraging participants to voice and act on their opposition within the institutional constraints of the system, they are one of the strongest forces operating in favor of the 1988 Constitution's "demos-constraining" effects (Stepan 2000). Further, this effect often operates in ways that privilege specific organized policy actors and political groups. From almost the instant it was promulgated, the Constitution was under the eye of reformers, but change was seriously compromised by the structure of the political system created by the Constitution itself. The controversies spawned by attempts at reform in a political environment characterized by an abundance of veto players—many of whom were not fully incorporated into policy deliberations in the executive and legislative branches—generated a healthy crop of cases for the judiciary, repeatedly placing courts, like it or not, at the center of the policy maelstrom. Further, the 1988 Constitution gave courts considerable potential power, and by extension, delegated great policy leverage to the groups best able to employ the courts to influence policy. Within the federal court system, many of the institutional characteristics of the broader political system were reproduced and at times accentuated, contributing new veto points beyond those already extant in the executive and legislative branches, and thereby constraining policy debate and slowing the process of policy implementation.

Regardless of whether one agrees with the federal government's policy priorities, the constraints imposed by courts have had visible implications for governance and for political participation. The judiciary has had a visible effect not only in individual legal cases, but on the policy process, on political debate, and, more broadly, on the structure of power within the Brazilian political system as a whole. The question, going forward, is whether and how this influence will be further democratized and made more broadly effective. Formal equality before the law exists, but effectual legal remedies, including the remedies against public policy that have been my focus here, are beyond the reach of most citizens and unequally distributed among policy actors. In the long run, then, the courts' most profound effect on the further deepening of democracy in Brazil is thus likely to come not from the expressed wisdom of judges' decisions in conflicts between majority and minority policy coalitions, or from the brilliance of their arbitration of constitutional conflicts, but from the extent to which they broaden the effective legal franchise.

Reference Matter

NOTES

Chapter 1

1. Throughout this book, *public policy* is defined as an action undertaken at least in part by government, with the implicit assumption that a public policy includes a particular long-term goal or objective, necessitates some action for implementation, and is intentional. *Policy reform* is a change in the intended goals, lines of action, and intent of a given public policy, and is used interchangeably with *policy change* (Ríos-Figueroa and Taylor 2006, 740; Dye 1972, 2; Ranney 1968; McCool 1995).

2. In a seminal essay written more than two decades ago, Verner (1984) created a typology of Latin American courts and noted that only one country—Costa Rica—had "independent activist courts" with a significant ability to alter government objectives. The list of courts with significant judicial power has grown in the wake of the region's democratic transformation to include countries as varied as Costa Rica, Colombia, Mexico, and—the focus of this book—Brazil. For reviews of the English-language literature on judicial politics in Latin America between Verner's article and the present, see Kapiszewski and Taylor 2006 and Taylor 2006c.

3. Notable published works by Brazilian scholars on the structure, history, politics, and policy relevance of the courts in contemporary Brazilian politics include Arantes 1997; Castro 1993; 1997a; 1997b; Favetti 2003; Koerner 1998; Sadek 1995b; 1999a; 1999b; 2000; Vilhena Vieira 2002; Werneck Vianna et al. 1999; and Werneck Vianna and Burgos 2002. In addition, a host of recent dissertations and articles by rising scholars, including Carvalho Neto 2005, Pacheco 2006, Oliveira 2006, and Oliveira 2005, have greatly expanded our understanding of courts' political role.

4. Research on Brazilian political institutions since the transition to democracy includes analyses of the institutional effects of the constitution (e.g., Martínez-Lara 1996; Reich 1998; Rosenn 1990; Souza 1997); of resulting electoral rules and the electoral system (e.g., Ames 1995a, 1995b; Palermo 2000); of political parties (e.g., Mainwaring 1993, 1995, 1999; Figueiredo and Limongi 1999); of federalism and especially its effects on economic policy (e.g., Castelar Pinheiro et al. 1999; Loureiro 2001; Souza 2001, 2003; Stepan 2000); of regulatory institutions and the Central Bank (e.g., Melo 2000; Mueller

2001; Sola and Whitehead 2006; Sola et al. 1998); and cross-institutional analyses of the overall political system (e.g., Ames 2001; Kingstone and Power 2000).

5. Courts provide services in three major areas: dispute resolution, social control, and policymaking (Hammergren 1998; Schor 2003; Shapiro 1981). Given my focus on the Brazilian federal courts' effects on policymaking, I largely leave aside outputs in the fields of social control and dispute resolution (generally the function of Brazil's state courts), which are the subject of a distinct and quite substantial literature in Brazil and Latin America (e.g., Agüero and Stark 1998; Brinks 2003; Caldeira 2000, 2002; Holston 1991; Pereira 2000; Mainwaring and Welna 2003; Méndez et al. 1999).

6. As one legal expert rebuked me when I told him about my research, "O judiciário não age por sim só . . . ele só age por provocacão [The judiciary doesn't act on its own . . . it only acts when provoked]" (Informal personal conversation with a University of São Paulo law professor, March 6, 2003). This statement, which was repeated to me more than once, closely echoes the thinking of prominent early twentieth-century legal scholar Pedro Lessa (1915), who formulated what Gonçalves Ferreira Filho (1994) terms the "classical legal doctrine" that the judiciary has three distinctive qualities: (1) it functions as an arbiter when conflict arises; (2) it only makes judgments about specific cases, rather than abstract precepts; and, most relevant here, (3) it has no initiative, acting only when provoked. Although the capacity of Brazilian courts to make decisions on abstract grounds has grown significantly over time, including in the 1988 Constitution, the residual doctrinal influence of Lessa's work remains quite pervasive.

7. Skepticism about the relevance of Latin America's courts is even more pronounced, with the potential for the judiciary to have any role at all called into question, as in one taxonomy of courts, which argued that in Latin America, "law in the professional term of the word is not absent, but is extremely marginalized and weak before other sources of social rule making (mainly political power)" (Mattei 1997). Studies of the overall performance of Latin American democracies also call into question the potential influence of courts. This ubiquitous gloom is reflected most eloquently in O'Donnell's doubts about the extent of horizontal accountability and in his observations about pervasive particularism, delegative rule, and "brown areas" where citizens are "legally poor"; "low intensity" citizenship prevails; and an intermittent, biased rule of law is the norm (1994, 1996, 2000, 2001a, 2001b). Other scholars have similar fears: Méndez et al. (1999) follow a long tradition of questioning the gap between the letter of the law and its practice; Hagopian (1990, 1994), Roett (1999), and others paint a bleak picture of the subversion of formal state institutions by patrimonial traditions; and yet others emphasize the importance of parallel polities that operate alongside the Latin American state (e.g., Leeds 1996; Arias and Rodrigues 2006).

8. This book is not an attempt to reveal the "judicialization of politics," a phrase that describes a visible trend in politics throughout much of the world, and one that has already been amply documented in Brazil (e.g., Arantes 1997, 2005; Werneck Vianna 2002; Werneck Vianna et al. 1999) and Latin America (Sieder et al. 2005). Rather, I aim to better understand—in part, motivated by the broad evidence of judicialization—how it is that courts are activated in policy debates. To avoid conceptual confusion, the term *judicialization* will be used sparingly and in accordance with Tate and Vallinder's (1995: 5) narrowest original conception, which is that the "judicialization of politics" refers to two phenomena: the increasing recourse to courts in political matters ("the global expansion of judicial power"), and the "less dramatic" instance of the "domi-nation of non-judicial decision-making arenas by quasi-judicial (legalistic) pro-cedures." I will use the term only in this first, conventionally assumed definition of *judicialization,* and the term will only be used to refer to an increase in court use, in contrast to the all-too-frequent practice (of which I have been guilty in the past) of referring to any use of the courts in political or policy matters as *judicialization.* On the many overlapping and even contradictory meanings ascribed to this trendy term, see, for example, Maciel and Koerner 2002.

9. Although the term *venue-shopping* is widely used, a good expression of its meaning can be found in Shapiro (1981, 32): "[T]he ultimate strategy for anyone wishing to get something out of government is to treat all agencies as multiple purpose, shopping among them until any one or any combination of them will yield what is desired."

10. This second factor approximates what Wilson and Rodriguez Cordero (2006, 326–7), drawing on the literature on social movements, label the "politi-cal opportunity structure." In their words, "both stable and contingent factors outline specific opportunity structures (formally and informally) that social movements and interest groups can exploit when pursuing their goals." How-ever, because the term *overall political environment* sounds slightly less prescrip-tive, and is less associated with a specific and established academic literature, I use it here.

11. Legal tactics employed thus will vary across different types of policy ac-tors in the same legal system, as well as across similar policy actors in different (national or subregional) legal systems. The focus of this book is primarily on the comparison of tactics across several policy players in the Brazilian federal case, although later in the book I apply the same arguments in comparative per-spective to three other Latin American nations undergoing similar policy reform.

Chapter 2

1. Courts with significant policy effects are also found in Costa Rica (e.g., Barker 2000; Verner 1984; Wilson 2005), Colombia (e.g., Cepeda Espinosa 2005; Rodriguez-Garavito et al. 2003; Uprimny 2004) and, increasingly,

Mexico (e.g., Domingo 2004, 2005; Finkel 2003, 2005; Lopez-Ayllon and Fix-Fierro 2003). A potential warning of the ephemeral nature of court power, however, comes from Venezuela: until recently, Venezuela's courts were considered potentially powerful policy actors (e.g., Pérez-Perdomo 2003, 2005), but the ability of judicial power to constrain the executive branch seems to have been considerably weakened in the wake of President Chavez's moves to consolidate executive power.

2. There were 452 *controversias constitucionales* and 152 *acciónes de inconstitucionalidad* over this period, for a combined total of 604. In 162 cases (27 percent) the Supreme Court altered the municipal, state, or federal constitution, law, or decree being questioned. I am grateful to Julio Ríos-Figueroa for his enormous help in tracking down the Mexican figures, collected by Guardado Rodríguez (2007) (author correspondence with Ríos-Figueroa, September 6–7, 2006; February 2–14, 2007).

3. GDP figures and tax collection figures are from Tendências Consultoria Integrada's economic database, available at www.tendencias.com.br. Calculations are by the author.

4. My reasoning here echoes that of many previous authors: Uprimny (2004, 66) notes in regard to Colombia that the "dramatic justice" of high court interventions—with media coverage, public hue and cry, and the involvement of major political actors—is just a part of the story, and may not even be the most important part. In fact, "the risk of dramatic justice is that it can hide the problems of the everyday or 'routine' justice, which can be more important for the lives of the citizens." Cepeda Espinosa (2005, 67) offers a further paradox from Colombia that has interesting parallels in the Brazilian case: "In a country associated with political violence and the drug trade, a strong tradition of judicial review may appear strange. It is as if there were two countries: one where force reigns, another based on the rule of law." As Magaloni (2003) suggests in the Mexican case, the Madisonian (checks and balances) and Hobbesian (personal security) dimensions of court performance are often out of sync in Latin America.

5. As noted in Chapter 1, courts are involved in policy in a number of different ways: they provide dispute resolution, protect individuals from government abuses, and provide an alternative locus for political debate, among other functions. Given my emphasis throughout this book on policymaking, this chapter focuses heavily on characteristics affecting civil cases, as well as on the courts' use for redress against federal public policies, with little attention given to criminal cases.

6. Most new institutionalist approaches to the courts have largely focused on the U.S. case (e.g., Smith 1988; Clayton and Gillman 1999), rather than the potentially riper target of Latin America's civil code systems (but see some of the more recent work in Ginsburg and Kagan 2005 and Sieder et al. 2005). At their base, these approaches share a view that political behavior, including the

behavior of courts, is given "shape, structure, and direction by particular institutional arrangements" (Clayton and Gillman 1999, 5).

7. As noted earlier, it has been commonplace since Dahl (1957) to argue that the means by which judges are recruited from among elites make them strongly favorable to the interests of dominant groups in policy-relevant decisions. Without rejecting this view in its entirety, it is worth noting that in some legal systems, such as Brazil's, the manner of judicial appointment from within the judicial career is such that ties to political majorities may be less direct. Even among politically appointed judges on the high courts, for example, Brazil's multiparty system means that there is room for potential policy disagreement on many distinct dimensions, even if justices are broadly loyal to those appointing them. This does not eliminate the common socioeconomic bonds that connect the elite, of course, but it does suggest that there is room for divergent policy preferences between the judiciary and the elected branches.

In terms of ideological bias on the STF, aside from a split between ministers appointed by the military regime, and those appointed by presidents during the democratic period, it is very difficult to identify any overarching ideological divide on the court, with the possible—and quite tenuous and largely unstudied—exception of the differences between ministers appointed by President Luis Inácio "Lula" da Silva and those appointed by his predecessors. Lula is the first president since the military regime who has appointed a majority of the eleven STF ministers. Prior to Lula, the post-transition STF included eight ministers appointed by military governments; five appointed by Sarney; four appointed by Collor; one by Itamar Franco; and three by Cardoso. Finally, recording practices in the STF are such that an accurate measure of each judge's vote cannot be reliably categorized as an indicator of attitudes. To conclude on a humorous note, the difficulty of attitudinal measures in Brazil is well reflected in an irreverent popular saying from the state of Minas Gerais, "de bumbum de nenê, barriga de grávida, e cabeça de juiz ninguém é capaz de prever o que pode sair," or roughly, "nobody can predict what can come out of babies' bottoms, pregnant bellies, and judges' heads."

8. "High court" is used here as shorthand for the highest court in the land, whether this is called a Constitutional Court, a Supreme Federal Tribunal, a Supreme Court, or something entirely different.

9. It should be noted, however, that the lack of independence does not necessarily mean that courts will always rule for the government: in some cases dependent courts may rule against the majority. Pereira (2005) notes that the Brazilian high court under the military regime was able to challenge the government on occasion precisely because it was so closely aligned with the military's objectives, in contrast to its counterparts in Argentina and Chile. Helmke (2005) provides a slightly different approach in her discussion of strategic decision making in the Argentine case, where justices have ruled strategically against the very incumbents who appointed them so as to curry favor with

incoming governments. However, given that (by definition) such experiences cannot be generalized to all, or even a majority of cases of policy intervention by dependent courts, I simply note their existence here.

10. For various definitions of independence drawn from the Latin American case, see Brinks 2005; Finkel 2003, 779; Iaryczower et al. 2002, 699; and Ríos-Figueroa 2006.

11. Whittington (2005, 593–94) offers a lucid argument for why it is that incumbents in federalist systems may benefit from activist courts, even when they rule against the government: "An ideologically friendly judiciary insulated from such competing pressures may be willing and able to act where elected officials temporize. In doing so, judges may well earn plaudits, or at least deference, from the political leaders whose hands were otherwise tied."

12. This is not always the case, however. In the Chilean case, for example, the constitutional tribunal may hand down its decisions *a priori,* permitting the legislature to revise legislation prior to implementation if necessary.

13. Abstract review refers to the ability of courts to hear cases that challenge a particular law or statute in the abstract, without a concrete case in which the plaintiff seeks redress against the actual consequences of that law's application.

14. As Koerner (2006, 272–75) notes with regard to Brazil, the law and its accumulated consensus, which he labels the "jurisprudential regime," is vital to understanding how judges make their decisions. Political debates between jurists are not usually framed in terms of judges' preferences, but instead take the form of controversies about judicial technique and legal rules. The "jurisprudential regime" refers to the "standardized form by which the courts approach each social problem, construct it as a juridical case and [make decisions] about it . . . " (272; translation mine).

15. The eleven ministers of the STF are appointed by the president and approved by the Senate, and they rule on most constitutional issues, as well as in cases involving conflicts between federal powers, between the federal government and the states, between different levels of the judicial system, and in cases involving foreign governments.

16. On the "political question" doctrine, it is worth noting that the Brazilian judiciary in the past has been more severely constrained—in theory at least—in its ability to act on political issues. The 1934 Constitution, for example, included an article reading, "the Judicial Branch is barred from recognizing exclusively political questions" ("É vedado ao Poder Judiciário conhecer de questões exclusivamente políticas"; Gonçalves Ferreira Filho 1994).

17. Cases from the federal small claims courts (*juizados especiais*), if challenged, are sent to a special appeals body made up of three judges, known as the *Colégio Recursal.* Any further appeals would occur only in special cases, such as if the decision is alleged to violate the Constitution (in which case it

would go to the STF). In practice, however, such an appeal is highly unlikely to be judged by the STF. I am grateful to Marco Antônio G. L. Lorencini for his help in understanding small claims courts, as well as for his patient explanation of many other aspects of the Brazilian legal system. As always, any ensuing errors are entirely my own.

18. Prillaman (2000, 92) notes, however, that some of these new forms of access were an "unfunded mandate" that did not materialize as expected. The law effectively putting the *juizados especiais* into operation at the state level was not passed until September 1995; at the federal level, not until July 2001. Since then, however, these *juizados* have become the most productive (in terms of cases decided by judge) and efficient (in terms of time to resolution per case) of all the courts in the federal court system (Cardoso 2006), even though they cost significantly less than other federal courts (Bottini 2006; *O Estado de São Paulo* 2006).

19. There are two distinct legal positions at the federal level that should not be confused: the prosecutor-general (*procurador geral*), who heads the highly autonomous *Ministério Público,* and the attorney general, who heads the executive branch's *Advocacia Geral da União.*

20. The ADIN mechanism was originally created in 1965, by an amendment to the 1946 Constitution. At its creation, only the prosecutor-general could use the ADIN to question the constitutionality of a given law. The goal was to bring greater efficiency to the judiciary, by limiting the number of constitutional challenges at all levels of the system and by creating an instrument that would be binding against all. This original efficiency goal was substantially undermined by the expansion of the right to use the ADIN in the 1988 Constitution. A very useful history of the expansion of the rights of constitutional challenge to new players, from the Portuguese colonial period forward, can be found in Sadek 1995a.

21. Throughout this book, I use the term *Ministério Público,* rather than the awkward translation Public Ministry, to highlight the distinctive nature of the Brazilian prosecutorial service. Useful references on the rather independent state and federal *Ministério Públicos* include Arantes 2002; Castilho and Sadek 1998; Ferraz 1997; Kerche 1999, 2003; Macedo Júnior 1995; McAllister 2008; and Sadek and Cavalcanti 2003.

22. Vilhena Vieira (2002, 151–170), for example, discusses the impact of Provisional Measure 173, of March 1990, by which the government sought to restrict the use of injunctions or writs against the Collor economic stabilization plan. He notes that while the STF did not rule directly on whether the provisional measure was constitutional, by failing to do so, it actually enabled lower-level courts to invalidate the provisional measure if they sought to.

23. STF Minister Moreira Alves, rapporteur's report on Direct Action of Unconstitutionality (ADIN) No. 896. Translation mine.

24. Personal conversation with policymaker, March 7, 2003.

25. Brazil followed the vogue for codification that began with the Napoleonic Code of 1804. Although it was a latecomer in the wave of Latin American codifications, Brazil drew creatively on French, German, and Swiss codes to develop its own in the late nineteenth century (Karst and Rosenn 1975, 46). Legislation under the new codes was seen as the sole source of the law, with no reason for judges to engage in law creation. It has been argued that, under the civil law tradition, "The judge becomes a kind of expert clerk. . . . His function is merely to find the right legislative provision, couple it with the fact situation, and bless the solution that is more or less automatically produced from the union" (Merryman 1985). But this is a rather unnuanced view, and there has long been a recognition that within civil code systems, the "creative role" of the judge is needed to overcome potential hurdles of human unpredictability, thereby adding a degree of discretion to the judge's role (David and Brierley 1968, 82–83). This degree of discretion is further augmented in the Brazilian case by the autonomy of lower court judges.

26. Reforms to the Civil Code in 2002 are still too embryonic for a reasoned evaluation of the effect of the reforms enacted, although the abundance of laws continues.

27. Exceptions to the "case-specific effects of most decisions" in the case of some constitutional review instruments have been noted. Among Brazilian observers, Nalini (2000) and Castelar Pinheiro (2000) have been among the many strong critics of the judiciary's tendency to avoid thinking outside the narrow confines of individual legal decisions.

28. Rosenn emphasizes the combination of formalism and paternalism among Brazilian judges and lawyers, noting, "Brazilian legal education has been overwhelmingly formalistic. . . . Generations of Brazilian law students have been taught that law is a science, and that the task of the legal scientist is to analyze and elaborate principles that can be derived from a careful study of positive legislation into a harmonious, systematic structure" (Rosenn 1984, 23; 1971; a critical review of this last piece is Lacerda Teixeira 1972).

29. Junqueira (2003, 88) notes that the reforms to the legal curriculum during the 1990s have in fact expanded these noncore curriculum classes beyond their previous scope. That said, they remain a rather small share of the total, as shown in the numbers given in the text, which draw on my review of the USP law school's curriculum in 2003.

30. The *provão* is an exam given to all college graduates. The test evaluates knowledge of basic concepts across a variety of fields, and is aimed at creating quality benchmarks that are comparable across universities nationally. As in most Latin American countries, college education in Brazil does not follow a liberal arts model. High school graduates enter college already enrolled in their major fields of study, such as law or medicine, and graduate four or five years

later as lawyers and doctors (pending approval on a bar or medical association practitioners' exam).

31. Candidates for federal judgeships are required to have worked for at least two years as lawyers. A recent poll of judges found that the average age at which they entered the bench was thirty-three (Associação dos Magistrados Brasileiros 2006, 9). Earlier polls have shown that 55 percent of judges began on the bench before turning thirty (Sadek 1999a, 310; see also Werneck Vianna et al. 1997).

32. According to data for 2000, using purchasing-power-parity-adjusted dollars, Brazil spent on the federal judiciary $3.81 million per 100,000 inhabitants, whereas Argentina spent $3.46 million per same, Mexico spent $2.65 million, and the "worldwide" average was $2.04 million (World Bank, Legal and Judicial Reform Working Group, "Worldwide Legal and Judicial Indicators 2000"). These World Bank figures do not include the other big federal system in the hemisphere, the United States, but given that the Brazilian federal court budget is nearly equal in dollar terms to that of the United States, despite a smaller population, Brazilian courts have the higher purchasing power parity budget. Brazil's federal courts' 2003 budget, at US$4.7 billion, was comparable to that of the United States federal court system, which had a US$4.9 billion budget in the same fiscal year. Brazilian figures are from National Treasury, "Relatorio Resumido da Execução Orçamentária do Governo Federal e Outros Demonstrativos," available at www.tesouro.fazenda.gov.br/, p. 63, accessed March 5, 2004. U.S. figures are from Administrative Office of the U.S. Courts, "The FY 2003 Budget and the Federal Courts," available at www.us courts.gov, accessed March 5, 2004.

33. Spending has been heavily biased toward the Labor Courts, which have consumed between 38 percent and 50 percent of the total judicial budget between 1995 and 2005, as opposed to the roughly one-third of the budget that has gone to the STF, STJ, and the rest of the courts in what I term the "federal judiciary" (electoral and military court systems account for the remainder). The high share of the budget going to the labor courts is due in part to the fact that the labor justice system has more courts than any other segment of the federal judiciary. But Vargas-era labor laws provide a continuous source of new cases for the courts to solve, and the practice of using "class-based" appointments to the labor courts as a pork barrel for political allies has also meant that until recently the labor courts accounted for a large share of judges. A 1999 labor court reform (Constitutional amendment No. 22) abolished the "class-based" judges, but the labor courts remain the largest single expenditure in the judicial budget, even though they deal with only half as many cases per year and a third as many cases per judge as their counterparts in the rest of the federal system (Cardoso 2006).

34. Data are from the Secretaria do Orçamento Federal (SOF), Ministry of Planning. Available at www.planejamento.gov.br/orcamento/index.htm, accessed November 2003. All calculations are mine.

35. Non-Brazil data are for 1995–96; Brazilian data are from 1999.

36. There were 9.5 million cases in the Justiça Comum, 790 thousand in the state appeals courts, and 1.9 million in state *juizados especiais* in 2001 (Supremo Tribunal Federal 2005).

37. It should be noted that although municipal governments have no standing to bring constitutional review cases via ADIN, they are frequent users of other legal instruments.

38. There may be little choice for government lawyers but to appeal: members of the *Advocacia Geral da União* have the "functional duty to appeal" ("*dever funcional de recorrer*") and could face sanctions if they did not.

39. Cardoso's attorney general, Gilmar Mendes, issued nearly twenty administrative acts forcing his office, the *Advocacia Geral da União*, to cease from appealing clearly lost cases ad infinitum, nearly halving the number of federal government appeals from 160,000 to 87,000. In 2000, the federal government decided not to file further appeals in cases related to the inflation adjustment of FGTS (*Fundo de Garantia do Tempo de Serviço*) labor service accounts, unilaterally readjusting sixty million FGTS accounts after losing the first cases at the STF in August 2000 (*Folha de São Paulo* 2004). A 2001 government decision forced the Caixa Econômica Federal, a major federal bank, to file motions in the STF giving up (via "*homologação de desistência*") on most cases relating to monetary correction in which it was a defendant; fifty thousand such cases were dismissed in 2003, explaining the significant—but temporary—drop in the extant case load that year. Simultaneously, the STF was implementing major administrative improvements aimed at speeding up the administrative processing of cases, in some cases reducing the time between receipt and judgment in the STF from months to days. I am grateful to Túlio Macedo for his assistance in untangling the STF caseload numbers, and his interpretation of the decline in cases received during 2003 (telephone conversation with Túlio Macedo, Núcleo da Qualidade, Secretaria do Tribunal, Supremo Tribunal Federal, March 16, 2004).

40. *Embargo de declaração* appeals accounted for 26.5 percent of distributed cases, while *agravo regimental* appeals accounted for a further 52.3 percent (Supremo Tribunal Federal 2006).

41. Presentation by Minister Sydney Sanches at the seminar "Como melhorar a justiça brasileira?" [How to Improve the Brazilian Judiciary?], Fernand Braudel Institute of World Economics, São Paulo, October 14, 2003.

42. This compares with ratios of 1.68:1 in Chile, 1.82:1 in Argentina, and a "worldwide" average of 2.49:1 in a survey of ninety-three countries by the World Bank Legal and Judicial Reform Working Group. "Worldwide Legal and Judicial Indicators 2000." Available at www4.worldbank.org/legal/database/justice/, accessed June 2006.

43. In 1998–99, a congressional inquiry found evidence of massive corruption in the construction of a São Paulo courthouse for the regional labor court,

finding that one labor court judge, known by his nickname "Lalau," had bilked the project of R$169.5 million (or roughly US$95 million, at the 1999 year-end exchange rate). For an analysis of this case and others like it, see Taylor and Buranelli 2007.

44. An engaging journalistic account of recent judicial corruption among both state and federal judges can be found in Vasconcelos 2005.

45. Although Brazilian courts are still more trusted than most of their counterparts in the rest of Latin America, by 2002, 63.9 percent of Brazilians claimed they had "little" or "no" confidence in the judiciary. The judiciary inspired less confidence than any other institution in Brazilian society save Congress (Toledo y Associados poll taken September 16–26, 2003, cited in Fleischer 2003).

46. The prevailing rules within the judiciary keep all investigations of judges' malfeasance secret (including the names of accused judges); allow for the impeachment only of STF ministers (judges on other courts can only be forcibly retired, but only after sentencing); and allow for the suspension of a judge only when his or her colleagues (from the same court) vote two-thirds in favor. All of this contributes to a perception of impunity accompanied by little transparency, best expressed by President Luis Inácio da Silva, who lashed out against the "black box" of the judiciary early in his term (Freitas 2003; Christofoletti 2003).

47. Some individuals are able to claim direct standing in the Supreme Federal Tribunal for their defense, if they are one of the few public authorities with the right to the so-called "*foro privilegiado*." Under Article 102 of the 1988 Constitution, these authorities are the president, the vice president, members of Congress, cabinet ministers, and the head of the *Ministério Público*.

Chapter 3

1. I focus solely on policies undertaken by the Cardoso government (1995–2002) as a way of reducing variance in other potential explanations of the judicialization of policy, such as significant changes in overall court composition or changes in the nature of relations between the political incumbent and the opposition.

2. As Collier et al. (2004, 251) note, case studies can detail a number of different phenomena, including "episodes of policy implementation."

3. For a robust defense of the use of case studies in political science research, see Collier et al. 2004; George and Bennett 2005; and Ragin 1987. Collier and colleagues' emphasis on the importance of the "detailed knowledge associated with thick analysis . . . [as] a major source of leverage for inference" (246); George and Bennett's emphasis on the case study as a methodological tool that can be used to complement both formal and statistical methods; and Ragin's notion that case-oriented comparative research can be a valid means of

developing causally complex explanations all undergird my reasoning here, which uses case studies as a way of both illustrating potential causal implications and describing current patterns of policy contestation. I do not claim to have exhausted all the cases that might be considered here, nor do I think such an approach would be viable, given the almost daily activation of Brazilian courts to policy ends. As for the potential conflict that some readers might find between the case studies used here and the statistical model developed in Chapter 4, I prefer to emphasize the complementarity of the statistical and case study methods, in line with George and Bennett's (2005, 3–5) exhortation for a more methodologically aware use of combined methods that "can accommodate various forms of causal complexity" (5). Simply put, the two chapters provide two distinct yet complementary perspectives on the policy ends to which the federal courts are frequently used. Statistical analysis provides the wherewithal to comprehensively study the use of particular legal instruments; policy case studies allow us to trace the path of a single policy through the full trajectory of judicial contestation.

4. Although Wilson and subsequent authors have created more eloquent titles for each of the cells—rather than the rather dull Type I, II, III, and IV used here—I have chosen the dull route because some of the alternative titles ("majoritarian," "entrepreneurial," and so on) may unnecessarily confuse matters.

5. In August 1995, ten landless farmers and two policemen died in the eviction of landless workers from a farm they had seized in Corumbiara, Roraima, and in April 1996, nineteen were killed when police charged a highway roadblock by landless farmers in Eldorado do Carajás, Pará.

6. These included a 1997 march on Brasília, annual "Scream of the Excluded" marches in various cities from 1995 onward, the "invasion" of the national development bank (BNDES) in 1998, and active campaigns for the resignation of various Cardoso ministers.

7. Evidence of this relationship is broad, including op-ed articles in favor of the MST by Church and PT leaders, as well as the joint organization of marches. The Church is placed in a difficult position by the illegality of the invasions, but as the president of the CNBB noted without condemning the invasions, "The MST has the merit of keeping agrarian reform permanently on the agenda" (*Folha de São Paulo* 1998a; translation mine).

The PT, on the other hand, argued flatly that "the occupations are a legitimate instrument of pressure," in an editorial by then-PT party president José Dirceu (1997; translation mine). Perhaps the best example of the shared political goals between the groups is the decline in land invasions by the MST in the run-up to the 2002 presidential elections, and the subsequent appointment of an MST sympathizer to run Lula's agrarian reform projects.

8. A 2002 federal government audit of the agrarian reform program, for example, found that only 3 percent of the resettled families had received final title to the lands they were "resettled" on.

9. ACOs are used to contest cases between members of the federation, such as individual states or the federal government. Litigants attempted unsuccessfully to contest land seizures by listing state governments as plaintiffs, claiming that the federal government was violating the rights of states by overturning states' land grants to individuals. Of the seventy-two ACOs published in the STF's *Revista Trimestral de Jurisprudência* (Supremo Tribunal Federal, 1989) between 1988 and 2002, twenty-two referred to expropriation for creation of Indian reserves, and only three referred to expropriation for purposes of agrarian reform. All three of these cases dated from the 1980s, and were not heard by the STF. Jurisprudence established that landowners could not claim a right to an ACO hearing by listing the state as a co-litigant.

10. Landowners' legal actions have thus included suits to question the size of compensation payments for farms that have been expropriated, especially when improvements have been made to the land; challenges to the government's right to inspect land prior to expropriation; challenges to the procedure by which expropriation was carried out; and so forth. But given the individual nature of each of these cases, the direct impact on policy implementation even in the rare circumstances in which the case was won has been local rather than universal.

11. I am grateful to Cliff Welch for highlighting this last point to me in personal conversation.

12. The most common complaint by the MST is that "the Judicial Power only works for the rich." See, for example, the MST's open letter to Cardoso (*Folha de São Paulo* 1997).

13. Provisional measures are decree laws, which can be issued by the president at any moment. Until limits on the use of provisional measures were passed in 2001, provisional measures expired at the end of thirty days. It was common practice, however, for presidents to "reissue" the provisional measures every thirty days with only minor changes in the text. The Real Plan, for example, relied on provisional measures that were consistently reissued for nearly a year before Congress was able to debate and approve enabling legislation. For further discussion of the use of these measures, and the controversy they generated, see Figueiredo and Limongi 1997 and Power 1998.

Other significant forms of legislation that have been commonly used to approve policy reforms include, in decreasing order of difficulty, constitutional amendments, complementary laws, and ordinary laws. In addition to committee votes, in order for an amendment to be approved, the Chamber and the Senate both must vote in favor of it twice, with 60 percent support from the members of the entire house (308 deputies or 49 senators) in each of the four votes. Complementary laws must be approved by an absolute majority in both the Chamber and the Senate (257 deputies or 41 senators); ordinary laws must be approved by a simple majority of those present, in both the Chamber and the Senate. For the rules governing the approval and veto of legislation, see the 1988 Constitution (Título IV, Seção VIII).

14. A second industrial federation, Sindipeças, is made up of the major car parts manufacturers. Given the size of the car parts sector, and the fact that policies related to car parts were often quite different from those implemented for the auto industry, I focus here only on the policies affecting auto manufacturers themselves.

15. This tariff was subsequently softened for local manufacturers: as of 1996, auto manufacturers with local investment plans or established factories were allowed to import at a 35 percent tariff. The increase in tariffs on automobiles was accompanied by a decrease in tariffs on auto parts, from 18 percent to 2 percent.

16. Under the new policy, sixteen new auto plants were planned for construction in Brazil from 1997 to 2000, with planned investment of US$8.8 billion aimed at increasing capacity by nearly a third (O'Keefe and Haar 2001, 8).

17. As one observer noted, the new agreement with the automotive sector was "the most flagrant privilege conceded to a single industry since the process of economic opening began" (Bedê 1996b; translation mine). But the gains were somewhat disparate. Local auto manufacturers gained protection, in contrast to auto parts producers, who faced assiduous competition from a large number of domestic firms and international competition driven by the March reduction in tariffs on auto parts from 18 percent to 2 percent. And despite the auto industry's reticence on the subject, proof that the policy package met with industry approval came in 1996, when the ANFAVEA hired international law firms to defend the policy at WTO hearings (*Folha de São Paulo* 1996a). Throughout 1997, further proof came in the form of ANFAVEA lobbying to extend the supposedly "temporary" tariff protection.

18. The bulk of judicial action was focused on interpreting the new tariff rules on imported cars that had been ordered, but not delivered to buyers at the time the tariffs went into effect, making the cars instantly 32 percent to 70 percent more expensive.

19. The provisional measure establishing the import tariff, quotas, and fiscal incentives was the subject of an ADIN filed by the Workers' Party (PT), but this ADIN was not filed to contest these policies per se. Instead, it was one of a series of ADINs filed by the PT against provisional measures between January and June 1995, filed to question the constitutionality of "re-editing" provisional measures before the previous version of the measure had expired.

20. I am indebted to Carlos Lopes, senior political analyst at Santafé Idéias, a political consultancy, for his helpful guidance on the many twists and turns of social security reform.

21. Wilson uses social security in the United States as an example of politics with diffuse costs and benefits. In the case of social security reform in Brazil, however, the issue is not so much addressing widespread benefits but reforming the high concentration of benefits in the hands of a concentrated minority, the civil service. I therefore put social security reform in the category

of concentrated costs and diffuse benefits, following Wilson's own enjoinder that "a distinction should be made between the adoption of a new policy and the amendment of a new one" (1995, 330); by this logic, Brazilian social security reform of the 1990s is in an entirely different class, for example, than the social security program initiated by the Vargas government of the 1930s.

22. Judges also played a not-insignificant role in the legislative debate over reform. In August 1997, for example, the College of Presidents of Justice Tribunals—the heads of the top state courts—announced their opposition to the proposed cap on public sector retirement benefits. After a three-day conference, twenty-four of these judges signed what became known as the "Letter from Manaus," complaining of the loss of "minimum guarantees" and "acquired rights," and warning about the loss of judicial independence that might result from the social security reform. Reports at the time suggested that a majority of STF ministers also supported special retirement benefits for judges, with only Celso de Mello and Marco Aurélio de Mello, of the eleven top judges, arguing against the "egotistical" "corporatism of the judiciary" (Freitas 1997b).

23. The ability of one judge to provide an injunction halting policy implementation was highly criticized after this decision, which was not Mello's first controversial injunction. See, for example, Ramos 1996.

24. In addition, supporters agreed with Minister Mello's contention that under the congressional rules, it was illegal for the author of an amendment proposal to also serve as its rapporteur, as Congressman Michel Temer had (Freitas 1996).

25. Marco Aurélio de Mello became widely known as the "*ministro vencido*," or "defeated minister," for his minority opinions on the court, where it was not unusual for Mello to be outvoted 10 to 1 (Galluci 2003).

26. The success rate for ADINs on these social security proposals was 3 percent on the merit and 9.1 percent on the injunctions, against an overall success rate for ADINs of 7.1 percent and 18.6 percent, respectively.

27. The first ADIN that led to an injunction was decided in April 1999, when the STF determined that the cap on pension benefits would not apply to maternity leave, which is also funded through the overall social security system (ADIN 1946, filed by the PSB, against Art. 14 of Constitutional Amendment 20). The other ADIN that led to an injunction, in November 1999, ruled that philanthropic organizations were exempt from social security contributions (ADIN 2028, filed by the Confederação Nacional da Saude, Hospitais, Estabelecimentos e Serviços, against Law 9732).

28. The Economist Intelligence Unit (2001, 23) estimated that the investment needs totaled US$4.4 to US$5.5 billion annually; in the same year, Ernst & Young calculated the annual investment needed at US$8 to US$10 billion a year (Ogier 2001, 114).

29. These were the electric regulatory board (ANEEL), the water regulatory board (ANA), and the petroleum regulatory board (ANP).

Notes to Pages 64–76

30. Small consumers, using under one hundred kilowatt hours per month, were exempted from the reduction, but were not allowed to increase consumption from the previous year. Suspension of service would begin with a three-day suspension, with further infractions leading to ever-increasing suspensions. One small carrot was provided to consumers: those who were able to reduce their consumption would receive a "bonus" on their electric bills.

31. Demand appears to have been reduced sharply; when rationing ended in 2002, consumption remained below its 2001 average. Meanwhile, supply was boosted: over 3000 MW in new supply came online in 2001, and another 9000 MW were projected for 2002 (Arce 2002).

32. This formulation of the problem drew on past jurisprudence, particularly challenges of the Collor Stabilization Plan's freezing of savings, which had been deemed "confiscation" by the STF early in the 1990s.

33. Thus, in Type I, the OAB's challenge to agrarian reform is excluded, and in Type II, the challenges to the IPI tax and the import tax are excluded, because in these cases, the element being challenged was in reality a Type III policy.

Chapter 4

1. The dichotomous nature of the debate on political institutions in Brazil is addressed in Palermo 2000, as well as in Pereira and Mueller 2003.

2. The ten policies were the Emergency Social Fund; the Real Plan; the "economic order" reforms; the National Privatization Program; the Fiscal Stabilization Fund; CPMF tax; civil service reform; social security reform; the civil service pension tax; and electricity rationing measures.

3. The literature on political decision making and policy outcomes in Brazil until very recently largely ignored the role of the judiciary. With the exception of Stepan (2000), who views the judiciary as one more "demos-constraining" factor in Brazil's counter-majoritarian political system, none of the authors cited in the debate on the executive and legislative branches in this section directly addresses the role of the courts in the policymaking process. Studies on the courts' policy effects, meanwhile, seldom are integrated into the discussion of the elected braches.

4. See also Andrews and Montinola 2004 and Haggard and McCubbins 2001 (5, fn. 10). For a thoughtful critique of the veto player literature, see Ganghof 2003.

5. Stone Sweet (2000, 53) offers an alternative definition: "A veto point is a formally organized opportunity for opponents of the governing majority to block legislative provisions they do not like from becoming law." The definition I give here is preferable for my purposes because it emphasizes not only the importance of the veto itself but also the importance of the veto threat in its own right.

6. For earlier uses of the concept of veto points, see, for example, Huber et al. 1993 and Birchfield and Crepaz 1998.

7. Readers who are acquainted with Tsebelis's work may question my use of the term *veto point*. I use the term *veto point* to avoid the semantic confusion between the process of decision making and the players involved in that decision making. Tsebelis addresses this issue in part by distinguishing between institutional and partisan veto players, depending on whether they are generated by the constitution or by the political game. But the semantic difficulties inherent in Tsebelis's distinction are further complicated by the Brazilian case: the 1988 Constitution created new rules that expressly benefited the very groups that participated in the constituent assembly, allowing them to share the characteristics of both institutional and partisan veto players.

8. Tsebelis briefly notes the role of the judiciary as a potential veto player, arguing that the judiciary is not a veto player when performing statutory interpretations (because it can be overruled) but is a veto player with respect to constitutional interpretation. He softens this, however, by arguing that most of the time, courts are "absorbed" by other political veto players; when they are not, the multiple decisions involved in judicial cases make it impossible to allocate judicial decisions to veto player policy positions (2002, 226–34). Alivizatos (1995) also addresses judges as veto players.

In the literature on Latin America, Stein et al. (2006) argue that Latin American courts perform four roles in the policymaking process (veto player, policy player, impartial referee, and societal representative), but veto point is not among them. The conceptual emphasis on courts as veto players rather than veto points carries over to Brazil. Ames (2001, 15, fn. 25) briefly suggests in a footnote that courts may act as veto players through judicial review of legislation, but does not extend this analysis. Sadek and Arantes (1994, 37), meanwhile, argue that the Brazilian political system is one of "multi-vetoes" across the branches of power. Within this system, the judiciary is able to exercise veto power, usually after a policy has been implemented by other political actors: "[the judiciary's] decentralized and de facto federalized structure allows it to paralyze policies, offer decisions in a non-uniform fashion and thus suspend, even if only temporarily, measures with national impact" (translation mine).

9. This reasoning is similar in some ways to that offered by "resource theory" (Haynie 1994). In contrast to the Philippine case addressed by Haynie, the Brazilian federal judiciary does not uniformly privilege those with the least resources, at least procedurally; in this case the resource in question is the ability to withstand long delays, which the government has in spades.

10. Of more than forty case types heard by the STF, it has original jurisdiction in ten. Of these, three are of particular potential interest: the Direct Action of Unconstitutionality (*Ação Direta de Inconstitucionalidade*, ADIN), the Direct Action of Constitutionality (*Ação Declaratória de Constitucionalidade*, ADC);

and the Original Civil Action (*Ação Civil Originária*, ACO). Two qualities distinguish these three types of cases for my purposes: all three are heard directly at the STF, and none is specifically focused on criminal malfeasance. Standing in all three is restricted to a select group of political actors. Of these three types of cases, however, only the ADIN has been used in sufficient quantity to enable broad analysis. Roughly 2,900 ADINs were filed addressing laws passed between 1988 and the end of 2002, as compared with 9 ADCs and 234 ACOs.

Three other case types might be of peripheral interest from a policy perspective, but are also excluded here. Federal intervention (*Intervenção Federal*) cases are excluded mainly because they involve a choice by the STF on the appropriateness of requests for federal government corrective intervention in state and municipal governments, rather than a challenge to the federal government's policies. Original actions (*Ações Originárias*) are also excluded, because they are primarily criminal in nature. Cases of "Accusations of Noncompliance with Fundamental Precepts" (*Argüição de Descumprimento de Preceito Fundamental, ADPF*) will definitely be of interest to future researchers, but because the case type was created only in 1999 (by Law 9882), relatively few ADPFs were filed during the period analyzed here.

11. The dataset begins with the 1988 Constitution, which significantly altered the rules for the ADIN, making it much more broadly used. It ends in 2002 because so many of the cases filed since 2003 remain pending, but future researchers could easily extend it. The full dataset is available at http://matthew macleodtaylor.googlepages.com/home.

12. The ADIN was created by the military regime in 1965, but at its creation, only the prosecutor-general was given the standing to bring ADINs. The original efficiency goals of the ADIN were clearly trumped by the expansion of standing in the 1988 Constitution, although ADINs remain far more expeditious than other legal instruments for challenging policy.

13. My analysis builds on two pioneering studies of the ADIN, by Werneck Vianna et al. (1999) and Castro (1993). My research—largely because it was carried out several years later—treats a larger sample of cases at the federal level. Other significant differences in my work include the following: (1) rather than adopt the STF's categorization of ADIN cases, as previous scholars did, I use my own policy-oriented descriptions to categorize topic areas; (2) given my focus on federal public policymaking, I focus solely on ADINs that challenge policies adopted at the federal government level; and (3) my binary logistic model of ADIN decisions permits a multivariate approach.

14. In a handful of cases, ADINs have also been filed for redress against "omission," or the failure of the relevant authority to actually implement a policy or take a legislative step required by the 1988 Constitution.

15. Injunction requests were filed in nearly 90 percent of the ADINs during this period.

16. When filing an ADIN petition, a plaintiff usually asserts his or her right to seek ADIN relief before the STF and details why the law in question is unconstitutional (or, in the far rarer case of "omission," the plaintiff explains why the absence of a law is unconstitutional), citing past cases, expert opinions, and constitutional interpretations to back his or her argument. The STF, in making its decision, names a rapporteur (*relator*) to provide a summary judgment of the case, and the rapporteur's report is voted up or down by the full STF. Any injunction request is decided upon by the rapporteur, and goes into effect immediately, but is then voted on by the full STF.

17. This total, 20.8 percent, is the proportion of all cases in which either the merit or the injunction, or both, was granted or partially granted (striking down the full legislation implementing policy, or a portion of it).

18. Readers may reasonably wonder why I did not categorize ADIN topics according to the typology in Chapter 3. Given the frequency of laws that include several separate policy types (e.g., the examples of the Type III elements of automotive policy), this would be an almost impossible and enormously subjective task. I rely on general topic categorization instead, which is not itself a simple task: to categorize each ADIN, I compiled two datasets that analyzed the primary topic of the laws and the ADINs in question. Though there may be overlap between subject categories (e.g., a law might focus on both taxation and fiscal transfers), by using broad categories, a close reading of both laws and ADINs, and external sources to verify subject matter, I believe I have generated a reliable and replicable rendering of the topics in question. On the laws in question, I have used the index of laws provided at www.soleis.adv.br and the presidential staff's legislation search engine (https://legislacao.planalto .gov.br/legislacao.nsf). On ADINs, I draw all ADINs from the STF's database, found at www.stf.gov.br/processos/adi/default.asp. I have also checked my topic categorization of ADINs against the *Ministério Público*'s subject index of ADINs (Ministério Público Federal 2003).

19. This percentage is not directly illustrated in Figure 4.1, because the members of the legal professions are categorized both under OAB and under professional unions.

20. As Ganghof (2003) notes, without the assumption of Euclidean preferences—in which each dimension is weighted equally—virtually nothing could be said about the importance of veto players. I have simplified to two policy dimensions, while recognizing that few cases—including this one—are quite so simplistic. That said, the explanatory value of this heuristic exercise is germane even under multiple preference dimensions.

Chapter 5

1. The PT gained legislative control in 2002 by building a coalition with other left and center-left parties to augment its 18 percent share of the Chamber.

It is worth noting that no political party had a legislative majority in Congress during the Cardoso administration; instead, the Cardoso administration cobbled together an amalgam of center and center-right parties for support. The Lula government has reversed this pattern by cobbling together a coalition with left and center-left parties that has provided it with an unstable legislative majority.

2. Throughout this chapter, in addition to primary and secondary sources, I rely on interviews conducted in November and December 2003 with PT party members, PT staff members and lawyers, and journalists based in Brasilia who were well acquainted with the PT's use of the courts. To obtain the interviews and address somewhat sensitive information in a manner that does not jeopardize interviewees' professional or personal standing, I pledged to maintain interviewees' anonymity. I use direct quotes only when citing particularly relevant points from these conversations. All the interviews were conducted in Portuguese, and all the translations are mine.

3. Other case types in which the STF had original jurisdiction were less attractive to plaintiffs such as the PT, either because the case type was not clearly regulated, or because it did not appear to offer the same chances of success, with the same speed. The *mandado de segurança coletivo,* included in the 1988 Constitution, was a potential alternative to the ADIN, as it also could be brought by political parties. But as interviewees noted, the *mandado de segurança coletivo* was infrequently used because of the complexities of getting the *mandado* admitted in court, and because it was usually heard more slowly than ADINs.

4. The decision to "share" ADINs by submitting ADIN requests in tandem with co-plaintiffs was largely tactical, as ADINs dealing with the same topic are usually funneled to the same rapporteur in the STF. By bringing ADINs jointly with other groups or parties, the PT thus prevented the rapporteur from becoming bogged down in various similar ADIN requests, and sped up the STF's consideration of the policy being questioned.

5. The exception to this rule occurs on weekends, when only one judge is normally on duty. Political parties occasionally took advantage of this fact to file cases before "weekend duty" judges believed to be sympathetic to their arguments, resulting in an injunction that went into effect over the weekend, before a random judge could be selected on Monday morning.

6. In some of the cases discussed here, state courts were also used, introducing a further element of potential variance.

7. A search of court cases from the STF, STJ, and 3rd Regional Federal Tribunal, in which leading national PT members and congressional representatives from the states of São Paulo and Mato Grosso do Sul were plaintiffs or defendants, found that PT party members were defendants in roughly twice as many suits as they were plaintiffs, most often in suits over alleged malfeasance in local government or in cases of alleged slander.

There are a few reasons to treat these figures with some skepticism: (1) the search engines for these courts are not always fully accurate (for example, not using the full name used in the court case may result in an incomplete search result); (2) the PT's suits against the government were not always filed by the leading party members used in my searches; and (3) appeals court cases often show one party as the appellant, but it is impossible to know whether they were the original defendant in the court of first instance. The search included all PT congressional representatives elected to the 1995–99 Chamber and the 1999–2003 Chamber, as well as the following prominent PT members: Luis Inácio Lula da Silva, Antônio Palocci, Eduardo Suplicy, Marta Suplicy, Guido Mantega, José Dirceu, Ricardo Berzoini, José Genoíno, Aloízio Mercadante, Luiz Dulci, and Tarso Genro.

8. A second legislative initiative by the departing Cardoso administration sought to neutralize another tactic in this regard: the spurious announcement of investigations (or leaks about such investigations) into public figures, oftentimes announced with great fanfare, but then not followed up with any legal action. The perjoratively nicknamed *Lei de Mordaça* (roughly, "gag-rule law"; known officially as the "Law Against the Abuse of Authority") prohibited judges, members of the *Ministério Público,* and police from commenting on ongoing investigations. The Cardoso government was responding to the common tactic of leaking alleged malfeasance to the press, which served to discredit policies and policymakers in the public mind as well as potentially turning up new information for the prosecution. The proposed *Lei de Mordaça* followed up on a provisional measure issued by the government in 2000 that sharply reduced the number of suits against the government by requiring judges to evaluate, prior to trial, whether the evidence presented by the *Ministério Público* was sufficient. The effectiveness of this provisional measure in reducing the number of case filings suggests there may have been some truth to the Cardoso administration's claims that not all cases previously brought by the *Ministério Público* against government officials had been backed by substantive legal claims, but instead represented fishing expeditions aimed at tarring policy, policymakers, or both (Brasil et al. 2001).

9. This figure is the result of my search of court cases in which Malan was named as a plaintiff, in these three courts. It is by no means exhaustive, and it is impossible to identify the party loyalties of all those who filed suit against Malan, but it provides a sense of the ubiquity of suits against policymakers.

10. The three categories of accusations listed here were *inquéritos civis, ações de improbidade administrativa,* and *açoes por crimes de responsabilidade.* There were also 60 such cases pending against congressmen, 17 against governors, 1,448 against mayors, and 65 against judges (author correspondence with the office of Gilda Pereira de Carvalho, Sub-Procuradora Geral da República, Ministério Público Federal, December 2003).

11. This situation has now been reversed, as Lula has appointed a majority of current STF ministers.

12. The PFL switched its name to "Democratas" in March 2007. During the entire period analyzed here, however, its official name remained "PFL," which is therefore used in the text.

13. I choose this period in 2003–2004 because the strictly policy use of the courts was not yet "contaminated" by the political scandal that ultimately toppled a portion of Lula's cabinet in 2005–2006. Furthermore, publicly available court records for more recent years were unfortunately incomplete at the time of writing.

14. The search includes the Regional Federal Court for the First District (Brasília), the *Superior Tribunal de Justiça*, and the *Supremo Tribunal Federal*. This replicates the method used in my search of cases against Pedro Malan.

15. Of these, two challenge laws implemented prior to Lula's inauguration, while the other two challenge Lula policies on genetically modified soybeans and congressional regulations on sports.

Chapter 6

1. I am grateful to a number of lawyers who shared their time and insights about the OAB with me, and especially to the members of the São Paulo OAB, who were extraordinarily generous. Any inadvertent errors are mine alone.

2. The OAB was created by Decree 19,408 of 1930, signed by Getúlio Vargas. But as Bonelli (2003) and Diniz (2003) note, the OAB had deep roots prior to Vargas: the *Instituto dos Advogados* was created by Emperor Don Pedro II in 1843, and creation of a bar association was a primary objective of the Instituto in the intervening decades. Bonelli (2003: 1059) argues convincingly that the founding of the OAB was not—as some have argued—"evidence of the new [Vargas] regime's corporatism," but rather the outcome of a long process of professionalization that had been under way for nearly a century. Nonetheless, even if the OAB's founding was clearly not a part of the Vargas regime's general push toward corporatist organization of Brazilian society, it can be fairly labeled as corporatist in that it is essential to intermediating lawyers' interests within the political system, as the conclusion to this chapter illustrates.

3. Skidmore's interview with Seabra Fagundes, OAB president at the time, suggests the bomb's timing was directly linked to the OAB's request for access to agents of the DOI-CODI intelligence service who were believed to have participated in the kidnapping of prominent opposition lawyer Dalmo Dallari (Skidmore 1988, 277, fn. 52).

4. Further rights that were listed in the Statute have since been suspended by suits filed at the STF, primarily by judges' and prosecutors' associations. These challenged various elements of the Statute such as an article that required an OAB representative to be present for any search of a lawyer's home

or if a lawyer were arrested in the course of professional duties, and another that required lawyers to be contracted by anyone using small claims courts.

5. State-level OABs are largely free of hierarchical oversight by the federal OAB, although on rare occasions, state organizations have come under intervention from the federal organization. In 2003, for example, the Federal Council intervened in the Rio Grande do Norte state OAB to ensure the inauguration of the candidate it believed had rightfully won the state election, against the protests of an opposition group (*Consultor Jurídico* 2003). Meanwhile, between elections, the ties between the state and federal OAB are tenuous: while the Federal Council is made up of state representatives, they are not directly tied to the leadership of the state organizations and have little operational responsibility in their home states.

6. Another small irony is that although the OAB has advocated at a national level for a nonobligatory vote, voting is mandatory for all OAB members.

7. The fee was approximately R$550, and there were 445,418 members of the OAB in 2004 (OAB 2004: 31).

8. In São Paulo, for example, article 40 of state law 10.394 ("Carteira de Previdência dos Advogados de São Paulo") states that lawyers will contribute R$4.80 for every *mandado judicial* filed.

9. Federal budget figures are available at www.oab.org.br; state budget figures are available at www.oabsp.org.br, both accessed February 17, 2005.

10. The OAB, both at the federal and state levels, has routinely complained to the federal Education Ministry about the proliferation of law schools—which more than tripled from 183 in 1993 to 763 in 2003 (OAB-SP 2004), leading to the doubling of the number of graduated law students during the 1990s—and the fact that many students are not being properly prepared for the bar exam or, for that matter, for the practice of law. Although the OAB theoretically plays an advisory role to the Education Ministry in selecting which law schools are authorized, its advice is not always heeded and it complains that the new law schools are training students not for the practice of law but for the Education Ministry's examinations. It is evident that there is a large disparity between top-of-the-line law schools, whose students routinely pass the bar exam with 70–75 percent approval ratings, and some of the upstart schools, whose approval numbers rank below 25 percent. The OAB became so incensed by the growth in numbers of law school students, which now total roughly 14 percent of all college students in Brazil, that in 2002 the OAB federal council successfully sought an injunction in the Superior Justice Tribunal (STJ) to curtail the Education Ministry's planned expansion of law school openings.

11. In an opinion piece, for example, one critic noted that some jailed drug traffickers in Rio had as many as twenty-four lawyers working for them at any given time, and that often these lawyers worked as "carrier pigeons," transmitting messages outside prison walls. Her main complaint, however, was that the

OAB, at both the state and federal levels, had done little to fight the problem of lawyers who had become "criminal" (Wolthers 2000).

12. Between 1987 and 1999, 39.8 percent of congressmen in the Chamber of Deputies were law school graduates (against 10.2 percent doctors, 11.2 percent engineers, 7.5 percent economists, 16.1 percent other, and 15.2 percent who had no college education). This represented a marked decline in the number of law school graduates, who represented 57 percent of congressmen in the 1946–67 period, and 61.3 percent in the 1967–87 period (Boschi et al. 2000: 98). By October 2003, when the Parliamentary Front of Lawyers was founded in the Chamber of Deputies, only eighty-eight deputies (17.15 percent) were members. In the Senate, law school graduates are the largest professional contingent, at 37 percent in 1999. This percentage fell steadily throughout the 1990s, however, from 42 percent in 1991 to 40 percent in 1995, and 37 percent in 1999 (Lemos and Ranincheski 2003).

13. As Riker (1986, 18–33) notes, the considerable agenda power of leaders often permits them to achieve their preferences by controlling the timing and content of decisions. As a result of exactly this dynamic, OAB presidents have exercised considerable influence over the Order's policy stances.

14. A fourth goal, which is too complex to discuss in great detail here, is personal ambition. A number of lawyers have used OAB state and federal leadership positions as a stepping-stone in their political and legal careers, running for Congress or simply boosting their professional status. This helps to explain the monumental sums spent on OAB elections, which reach into the millions of *reais*. Suffice it to note that, as in any institution, leadership goals are not always fully aligned with the full membership's goals. It is difficult to assign political labels to the various presidents of the OAB. Batocchio and Uchoa Lima both held office, the first as a PDT congressman and the latter as an ARENA/UDN senator under the military regime (Uchoa Lima was a *suplente*, a kind of vice-senator, who took office when the titular senator, Wilson Gonçalves, resigned in 1978). The supposed ideological differences between these two parties—the leftist PDT and the conservative UDN—did not prevent Batocchio from supporting Uchoa Lima's candidacy. Their two successors, Reginaldo Oscar de Castro and Rubens Approbato, did not hold political office. Castro worked as a legal advisor to President Cardoso's first presidential campaign, in 1994, but this did not prevent him from publicly criticizing Cardoso administration policy later. He ran for the Brasília Senate seat in 2002 with the leftist PSB, but resigned his candidacy before the election.

15. The term *federal intervention* has a very specific constitutional meaning in Brazil. According to the constitution, under very specific circumstances, and at the request of the STF and with congressional approval, the President can decree federal intervention in any of the twenty-seven states. These include cases in which judicial decisions are not carried out and the STF or STJ requests intervention; or if federal law is not carried out. Examples of cases in

which the OAB called for intervention include in Alagoas, after police killed
a man who had complained earlier of torture; in Mato Grosso do Sul, where
court workers went on strike after the state government failed to pay them,
and then again, after a spate of political killings; in Piauí, where organized
crime was reaching startling levels; in Roraima, where state payrolls had been
misappropriated; and in Espírito Santo, where the OAB led an investigation
into the role of organized crime in state government and called for intervention after a prominent lawyer was murdered.

16. After then STF president Maurício Corrêa suggested that the OAB's
accounts should be more rigorously and transparently controlled, the Association of Brazilian Federal Judges (AJUFE) sent a letter of support, in which its
president noted, "We are favorable to transparency at all levels, including in
the Judiciary, and there is no reason [to give] different treatment to the OAB,
which is the only federal council of professional supervision that refuses to
account for [its revenues]" (quoted in a letter of support to Minister Maurício
Corrêa, "AJUFE também defende controle das contas da OAB," cited in the
STF press release, "Presidente do STF recebe nota de apoio da AJUFE," February 19, 2004, STF daily press briefing, at www.stf.gov.br/noticias/imprensa,
accessed on February 20, 2004; translation mine).

17. The *Tribunal de Contas da União* (TCU), despite the name *Tribunal*, is
not a part of the judiciary. Rather, it is an audit body loosely (but constitutionally) tied to the Congress, with the responsibility to audit public entities in
Brazil. The *Ministério Público* had urged that the OAB, as a quasi-public institution, should be subject to TCU audits.

18. All of the OAB presidents during this period, from José Roberto
Batocchio through his successors Ernando Uchoa Lima and Reginaldo Oscar
de Castro, followed the same critical line regarding provisional measures.

19. As former OAB president Approbato Machado noted, on rare occasions when speed was of the essence, he filed suit without going through the
full formal process of approval on the Federal Council. However, this was ex-
ceedingly rare (author interview, April 29, 2004).

Chapter 7

1. My choice of pension reform as the policy analyzed here follows the
logic explored in Chapter 3, namely, that different policy arenas may generate
different forms of policy contestation: Type III policies such as pension reform
that concentrate costs among a particular interest group will likely face intense
opposition, because a small group of reform "losers" will be motivated to collective action.

2. Although reformers argued otherwise, skepticism regarding the economic outcomes of pension reform is widespread: for an overview, see Orszag
and Stiglitz 2001. In a review of the literature on pension reform, Kay (1998,

142) praises the dose of realism that permits the authors to recognize that "pension reform does not automatically increase national savings and that it is just one of many reforms that contribute to the development of capital markets."

3. In all four countries, various groups were exempted from the pension reforms, usually the armed forces and often local-level civil servants. As in Chile, the armed forces pension system remained unprivatized in Mexico; Mexico also maintained separate pension schemes for federal civil servants and oil workers.

4. The most prominent case that established jurisprudence in this regard was the 1986 Rolón Zappa case, in which the Supreme Court rejected the government's claims that the economic emergency allowed it to reduce payments to pensioners without Congressional approval. I am grateful to Diana Kapiszewski for highlighting this case.

5. President Sanguinetti, for example, kept all top posts in his administration vacant until reform had passed (Kay 1999). Meanwhile, the timing of the reform vote was purposely scheduled early in the presidential term to allow opposition to cool before a plebiscite, which could not take place until the following national election in 1999, by which time "the system would be in place and functioning" (Bergara et al. 2004, 55).

6. As Figueiredo and Limongi (1999) and Amorim Neto et al. (2003) illustrate, governments have at times—including during pension reform—been able to construct a highly effective majoritarian governing coalition. But these coalitions have not been able to overcome the consensual elements (in the sense of *consensual* used by Lijphart 1999) of the political system outside the executive-legislative axis, such as the court system itself, and this in part explains the difficulty of approving some of the more contentious policy initiatives.

7. As Stone (1992, 49) notes in reference to France, the mere possibility of filing suit changes the political dynamic of relations between government and the parties privileged to bring suit: "Because governments can not prevent such petitions, they are obliged either to work on the assumption that opposition will refer important projects to constitutional judges or to risk court censure, embarrassment, and lost time."

The existence of the veto point provided by the courts in Brazil might have similarly permitted earlier inclusion or incorporation of opposition groups' views and the modification of policy reforms to limit contestable positions. Of course, this assertion is extraordinarily difficult to prove, and given the "parliamentary agenda cartel" prevalent during the Cardoso administration (Amorim Neto et al. 2003), it may have made little sense to executive and legislative negotiators to incorporate the unknown preferences of veto players external to the cartel. Furthermore, the surprise with which both governments and markets greeted court decisions (Taylor 2006a) may be a reflection that some potential veto players were unable to use the threat of a veto to leverage their policy opposition earlier in the process, or that the dominant coalition paid no attention to warning signals, at least early in the Cardoso presidency, before it had experience with the increasingly predominant practice of judicial policy contestation.

8. Larkins (1998) notes that the institutional scope of judicial authority was not reduced in Argentina, because judges' partiality and lack of insulation from political pressures meant that the court generally ruled in the government's favor. Larkins notes, "Particularly, the court has set solid precedents on the extent of the president's decree authority, civil-military and federal-provincial relations, the validity of decrees issued by de facto governments, and the validity of government contracts. The key difference, of course, is that on virtually all of these occasions the supreme court's decisions either supported or strongly favored the president's policies."

9. The widespread use of instruments such as referenda in Uruguay suggests courts may remain only a second-best alternative after other more effective and commonly used mechanisms of popular representation. Altman (2002), for example, argues that Uruguay is one of the most prolific users of direct democratic devices at the national level.

10. ADINs No. 319, 414, 427, 768, 1102, 1108, and 1153, among others.

11. ADIN No. 975.

12. ADIN No. 2332.

13. ADINs No. 1127 and 1194, among others.

14. ADIN No. 1659.

15. ADINs No. 1417, 2178, and 2556.

16. ADINs No. 1361, 1675, 1849, and 1861, among others.

Chapter 8

1. *Democratic consolidation* is a term frequently used with only loose definition. In its simplest form it is when a democracy is "truly the only viable political system and method for the foreseeable future" (Diamond 1997). I avoid the term *democratic consolidation* here as much as possible, preferring to refer to the deepening of democratic practices. This deepening is very much in line with Linz and Stepan's (1996) view of the need to provide both economic and political baskets of goods that improve the quality of life, as well as the emphasis given by Sen (1999) to the interactive nature of development, composed of mutually dependent advances in providing economic opportunities, political freedoms, social facilities, transparency guarantees, and protective security. Both new and old democracies are engaged in an ongoing process of deepening democratic processes, making distinctions between "consolidating" democracies such as Brazil and Spain, for example, less a matter of time (a difference of roughly a decade) and more a difference in degree and scope.

2. In a 2002 case, for example, the STJ ruled that the readjustments in residential mortgages during the Collor Plan were tied to the wrong price index,

a decision that could have serious fiscal implications, with a cost as high as R$87 billion for the government, if upheld by the STF. Other pending decisions with significant potential repercussions include sugar and alcohol producers' suits, and hospitals and health clinics' suits, seeking compensation for the costs of past economic plans (with estimated total potential costs of as much as R$65 billion).

3. Perhaps the most important decision was the November 2005 STF decision overturning a 1998 government rate increase in the pension contributions paid by businesses (mentioned in Chapter 2). The court has also ruled in favor of the government, however, the most important being in August 2004, when it upheld the constitutionality of the 11 percent social security levy on retired public employees, rejecting an ADIN filed by the OAB.

4. Several states have sued the federal government for failing to make what they claim were required transfers related to its share of education spending, for example, and the national industrial federation has filed suit against a federal law that parceled out state governments' payments of *precatórios* (judicially mandated debt payments) over ten years. In addition, the federal courts have heard several cases in which state executive and legislative branches fought over the proper role and jurisdiction of new regulatory agencies controlling electricity, gas, water, and telecommunications services at the state level.

5. Perhaps most spectacularly, the STF has been called into the political fray to rule several times on whether parliamentary committees of inquiry (CPIs) and congressional votes can proceed in the scandal that engulfed Lula's former presidential chief of staff, José Dirceu, and many members of Congress. It was also asked to rule on whether minority parties in Congress can call their own CPIs, even without majority support, as well as on more mundane issues such as whether Central Bank presidents should have ministerial status (which confers privileged legal standing).

6. The federal courts have been called upon to rule on the new regulatory model for the electricity industry proposed by Lula; in a significant vote, the STF overturned the CADE anti-monopoly board's decision rejecting Nestlé's acquisition of a large Brazilian candy maker; and judges on the STJ have been asked to rule on the legality of rate increases proposed by the ANATEL telecommunications regulatory board.

7. The judicial reform of 2004 has already been contested by the AMB and AJUFE judges' associations, in suits that are pending. Other issues related to the functioning of the legal system have also been taken up in the courts, such as the 2003 ADIN filed by the OAB to contest the use of the *Advocacia Geral da União* to defend public servants in court.

8. As Stein et al (2006: 259) note, this is not an insignificant concern: the legitimacy of the policymaking process is frequently more relevant to policy sustainability than technical correctness.

9. While it has not been my focus here, this concern also extends to the social control function of courts in democracies. As noted in Chapters 1 and 2, a large gap exists between the letter of the law and its application, as noted by Brinks (2003); Caldeira (2000, 2002); Caldeira and Holston (1999); Holston (1991); Holston and Caldeira (1998); and Pereira (2000).

10. Law No. 11.417, of December 19, 2006, Art. 3.

REFERENCES

Abrucio, Fernando Luiz. 1998. *Os Barões da Federação: Os governadores e a redemocratização brasileira.* São Paulo: Hucitec.

Agência Estado. 28 November 2006. "Chefe do STF ganha 79% mais que equivalente nos EUA."

Agüero, Felipe, and Jeffrey Stark, eds. 1998. *Fault Lines of Democracy in Post-Transition Latin America.* Miami: North-South Center Press.

Alencar, Kennedy. 22 September 2002. FHC prioriza aprovação de proteção à ex-autoridade. *Folha de São Paulo,* p. Brasil A9.

Alivizatos, Nicos C. 1995. Judges as Veto Players. In *Parliaments and Majority Rule in Western Europe,* ed. Herbert Doring, 566–91. New York: St. Martin's.

Almeida, Maria Herminia Tavares de. 2004. Privatization: Reform Through Negotiation. In *Reforming Brazil,* eds. Mauricio A. Font and Anthony Peter Spanakos, 53–70. Lanham, Md.: Lexington Books.

Altman, David. 2002. Popular Initiatives in Uruguay: Confidence Votes on Governments or Political Loyalties? *Electoral Studies* 21, no. 4: 617–30.

Ames, Barry. 1995a. Electoral Rules, Constituency Pressures and Pork Barrel: Bases of Voting in the Brazilian Congress. *Journal of Politics* 57, no. 2: 324–43.

———. 1995b. Electoral Strategy Under Open-List Proportional Representation. *American Journal of Political Science* 39: 406–33.

———. 2001. *The Deadlock of Democracy in Brazil.* Ann Arbor: University of Michigan Press.

Amorim Alves, Paulo César. 2006. "O tempo como ferramenta de decisão no STF: Um mapeamento da seletividade do tribunal nos tempos processuais das ações diretas de inconstitucionalidade." Thesis, Escola de Formação da Sociedade Brasileira de Direito Público.

Amorim Neto, Octavio, Gary W. Cox, and Mathew D. McCubbins. 2003. Agenda Power in Brazil's Camara dos Deputados, 1989–98. *World Politics* 55: 550–78.

Andrews, Josephine T., and Gabriella R. Montinola. 2004. Veto Players and the Rule of Law in Emerging Democracies. *Comparative Political Studies* 37, no. 1: 55–87.

Arantes, Rogério Bastos. 1997. *Judiciário e Política no Brasil.* São Paulo: IDESP.

————. 2000. The Judiciary, Democracy, and Economic Policy in Brazil. In *Handbook of Global Legal Policy*, ed. Stuart Nagel, 335–49. New York: Marcel Dekker.

————. 2002. *Ministério Público e Política no Brasil*. São Paulo: EDUC.

————. 2005. Constitutionalism, the Expansion of Justice and the Judicialization of Politics in Brazil. In *The Judicialization of Politics in Latin America*, eds. Rachel Sieder, Line Schjolden, and Alan Angell. New York: Palgrave Macmillan.

————. 2006. Justice and Politics in Brazil: The Circular Journey from and Back to Normative Models of Democracy. Paper presented at the 2006 Meeting of the American Political Science Association, Philadelphia, Pennsylvania, August 31–September 4.

Arce, Mauro. 23 February 2002. O fim do racionamento. *Folha de São Paulo*.

Arias, Enrique Desmond, and Corinne Davis Rodrigues. 2006. The Myth of Personal Security: Criminal Gangs, Dispute Resolution, and Identity in Rio de Janeiro's Favelas. *Latin American Politics and Society* 48, no. 4: 53–81.

Arjomand, Said Amir. 1992. Constitutions and the Struggle for Political Order: A Study in the Modernization of Political Traditions. *European Archives of Sociology* XXXIII: 39–82.

Armijo, Leslie Elliott, Philippe Faucher, and Magdalena Dembinska. 2006. Compared to What? Assessing Brazil's Political Institutions. *Comparative Political Studies* 39, no. 6: 759–86.

Associação dos Magistrados Brasileiros (AMB). 2006. *Pesquisa AMB 2006: A palavra está com você*. Curitiba, PR: AMB.

Ballard, Megan J. 1999. The Clash Between Local Courts and Global Economics: The Politics of Judicial Reform in Brazil. *Berkeley Journal of International Law* 17, no. 2, pp. 230–76.

Barahona De Brito, Alexandra, Carmen Gonzalez-Enríquez, and Paloma Aguilar, eds. 2001. *The Politics of Memory: Transitional Justice in Democratizing Societies*. Oxford: Oxford University Press.

Barker, Robert S. 2000. Judicial Review in Costa Rica: Evolution and Recent Developments. *Southwestern Journal of Law and Trade in the Americas* 7, no. 2: 267–90.

Barros, Guilherme. 7 December 2002. Ex e atuais dirigentes do BC respondem a 68 ações. *Folha de São Paulo*, p. Brasil A5.

Bedê, Marco Aurélio. 1996a. A indústria automobilística no Brasil nos anos 90: Proteção efetiva, reestruturação e política industrial. Ph.D. dissertation, Faculdade de Economia e Administração da Universidade de São Paulo.

————. 25 October 1996b. O regime automotive em cheque. *Folha de São Paulo*, p. Dinheiro 2.

Bergara, Mario, Andrés Pereyra, Ruben Tansini, Adolfo Garcé, Daniel Chasquetti, Daniel Buquet, and Juan A. Moraes. 2004. "Political Institutions, Policymaking Processes and Policy Outcomes: The Case of Uruguay." Inter-

American Development Bank, Latin American Research Network, Research Network Working Paper #R-510.

Birchfield, Vicki, and Markus M. L. Crepaz. 1998. The Impact of Constitutional Structures and Collective and Competitive Veto Points on Income Inequality in Industrialized Democracies. *European Journal of Political Research* 34, no. 2: 175–200.

Blyth, Mark. 2003. Structures Do Not Come with an Instruction Sheet: Interests, Ideas, and Progress in Political Science. *Perspectives on Politics* 1, no. 4: 695–706.

BNDES, Área de Desestatização e Reestruturação. 2002. *Privatização No Brasil, 1990–94; 1995–2002.* Rio de Janeiro: Banco Nacional de Desenvolvimento Econômico e Social.

Bonelli, Maria da Glória. 2002. *Profissionalismo e política no mundo do direito.* São Carlos: Sumaré/Edufscar/Fapesp.

———. 2003. Lawyers' Associations and the Brazilian State, 1843–1997. *Law & Social Inquiry* 28, no. 4: 1045–73.

Boschi, Renato, Eli Diniz, and Fabiano Santos. 2000. *Elites políticas e econômicas no Brasil contemporâneo: A desconstrução da ordem corporativa e o papel do legislativo no cenário pós-reformas.* São Paulo: Konrad Adenauer Stiftung.

Bottini, Pierpaolo Cruz. 27 July 2006. Diagnóstico dos Juizados Especiais. *O Estado De São Paulo,* p. A-2.

Brasil, República Federativa do. 1988. *Constituição da República Federativa do Brasil.* Brasília: Centro Gráfico do Senado Federal.

Brasil, Sandra, Cristina Ramalho, and Luciana Costa. 4 June 2001. Coluna Mônica Bergamo. *Folha de São Paulo,* p. Ilustrada E2.

Brinks, Daniel M. 2003. Informal Institutions and the Rule of Law: The Judicial Response to State Killings in Buenos Aires and São Paulo in the 1990s. *Comparative Politics* 36, no. 1: 1–19.

———. 2005. Judicial Reform and Independence in Brazil and Argentina: The Beginning of a New Millenium? *Texas International Law Journal* 40: 595–622.

Buscaglia, Edgardo, and Thomas Ulen. 1997. A Quantitative Assessment of the Efficiency of the Judicial Sector in Latin America. *International Review of Law and Economics* 17: 275–91.

Caldeira, Teresa. 2000. *Cidade de muros: Crime, segregação e cidadania em São Paulo.* São Paulo: Editora da Universidade de São Paulo.

———. 2002. The Paradox of Police Violence in Democratic Brazil. *Ethnography* 3, no. 3: 235–64.

Caldeira, Teresa, and James Holston. 1999. Democracy and Violence in Brazil. *Comparative Studies in Society and History* 41, no. 4: 691–730.

Campos, Roberto. 26 May 1996. O pior corporativismo. *Folha de São Paulo,* p. Brasil 4.

Cardoso, Fernando Henrique. 13 April 1997. Reforma agrária: compromisso de todos. *Folha de São Paulo,* p. Brasil 11.

Cardoso, Maurício. 15 February 2006. Números da Justiça: Para cada 100 processos julgados há 13 recursos. *Consultor Jurídico.*

———. 2 January 2007a. Retrospectiva 2006: A Constituição e o Supremo na visão de seus Guardiões. *Consultor Jurídico.*

———. 14 February 2007b. Justiça em números: Apesar dos esforços, cresce quantidade de processos. *Consultor Jurídico.*

Carvalho Neto, Ernani Rodrigues de. 2005. "Revisão abstrata da legislação e a judicialização da política no Brasil." Ph.D. dissertation, Universidade de São Paulo.

Castelar Pinheiro, Armando, ed. 2000. *Judiciário e economia no Brasil.* São Paulo: Editora Sumare.

———. 2003a. Judiciário, reforma e economia: A visão dos magistrados. In *Reforma do judiciário: Planos, propostas e perspectivas,* ed. Armando Castelar Pinheiro. Campinas: Booklink Publicações.

———, ed. 2003b. *Reforma do judiciário: Planos, propostas e perspectivas.* Campinas: Booklink Publicações.

Castelar Pinheiro, Armando, Fabio Giambiagi, and Joana Gostkorzewicz. 1999. O desempenho macroeconômico do Brasil nos anos 90. In *A economia brasileira nos anos 90,* eds. Fabio Giambiagi and Maurício Mesquita Moreira. Rio de Janeiro: Banco Nacional de Desenvolvimento Econômico e Social.

Castiglioni, Rossana. 2000. Welfare State Reform in Chile and Uruguay: Cross-Class Coalitions, Elite Ideology, and Veto Players. Paper presented at 2000 Meeting of the Latin American Studies Association, Miami, Florida, March 16–18.

Castilho, Ela Wiecko, and M. Tereza Sadek. 1998. *O Ministério Público Federal e a administração da justiça no Brasil.* São Paulo: Editora Sumaré.

Castro, Marcus Faro de. 1993. Política e economia no judiciário: As ações diretas de inconstitucionalidade dos partidos políticos. *Cadernos De Ciência Política 7.*

———. 1997a. The Courts, Law, and Democracy in Brazil. *International Social Science Journal* 49, no. 152: 241–52.

———. 1997b. O Supremo Tribunal Federal e a judicialização da política. *Revista Brasileira De Ciências Sociais* 12, no. 34: 147–56.

Castro, Marcus Faro de, and Rochelle Pastana Ribeiro. 2006. Tribunais e políticas públicas: Um estudo comparado. Paper prepared for the 2006 Meeting of ALACIP, Campinas, São Paulo, September 4–6.

Castro, Reginaldo Oscar de. 2 February 1999. A crise da credibilidade. *Folha de São Paulo,* pp. Opinião 1–3.

———. 3 November 2000. Insegurança jurídica. *Folha de São Paulo,* p. Opinião A3.

Catanhêde, Eliane. 20 May 2001. Ministro soube da crise dois meses atrás. *Folha de São Paulo,* p. Dinheiro B4.

Cavalcanti, Carlos Povina. 1964. Speech by OAB national president Carlos Povina Cavalcanti to the 1115th session of the OAB, April 7, 1964. Speech cited in the history of the Brazilian Bar Association (OAB), at the OAB Website: www.oab.org.br, accessed February 16, 2004.

Ceneviva, Walter. 3 February 2001. OAB: História e representatividade. *Folha de São Paulo,* p. Cotidiano C2.

CEPAC—Pesquisa e Comunicação. 2002. Análise de Pesquisa Ibope-CNI. www.cni.org.br/produtos/diversos/src/cnibope_polit0302.pdf, accessed October 22, 2004.

Cepeda Espinosa, Manuel José. 2005. The Judicialization of Politics in Colombia: The Old and the New. In *The Judicialization of Politics in Latin America,* eds. Rachel Sieder, Line Schjolden, and Alan Angell. New York: Palgrave Macmillan.

Chavez, Rebecca Bill. 2004. *Rule of Law in Nascent Democracies: Judicial Politics in Argentina.* Stanford, Calif.: Stanford University Press.

Christofoletti, Lilian. 23 April 2003. Sombra do Poder. *Folha de São Paulo.*

Clayton, Cornell W., and Howard Gillman, eds. 1999. *Supreme Court Decision-Making: New Institutional Approaches.* Chicago: University of Chicago Press.

Collier, David, Henry E. Brady, and Jason Seawright. 2004. Sources of Leverage in Causal Inference: Toward an Alternative View of Methodology. In *Rethinking Social Inquiry: Diverse Tools, Shared Standards,* eds. Henry E. Brady and David Collier. Lanham: Rowman & Littlefield.

Consultor Jurídico. 24 January 2002. República dos bacharéis: Direito formou 50.933 bacharéis no ano passado.

———. 23 December 2003. Approbato decreta intervenção na OAB do Rio Grande do Norte.

Cox, Gary, and Mathew D. McCubbins. 2001. The Institutional Determinants of Economic Policy Outcomes. In *Presidents, Parliaments, and Policy,* eds. Stephan Haggard and Mathew D. McCubbins. Cambridge: Cambridge University Press.

Dahl, Robert A. 1957. Decision-Making in a Democracy: The Supreme Court as a National Policy-Maker. *Journal of Public Law* 6: 279–95.

Dakolias, Maria. 1999. Court Performance Around the World: A Comparative Perspective. *World Bank Technical Papers* 430.

David, René, and John E. C. Brierley. 1968. *Major Legal Systems in the World Today: An Introduction to the Comparative Study of Law.* London: The Free Press.

Diamond, Larry. 1997. Introduction: In Search of Consolidation. In *Consolidating the Third Wave Democracies: Themes and Perspectives,* eds. Larry Diamond, Marc F. Plattner, Yun-han Chu, and Hung-mao Tien. Baltimore: Johns Hopkins University Press.

Diniz, Carlos Roberto Faleiros. 2003. *A subsecção da OAB e a advocacia.* Rio de Janeiro: Editora Nacional de Direito.

Dipp, Gilson. 2001. A realidade da administração da justiça federal. *Revista do Centro de Estudos Judiciários*, no. 13: 103–7.

Dirceu, José. 18 March 1997. O PT e a via institucional. *Folha de São Paulo*, p. Opinião 3.

Domingo, Pilar. 1999. Rule of Law, Citizenship, and Access to Justice in Mexico. *Mexican Studies—Estudios Mexicanos* 15, no. 1: 151–91.

———. 2000. Judicial Independence: The Politics of the Supreme Court in Mexico. *Journal of Latin American Studies* 32, no. 3: 705–35.

———. 2004. Judicialization of Politics or Politicization of the Judiciary: Recent Trends in Latin America. *Democratization* 11, no. 1: 104–26.

———. 2005. Judicialization of Politics: The Changing Political Role of the Judiciary in Mexico. In *The Judicialization of Politics in Latin America,* eds. Rachel Sieder, Line Schjolden, and Alan Angell. New York: Palgrave Macmillan.

Dye, Thomas. 1972. *Understanding Public Policy.* Englewood Cliffs, NJ: Prentice-Hall.

The Economist. 7 August 1999. The Gavel and the Robe, pp. 43–44.

———. 26 May 2001a. The Americas: St. Peter Is Innocent.

———. 7 July 2001b. The Favoured Few.

———. 2 February 2002. The Americas: A Struggle for Power; Brazil's Energy Crisis.

———. 25 March 2004. Not-So-Swift Justice.

Economist Intelligence Unit. 2001. *Brazil: Country Profile 2001.* London: EIU.

Epp, Charles R. 1998. *The Rights Revolution: Lawyers, Activists, and Supreme Courts in Comparative Perspective.* Chicago: University of Chicago Press.

Epstein, Lee, and Jack Knight. 2000. Toward a Strategic Revolution in Judicial Politics: A Look Back, A Look Ahead. *Political Research Quarterly* 53, no. 3: 625–61.

Erdelyi, Maria Fernanda. 19 December 2006. Lula sanciona leis para racionalizar o Judiciário. *Consultor Jurídico.*

———. 2 February 2007. Início de tudo: Súmula vinculante é novidade no ano novo do Judiciário. *Consultor Jurídico.*

Falcão, Joaquim. 26 April 1995. OAB, uma herança preocupante. *Folha de São Paulo,* p. Opinião 3.

Faundez, Julio. 2005. Democratization Through Law: Perspectives from Latin America. *Democratization* 12, no. 5: 749–65.

Favetti, Rafael Thomaz. 2003. *Controle de constitucionalidade e política fiscal.* Porto Alegre: Sergio Antonio Fabris Editor.

Ferejohn, John A. 2002. Judicializing Politics, Politicizing Law. *Law and Contemporary Problems* 65, no. 3: 41–69.

Ferraz, Antonio A. M. de Camargo, ed. 1997. *Ministério Público: Instituição e processo.* São Paulo: Atlas.

Figueiredo, Argelina Cheibub. 2001. Instituições e política no controle do Executivo. *Dados—Revista De Ciências Sociais* 44, no. 4: 689–727.

Figueiredo, Angelina Cheibub, and Fernando Limongi. 1997. O Congresso e as Medidas Provisórias: Abdicação ou Delegação? *Cadernos de Pesquisa* (CEBRAP) 47, pp. 127–54.

———. 1999. *Executivo e legislativo na nova ordem constitucional.* Rio de Janeiro: Editora FGV.

———. 2002. Incentivos eleitorais, partidos e política orçamentária. *Dados—Revista De Ciências Sociais* 45, no. 2: 303–44.

Finkel, Jodi. 2003. Supreme Court Decisions on Electoral Rules After Mexico's 1994 Judicial Reform: An Empowered Court. *Journal of Latin American Studies* 35: 777–99.

———. 2005. Judicial Reform as an "Insurance Policy" in Mexico in the 1990s: A Supreme Court Willing and Able to Enter the Political Fray. *Latin American Politics and Society* 47, no. 1: 87–113.

———. 2008. *Judicial Reform as Political Insurance: Argentina, Peru, and Mexico in the 1990s.* Notre Dame: University of Notre Dame Press.

Fleischer, David. 1998. Review of *Constitutional Engineering in Brazil* by Celina Souza. *Journal of Interamerican Studies and World Affairs* 40, no. 4: 145–47.

———. 14 November 2003. *Brazil Focus: Weekly Report.*

———. 9 April 2004. *Brazil Focus: Weekly Report.*

Folha de São Paulo. 3 April 1995. Presidente da OAB assume com ataque à reforma, p. Brasil 4.

———. 13 April 1996a. No mínimo, surpresa, p. Opinião 2.

———. 13 July 1996b. Reprovação chega a 70% hoje, p. Cotidiano 1.

———. 19 April 1997. Leia a íntegra das cartas, p. Brasil 6.

———. 15 January 1998a. CNBB cobra ação dos Poderes, p. Brasil 6.

———. 15 January 1998b. O MST tem o mérito de deixar a reforma agrária em pauta constante, p. Brasil 6.

———. 3 February 1998c. Presidente da OAB critica uso de MPs, p. Brasil 4.

———. 11 April 1998d. Injustiça ou desordem? p. Dinheiro 2.

———. 15 December 1998e. Reforma da Previdência começa a vigorar, p. Brasil 6.

———. 9 January 1999a. Inscrição no exame da OAB triplica, mas só 30% passam, p. Cotidiano 2.

———. 19 January 1999b. OAB ameaça ir à Justiça contra projeto, p. Brasil 5.

———. 5 September 1999c. Documento da OAB critica uso excessivo de MPs pelo governo, p. Brasil 6.

———. 28 May 2001a. Promotores decidem atacar racionamento, p. Brasil A9.

———. 2 June 2001b. Presidente da OAB volta a enfrentar Executivo, p. Brasil A4.

———. 9 November 2003. Painel, p. Brasil A4.

204   *References*

————. 15 February 2004. Governo federal é maior cliente do STF, p. A6.

Franzese, Robert J. 2003. Quantitative Empirical Methods and Context Conditionality. *CP: Newsletter of the Comparative Politics Organized Section of the American Political Science Association* 14, no. 1: 20–24.

Freitas, Janio de. 16 April 1996. A fraternidade do alto. *Folha de São Paulo,* p. Brasil 5.

Freitas, Silvana de. 16 April 1997a. OAB move ação contra venda. *Folha de São Paulo,* p. Brasil 10.

————. 12 September 1997b. Privilégio a juízes causa divisão no STF. *Folha de São Paulo,* p. Brasil 10.

————. 16 November 1997c. Oposição usa STF para barrar governistas. *Folha de São Paulo,* p. Brasil 18.

————. 22 May 2001. FHC pode sofrer impeachment, diz Tourinho Neto. *Folha de São Paulo,* p. Dinheiro B3.

————. 16 June 2003. Ações penais contra magistrados correm em sigilo, impeachment só atinge ministros do STF e não existe controle externo. *Folha de São Paulo,* p. Brasil A11.

Freitas, Silvana de, and Wilson Silveira. 19 May 2001. Para STF, sobretaxa na conta é "confisco." *Folha de São Paulo,* p. Dinheiro B5.

Freitas, Silvana de, and Leila Suwwan. 21 June 2002. Mendes critica oposição ao governo. *Folha de São Paulo,* p. Brasil A10.

Freitas, Silvana de, Augusto Gazir, and Marta Salomon. 27 October 1999. Governo reage ao alerta do presidente do Supremo. *Folha de São Paulo,* p. Brasil 4.

Friedman, Barry. 2005. The Politics of Judicial Review. *Texas Law Review* 84, no. 2: 257–337.

Friedman, Lawrence. 1975. *The Legal System: A Social Science Perspective.* New York: Russell Sage Foundation.

Galluci, Mariângela. 28 September 2003. Ex-petista faz crescer "minoria" no Supremo. *O Estado De São Paulo,* p. Nacional, A14.

Ganghof, Steffen. 2003. Promises and Pitfalls of Veto Player Analysis. *Swiss Political Science Review* 9, no. 2: 1–25.

George, Alexander L., and Andrew Bennett. 2005. *Case Studies and Theory Development in the Social Sciences.* Cambridge, MA: MIT Press.

Gerring, John. 2004. What Is a Case Study and What Is It Good For? *American Political Science Review* 98, no. 2: 341–54.

Giannetti, Eduardo. 26 February 1998. O sistema de castas da previdência. *Folha de São Paulo,* p. Ilustrada 7.

Ginsburg, Tom, and Robert A. Kagan, eds. 2005. *Institutions and Public Law: Comparative Approaches.* New York: Peter Lang.

Gloppen, Siri, Robert Gargarella, and Elin Skaar, eds. 2004. *Democratization and the Judiciary: The Accountability Function of Courts in New Democracies.* London: Frank Cass.

Godinho, Fernando. 13 April 2000. Parcelamento de precatórios é aprovado. *Folha de São Paulo,* p. Brasil 11.

Godoy, Paulo. 2 January 1998. SOS Previdência. *Folha de São Paulo,* p. Dinheiro 2.

Gonçalves Ferreira Filho, Manoel. 1994. Poder Judiciário na Constituição de 1988: Judicialização da política e politicização da justiça. *Revista de Direito Administrativo* 198: 1–17.

Gondim, Abnor. 22 January 1998. OAB e juízes criticam efeito vinculante. *Folha de São Paulo,* p. Brasil 4.

Guardado Rodríguez, Jenny. 2007. "¿Activismo Judicial? Controversias constitucionales y acciones de inconstitucionalidad en México, 1995–2005." Unpublished B.A. Thesis. Centro de Investigación y Docencia Económicas (CIDE), México, D.F.

Habermas, Jürgen. 1998. *Between Facts and Norms: Contributions to a Discourse Theory of Law and Democracy,* trans. William Rehg. Cambridge, MA: MIT Press.

Haggard, Stephan, and Mathew D. McCubbins, eds. 2001. *Presidents, Parliaments, and Policy.* Cambridge: Cambridge University Press.

Hagopian, Frances. 1990. "Democracy by Undemocratic Means"? Elites, Political Pacts, and Regime Transition in Brazil. *Comparative Political Studies* 23, no. 4: 147–70.

———. 1994. Traditional Politics Against State Formation in Brazil. In *State Power and Social Forces,* eds. Joel S. Migdal, Atul Kholi, and Vivienne Shue, 37–64. Cambridge: Cambridge University Press.

———. 1996. *Traditional Politics and Regime Change in Brazil.* Cambridge: Cambridge University Press.

Hall, Peter A. 1997. The Role of Interests, Institutions, and Ideas in the Comparative Political Economy of the Industrialized Nations. In *Comparative Politics: Rationality, Culture, and Structure,* eds. Mark Irving Lichbach and Alan S. Zuckerman, 174–207. Cambridge: Cambridge University Press.

Hall, Peter A., and Rosemary Taylor. 1996. Political Science and the Three New Institutionalisms. *Political Studies* 44: 936–57.

Hammergren, Linn A. 1998. *The Politics of Justice and Justice Reform in Latin America: The Peruvian Case in Comparative Perspective.* Boulder, Colo.: Westview Press.

———. 2006. Running Faster and Still Losing Ground? Some Emerging Paradoxes of Latin America's Judicial Reform Movement. Paper presented at the 3rd Congress of the ALACIP, Campinas, Brazil, September 4–6, 2006.

———. 2007. *Envisioning Reform: Conceptual and Practice Obstacles to Improving Judicial Performance in Latin American.* University Park, Pa.: Penn State Press.

Haynie, Stacia L. 1994. Resource Inequalities and Litigation Outcomes in the Philippine Supreme Court. *The Journal of Politics* 56, no. 3: 752–72.

Helmke, Gretchen. 2005. *Courts Under Constraints: Judges, Generals, and Presidents in Argentina*. Cambridge: Cambridge University Press.

Hernández, Cristian, ed. 2006. *Reporte sobre el Estado de la Justicia en las Américas, 2004–2005*. Santiago, Chile: Centro de Estudios de Justicia de las Américas.

Hilbink, Lisa. 2003. An Exception to Chilean Exceptionalism? In *What Justice? Whose Justice? Fighting for Fairness in Latin America*, eds. Susan Eva Eckstein and Timothy P. Wickham-Crowley, 64–97. Berkeley, Calif.: University of California Press.

———. 2007. *Judges Beyond Politics in Democracy and Dictatorship: Lessons from Chile*. Cambridge: Cambridge University Press.

Holston, James. 1991. The Misrule of Law: Land and Usurpation in Brazil. *Comparative Studies in Society and History* 33, no. 4: 695–725.

Holston, James, and Teresa Caldeira. 1998. Democracy, Law, and Violence: Disjunctions of Brazilian Citizenship. In *Fault Lines of Democracy in Post-Transition Latin America*, eds. Felipe Agüero and Jeffrey Stark. Miami: North-South Center Press.

Huber, Evelyne, and John D. Stephens. 2000. The Political Economy of Pension Reform: Latin America in Comparative Perspective. *United Nations Research Institute for Social Development Occasional Working Paper* 7.

Huber, Evelyne, Charles Ragin, and John D. Stephens. 1993. Social Democracy, Christian Democracy, Constitutional Structure, and the Welfare State. *American Journal of Sociology* 99, no. 3: 711–49.

Human Rights Watch World Report. 1996 through 2002 (inclusive). New York: Human Rights Watch.

Iaryczower, Matías, Pablo T. Spiller, and Mariano Tommasi. 2002. Judicial Independence in Unstable Environments, Argentina 1935–1998. *American Journal of Political Science* 46, no. 4: 699–716.

Immergut, Ellen. 1992. *The Political Construction of Interests: National Health Insurance Politics in Switzerland, France, and Sweden, 1930–1970*. New York: Cambridge University Press.

Jackson, Donald W., and C. Neal Tate, eds. 1992. *Comparative Judicial Review and Public Policy*. Westport, Conn.: Greenwood Press.

Jobim, Nelson. 2003. O processo da reforma sob a ótica do Judiciário. In *Reforma do Judiciário: Planos, Propostas e Perspectivas*, ed. Armando Castelar Pinheiro. São Paulo: IDESP.

Jungmann, Raul. 15 June 1997. A agonia do latifúndio improdutivo. *Folha de São Paulo*, p. Opinião 3.

Junqueira, Eliane Botelho. 2003. Brazil: The Road of Conflict Bound for Total Justice. In *Legal Culture in the Age of Globalization: Latin America and Latin Europe*, eds. Lawrence Friedman and Rogelio Pérez-Perdomo. Stanford, Calif.: Stanford University Press.

Kapiszewski, Diana. 2007. "Challenging Decisions: High Court Politics in Argentina and Brazil." Ph.D. dissertation, University of California, Berkeley.

Kapiszewski, Diana, and Matthew M. Taylor. 2006. Doing Courts Justice? Studying Judicial Politics in Latin America. Paper presented at the Annual Meeting of the American Political Science Association. Philadelphia, August 29 to September 2.

Karst, Kenneth L., and Keith S. Rosenn, eds. 1975. *Law and Development in Latin America*. Berkeley, Calif.: University of California Press.

Kay, Stephen J. 1998. "Politics and Social Security Reform in the Southern Cone and Brazil." Ph.D. dissertation, University of California at Los Angeles.

———. 1999. Unexpected Privatizations: Politics and Social Security Reform in the Southern Cone. *Comparative Politics* 31, no. 4: 403–22.

Kerche, Fábio. 1999. O Ministério Público e a Constituinte de 1987/88. In *O Sistema de Justiça*, ed. Maria Tereza Sadek, 61–77. São Paulo: Editora Sumaré.

Kerche, Fábio. 2003. "O Ministério Público no Brasil." Ph.D. dissertation, Department of Political Science, University of São Paulo.

Kingstone, Peter, and Timothy Power, eds. 2000. *Democratic Brazil: Actors, Institutions and Processes*. Pittsburgh: University of Pittsburgh Press.

Kinzo, Maria D'Alva G. 1997. Governabilidade, estrutura institucional e processo decisório no Brasil. *Parcerias Estratégicas* 1, no. 3: 19–53.

———. 2001. A Democratização Brasileira. *São Paulo Em Perspectiva* 15, no. 4: 3–12.

Koelble, Thomas A. 1995. The New Institutionalism in Political Science and Sociology. *Comparative Politics* 27, no. 2: 231–43.

Koerner, Andrei. 1998. *Judiciário e Cidadania na Constituição da República Brasileira*. São Paulo: Hucitec.

———. 2006. Decisão judicial, instituições e estrutura socioeconômica: Por uma análise política do pensamento jurídico brasileiro. In *História da Justiça Penal no Brasil: Pesquisas e Análises*, ed. Andrei Koerner, 259–81. São Paulo: IBCCRIM.

Lacerda Teixeira, Egberto. 1972. O Jeito: Instituição jurídica brasileira com foros internacionais. *Revista dos Tribunais* 437: 473–75.

Lamounier, Bolívar, and Amaury de Souza. 2002. *As elites brasileiras e o desenvolvimento nacional: Fatores de consenso e dissenso*. São Paulo: IDESP.

Larkins, Christopher M. 1998. The Judiciary and Delegative Democracy in Argentina. *Comparative Politics* 30: 423–43.

Lasswell, Harold D. 1936. *Politics: Who Gets What, When, How.* New York: McGraw-Hill.

Leeds, Elizabeth. 1996. Cocaine and Parallel Polities in the Brazilian Urban Periphery: Constraints on Local-Level Democratization. *Latin American Research Review* 31, no. 3, pp. 47–83.

Leitão, Miriam. 22 June 2003. Senhor Juiz. *O Globo*.

Lemos, Leany Barreiro de Sousa, and Sonia Ranincheski. 2003. Carreras políticas en el Senado brasileño: Un estudio de las composiciones del Pleno y de la Comisión de Constitución, Justicia y Ciudadanía en la década de 90. *Lateinamerika Analysen* 4.

Lessa, Pedro. 1915. *Do Poder Judiciário.* Rio de Janeiro: Francisco Alves.

Lijphart, Arend. 1999. *Patterns of Democracy: Government Forms and Performance in Thirty-Six Countries.* New Haven, Conn.: Yale University Press.

Linz, Juan J., and Alfred Stepan. 1996. *Problems of Democratic Transition and Consolidation: Southern Europe, South America, and Post-Communist Europe.* Baltimore: Johns Hopkins University Press.

Lopez–Ayllon, Sergio, and Hector F. Fix-Fierro. 2003. "Faraway, So Close!" The Rule of Law and Legal Change in Mexico 1970–2000. In *Legal Culture in the Age of Globalization: Latin America and Latin Europe,* eds. Lawrence Friedman and Rogelio Pérez-Perdomo. Stanford, Calif.: Stanford University Press.

Loureiro, Maria Rita. 2001. Instituições, política e ajuste fiscal. *Revista Brasileira De Ciências Sociais,* no. 47: 75–96.

Lowi, Theodore J. 1964. American Business, Public Policy, Case-Studies, and Political Science. *World Politics* 16: 677–715.

———. 1972. Four Systems of Policy, Politics, and Choice. *Public Administration Review* 33: 298–310.

Loyola, Gustavo. 16 September 2002. Brazil: Where the Past Gets Everyday More Uncertain. *Inside Brazil (Tendências Consultoria Integrada):* 1.

Lozano, André. 14 January 1999. Metade dos advogados deve à OAB. *Folha de São Paulo,* p. Cotidiano 1.

Macedo Júnior, Ronaldo Porto. 1995. A evolução institucional do Ministério Público brasileiro. In *Uma Introdução ao Estudo da Justiça,* ed. Maria Tereza Sadek. São Paulo: Editora Sumaré.

Maciel, Débora Alves, and Andrei Koerner. 2002. Sentidos da judicialização da política: Duas Análises. *Lua Nova* 57, 113–33.

Madison, James, Alexander Hamilton, and John Jay. 1961. *The Federalist Papers,* ed. Clinton Rossiter. New York: New American Library.

Madrid, Raúl. 1999. "The New Logic of Social Security Reform: Politics and Pension Reform in Latin America." Ph.D. dissertation, Stanford University.

———. 2002. The Politics and Economics of Pension Privatization in Latin America. *Latin American Research Review* 37, no. 2: 159–82.

———. 2005. Ideas, Economic Pressures, and Pension Privatization. *Latin American Politics and Society* 47, no. 2: 23–50.

Madueño, Denise. 6 November 1998. Promulgação depende da votação de MP. *Folha de São Paulo,* p. Caderno Especial 4.

Magaloni, Beatriz. 2003. Authoritarianism, Democracy and the Supreme Court: Horizontal Exchange and the Rule of Law in Mexico. In *Democratic Accountability in Latin America,* eds. Scott Mainwaring and Christopher Welna, 266–306. Oxford: Oxford University Press.

Mainwaring, Scott. 1993. Brazilian Party Underdevelopment in Comparative Perspective. *Political Science Quarterly* 107, no. 4: 677–708.

———. 1995. Brazil:Weak Parties, Feckless Democracy. In *Building Democratic Institutions: Party Systems in Latin America,* eds. Scott Mainwaring and Timothy R. Scully. Stanford, Calif.: Stanford University Press.

———. 1999. *Rethinking Party Systems in the Third Wave of Democratization:The Case of Brazil.* Stanford, Calif.: Stanford University Press.

Mainwaring, Scott, and Christopher Welna, eds. 2003. *Democratic Accountability in Latin America.* Oxford: Oxford University Press.

Malloy, James, ed. 1977. *Authoritarianism and Corporatism in Latin America.* Pittsburgh: University of Pittsburgh Press.

Martínez-Lara, Javier. 1996. *Building Democracy in Brazil:The Politics of Constitutional Change 1985–1995.* New York: St. Martin's Press.

Maschio, José, and Eduardo Scolese. 19 December 2002. No campo, governo enfrentou o radicalismo dos sem-terra. *Folha de São Paulo,* p. Caderno Especial 13.

Mattei, Ugo. 1997. Three Patterns of Law: Taxonomy and Change in the World's Legal Systems. *American Journal of Comparative Law* 45: 5–43.

McAdams, A. James, ed. 1997. *Transitional Justice and the Rule of Law in New Democracies.* South Bend, Ind.: University of Notre Dame Press.

McAllister, Lesley K. 2008. *Making Law Matter: Environmental Protection and Legal Institutions in Brazil.* Stanford, Calif.: Stanford University Press.

McCool, Daniel C., ed. 1995. *Public Policy Theories, Models, and Concepts:An Anthology.* Englewood Cliffs, N.J.: Prentice-Hall.

Melnick, R. Shep. 2005. "One Government Agency Among Many":The Political Juris-Prudence of Martin Shapiro. In *Institutions and Public Law: Comparative Approaches,* eds. Tom Ginsburg and Robert A. Kagan, 19–44. New York: Peter Lang.

Melo, Marcus André. 2000. Política regulatória: Uma revisão da literatura. *BIB. Boletim Informativo e Bibliográfico de Ciências Sociais* 50, no. 2: 7–43.

———. 2002. *Reformas constitucionais no Brasil. Instituições políticas e processo decisório.* Rio de Janeiro: Revan.

———. 2003. When Institutions Matter: A Comparison of the Politics of Social Security, Administrative and Tax Reforms. In *Reinventing Leviathan: The Politics of Administrative Reform in Developing Countries,* eds. Ben Ross Schneider and Blanca Heredia, 297–319. Miami: North-South Center Press.

———. 2004. Institutional Choice and the Diffusion of Policy Paradigms: Brazil and the Second Wave of Pension Reforms. *International Political Science Review* 25, no. 3: 297–319.

Mendes, Gilmar Ferreira. 2002. Juizados Especiais Federais: O resgate de uma dívida social. *Caderno Virtual: Instituto Brasiliense De Direito Público.*

Méndez, Juan, Guillermo O'Donnell, and Paulo Sérgio Pinheiro, eds. 1999. *The (Un)Rule of Law and the Underprivileged in Latin America.* Notre Dame, Ind.: University of Notre Dame Press.

210   *References*

Merryman, John Henry. 1985. *The Civil Law Tradition: An Introduction to the Legal Systems of Western Europe and Latin America*, 2nd ed. Stanford, Calif.: Stanford University Press.

Mesa-Lago, Carmelo. 1978. *Social Security in Latin America: Pressure Groups, Stratification, and Inequality*. Pittsburgh: University of Pittsburgh Press.

————. 1997. Social Welfare Reform in the Context of Economic-Political Liberalization: Latin American Cases. *World Development* 25, no. 4: 497–517.

Mesa-Lago, Carmelo, and Katharina Müller. 2002. The Politics of Pension Reform in Latin America. *Journal of Latin American Studies* 34: 687–715.

Ministério Público Federal. 2003. *Informativo ADIN*. Brasília: Ministério Público Federal, Secretaria Geral, Coordenação de Documentação e Biblioteca.

Ministério da Justiça. 2004. *Diagnóstico do Poder Judiciário*. Brasília: Ministério da Justiça.

Ministério da Previdência Social. 1997. *Livro branco da previdência social*. Brasília: Ministério da Previdência.

Ministério da Previdência Social, Assessoria de Comunicação Social. 2003. *Mudar a previdência: Uma questão de justiça*. Brasília: Ministério da Previdência.

Moe, Terry M. 2005. Power and Political Institutions. *Perspectives on Politics* 3, no. 2: 215–33.

Monken, Mario Hugo. 22 May 2001. Saem as primeiras liminares contra o plano. *Folha de São Paulo*, p. Dinheiro B1.

Montesquieu, Charles de Secondat Baron de. 1990. *The Spirit of Laws*, trans. Thomas Nugent. Chicago: Encyclopaedia Britannica.

Morton, Yara. 16 January 1998. Tangled Law. *Brazzil*, www.brazzil.com/pages/p16jan98.htm, accessed February 2003.

Mueller, Bernardo. 2001. Institutions for Commitment in the Brazilian Regulatory System. *The Quarterly Review of Economics and Finance* 41: 621–43.

Murphy, Walter F., C. Herman Pritchett, and Lee Epstein, eds. 2002. *Courts, Judges, and Politics: An Introduction to the Judicial Process*, 5th ed. New York: Random House.

Nalini, José Renato. 2000. O juiz e a privatização. In *A privatização no Brasil: O caso dos serviços de utilidade pública*, eds. Armando Castelar Pinheiro and Fabio Giambiagi. Rio de Janeiro: BNDES.

————. 15 September 2006. Termômetro democrático. *O Estado De São Paulo*, p. A2.

Nascimento, Elimar Pinheiro, and Ivônio Barros Nunes. 1995. *A opinião da sociedade civil organizada a respeito da Justiça Federal*, ed. Série Monografias do CEJ. Brasília: Conselho da Justiça Federal.

Nassif, Luis. 11 May 1995. A OAB e o Idec. *Folha de São Paulo*, p. Dinheiro 3.

————. 8 December 1996. A crise anunciada das autopeças. *Folha de São Paulo*, p. Dinheiro 3.

―――. 8 January 1998a. O Latifúndio Acabou? *Folha de São Paulo*, p. Dinheiro 3.

―――. 15 April 1998b. A OAB e a reforma do Judiciário. *Folha de São Paulo*, p. Dinheiro 3.

Navia, Patricio, and Julio Ríos-Figueroa. 2005. The Constitutional Adjudication Mosaic of Latin America. *Comparative Political Studies* 38, no. 2: 189–217.

Netto Lôbo, Paulo Luiz. 1996. *Comentários ao estatuto da advocacia*, 2nd ed. Brasília: Brasília Jurídica.

North, Douglass C. 1990. *Institutions, Institutional Change, and Economic Performance*. Cambridge: Cambridge University Press.

Nunes, Eunice. 5 December 1998. Sociedade acha que falta ética a advogados, diz estudo. *Folha de São Paulo*, p. Cotidiano 2.

Nóbrega, Mailson da. 2000. *O Brasil em transformação*. São Paulo: Editora Gente.

O'Donnell, Guillermo. 1994. Delegative Democracy. *Journal of Democracy* 5: 55–69.

―――. 1996. Illusions About Consolidation. *Journal of Democracy* 7: 45–57.

―――. 2000. The Judiciary and the Rule of Law. *Journal of Democracy* 11, no. 1: 25–31.

―――. 2001a. Reflections on Contemporary South American Democracies. *Journal of Latin American Studies* 33: 599–609.

―――. 2001b. Democracy, Law, and Comparative Politics. *Studies in Comparative International Development* 36, no. 1: 7–36.

O Estado de São Paulo. 31 July 2006. A Reforma dos Juizados.

Ogier, Thierry. 14 May 2001. Did the Lights Just Flicker in São Paulo? Brazil Is Scrambling to Stave Off Power Outages. *Business Week*.

O'Keefe, Thomas A., and Jerry Haar. 2001. The Impact of Mercosur on the Automobile Industry. *North-South Agenda Papers* 50.

Oliveira, Fabiana Luci de. 2006. "Justiça, profissionalismo e política: O Supremo Tribunal Federal e o controle da constitucionalidade das leis no Brasil (1998–2003)." Ph.D. dissertation, Universidade Federal de São Carlos.

Oliveira, Vanessa Elias de. 2005. Judiciário e privatizações no Brasil: Existe uma judicialização da política? *Dados—Revista De Ciências Sociais* 48, no. 3: 559–87.

Ordem dos Advogados do Brasil (OAB). 2004. *Relatório De Gestão, OAB Conselho Federal, 2001–2004*. Brasília.

―――. 2005. "História da OAB." www.oab.org.br/hist_oab/, accessed October 18, 2005.

Ordem dos Advogados do Brasil, São Paulo (OAB-SP). "Diretores Da OAB SP e CAASP Tomam Posse Solene Hoje." www.oabsp.org.br/, accessed March 10, 2004.

Orszag, Peter R., and Joseph E. Stiglitz. 2001. Rethinking Pension Reform: Ten Myths About Social Security Systems. In *New Ideas about Old Age*

Security: Toward Sustainable Pension Systems in the 21st Century, eds. Robert Holzmann and Joseph E. Stiglitz. Washington, D.C.: World Bank.

Pacheco, Cristina Carvalho. 2006. "O Supremo Tribunal Federal e a reforma do Estado: Uma análise das Ações Diretas de Inconstitucionalidade julgadas no primeiro governo de Fernando Henrique Cardoso (1995–1998)." Ph.D. dissertation, Universidade Estadual de Campinas.

Palermo, Vicente. 2000. Como se Governa o Brasil? O debate sobre instituições políticas e gestão de governo. *Dados—Revista De Ciências Sociais* 43, no. 3: 521–57.

Papadopulos, Jorge. 1998. The Pension System in Uruguay: A Delayed Reform. In *Do Options Exist? The Reform of Pension and Health Care Systems in Latin America,* eds. María Amparo Cruz-Saco and Carmelo Mesa-Lago. Pittsburgh: University of Pittsburgh Press.

Pastoral Land Commission, Documentation Center, "Land Conflicts, Brazil 2002." www.cptnac.com.br, accessed September 15, 2003.

Patú, Gustavo, Kennedy Alencar, and Fábio Zanini. 6 December 2002. Lula se encontra com Armínio após rejeitar sua permanência no cargo. *Folha de São Paulo,* p. Brasil A4.

Pereira, Anthony W. 2000. An Ugly Democracy: State Violence and the Rule of Law in Postauthoritarian Brazil. In *Democratic Brazil: Actors, Institutions and Processes,* eds. Peter Kingstone and Timothy Power. Pittsburgh: University of Pittsburgh Press.

———. 2005. *Political (In)Justice: Authoritarianism and the Rule of Law in Brazil, Chile, and Argentina.* Pittsburgh: University of Pittsburgh Press.

Pereira, Carlos, and Bernardo Mueller. 2003. Partidos fracos na arena eleitoral e partidos fortes na arena legislativa: A conexão eleitoral no Brasil. *Dados— Revista De Ciências Sociais* 46, no. 4: 735–71.

Pereira Filho, Arthur. 12 August 1995. Indústria faz acordo sobre MP das cotas. *Folha de São Paulo,* p. Dinheiro 8.

Pérez-Perdomo, Rogelio. 2003. Venezuela 1958–1999: The Legal System in an Impaired Democracy. In *Legal Culture in the Age of Globalization: Latin America and Latin Europe,* eds. Lawrence Friedman and Rogelio Pérez-Perdomo. Stanford, Calif.: Stanford University Press.

———. 2005. Judicialization and Regime Transformation: The Venezuelan Supreme Court. In *The Judicialization of Politics in Latin America,* eds. Rachel Sieder, Line Schjolden, and Alan Angell. New York: Palgrave Macmillan.

Pérez-Perdomo, Rogelio, and Lawrence Friedman. 2003. Latin Legal Cultures in the Age of Globalization. In *Legal Culture in the Age of Globalization: Latin America and Latin Europe,* eds. Lawrence Friedman and Rogelio Pérez-Perdomo. Stanford, Calif.: Stanford University Press.

Pierson, Paul. 1996. The New Politics of the Welfare State. *World Politics* 48, no. 2: 143–79.

Power, Timothy J. 1998. The Pen Is Mightier Than the Congress: Presidential Decree Power in Brazil. In *Executive Decree Authority*, eds. John Carey and Matthew Soberg Shugart. Cambridge: Cambridge University Press.

———. 2000. Political Institutions in Democratic Brazil: Politics as a Permanent Constitutional Convention. In *Democratic Brazil: Actors, Institutions and Processes*, eds. Peter R. Kingstone and Timothy J. Power, 17–35. Pittsburgh: University of Pittsburgh Press.

Power, Timothy J., and Mahrukh Doctor. 2004. Another Century of Corporatism? Continuity and Change in Brazilian Corporatist Structures. In *Authoritarianism and Corporatism in Latin America, Revisited*, ed. Howard J. Wiarda. Gainesville: University Press of Florida .

Prillaman, William C. 2000. *The Judiciary and Democratic Decay in Latin America: Declining Confidence in the Rule of Law*. Westport: Praeger.

Przeworski, Adam. 1988. Democracy as a Contingent Outcome of Conflicts. In *Constitutionalism and Democracy*, eds. Jon Elster and Rune Slagstad. Cambridge: Cambridge University Press.

Ragin, Charles. 1987. *The Comparative Method*. Berkeley, Calif.: University of California Press.

Ramos, Saul. 10 May 1996. Nova goleada do Supremo Tribunal. *Folha de São Paulo*, p. Opinião 3.

Ranney, Austin. 1968. The Study of Policy Content: A Framework for Choice. In *Political Science and Public Policy*, ed. Austin Ranney. Chicago: Markham.

Rehnquist, William. 2002. *2001 Year-End Report on the Federal Judiciary*. Washington, D.C.: Supreme Court of the United States.

Reich, Gary M. 1998. The 1988 Constitution a Decade Later: Ugly Compromises Reconsidered. *Journal of Interamerican Studies and World Affairs* 40, no. 4: 5–24.

Richardson, Henry S. 2002. *Democratic Autonomy: Public Reasoning About the Ends of Policy*. Oxford: Oxford University Press.

Ricupero, Rubens. 11 April 1998. Injustiça ou desordem? *Folha de São Paulo*, p. Dinheiro 2.

Riker, William H. 1986. *The Art of Political Manipulation*. New Haven, Conn.: Yale University Press.

Ríos-Figueroa, Julio. 2003. A Minimum Condition for the Judiciary to Become an Effective Power: The Mexican Supreme Court, 1994–2002. Paper presented at the annual meeting of the Latin American Studies Association, Dallas, Texas, March 27–29.

———. 2006. "Institutional Models of Judicial Independence and Corruption in Latin America." Ph.D. dissertation, New York University.

———. 2007. The Emergence of an Effective Judiciary in Mexico, 1994–2002. *Latin American Politics & Society* 49, no. 1: 31–57.

Ríos-Figueroa, Julio, and Matthew M. Taylor. 2006. Institutional Determinants of the Judicialization of Policy in Brazil and Mexico. *Journal of Latin American Studies* 38, no. 4: 739–66.

Rodrigues, Fernando. 2 June 2001. O dia em que perderam o respeito. *Folha de São Paulo,* p. Opinião A2.

Rodríguez-Cordero, Juan Carlos. 2002. (Re)equilibrios políticos en Costa Rica: El poder constituyente y el control de constitucionalidad. *The Latin Americanist* XLV, no. 3–4: 15–28.

Rodriguez-Garavito, César A., Rodrigo Uprimny, and Mauricio García-Villegas. 2003. Justice and Society in Colombia: A Sociolegal Analysis of Colombian Courts. In *Legal Culture in the Age of Globalization: Latin America and Latin Europe,* eds. Lawrence Friedman and Rogelio Pérez-Perdomo, 134–83. Stanford, Calif.: Stanford University Press.

Roett, Riordan. 1999. *Politics in a Patrimonial Society,* 5th ed. Westport, Conn.: Praeger.

Rosenberg, Gerald N. 1991. *The Hollow Hope: Can Courts Bring About Social Change?* Chicago: University of Chicago Press.

Rosenberg, Luís Paulo. 18 February 1997. Cadê o Cade? *Folha de São Paulo,* p. Dinheiro 2.

Rosenn, Keith S. 1971. The Jeito: Brazil's Institutional Bypass of the Formal Legal System and Its Developmental Implications. *American Journal of Comparative Law* 19: 514–49.

———. 1984. Brazil's Legal Culture: The Jeito Revisited. *Florida International Law Journal* I, no. 1: 1–43.

———. 1990. Brazil's New Constitution: An Exercise in Transient Constitutionalism for a Transitional Society. *American Journal of Comparative Law* 38, no. 4: 773–802.

Rossi, Clovis. 5 July 1995. Cavallo diz que Brasil vai retirar cota para Argentina. *Folha de São Paulo,* p. Brasil 5.

———. 8 May 1997. Fundo Soros vê "tragicomedia." *Folha de São Paulo,* p. Brasil 8.

Rousseau, Jean Jacques. 1957 [1762]. *The Social Contract.* New York: Hafner.

Roux, Theunis. 2004. Legitimating Transformation: Political Resource Allocation in the South African Constitutional Court. In *Democratization and the Judiciary: The Accountability Function of Courts in New Democracies,* eds. Siri Gloppen, Robert Gargarella, and Elin Skaar. London: Frank Cass.

Sadek, Maria Tereza. 1995a. A crise do Judiciário vista pelos juízes: Resultados da pesquisa quantitativa. In *Uma introdução ao estudo da justiça,* ed. Maria Tereza Sadek. São Paulo: Editora Sumaré.

———. 1995b. A Organização do Poder Judiciário no Brasil. In *Uma introdução ao estudo da justiça,* ed. Maria Tereza Sadek. São Paulo: Editora Sumaré.

————. 1999a. O Poder judiciário na reforma do Estado. In *Sociedade e Estado em transformação,* eds. Luiz Carlos Bresser Pereira, Jorge Wilheim, and Lourdes Sola, 293–324. São Paulo: Editora UNESP.

————. 1999b. O sistema de justiça. In *O sistema de justiça,* ed. Maria Tereza Sadek, 1–18. São Paulo: Editora Sumaré.

————, ed. 2000. *Justiça e cidadania no Brasil.* São Paulo: Editora Sumaré.

Sadek, Maria Tereza, and Rogério B. Arantes. 1994. A crise do judiciário e a visão dos juízes. *Revista USP* 21: 34–45.

Sadek, Maria Tereza, and Rosângela Batista Cavalcanti. 2003. The New Brazilian Public Prosecution: An Agent of Accountability. In *Democratic Accountability in Latin America,* eds. Scott Welna and Christopher Mainwaring, 201–27. Oxford: Oxford University Press.

Samuels, David. 2004. From Socialism to Social Democracy: Party Organization and the Transformation of the Workers' Party in Brazil. *Comparative Political Studies* 37, no. 9: 999–1024.

Santafé Idéias. 30 December 2004. Judiciário propõe securitização dos precatórios. *Daily Client Newsletter,* no. 2432.

————. 4 January 2007. Judiciário—principais processos. *Daily Client Newsletter,* no. 2936.

Santos, Angela M., and João Renildo Jornada Gonçalves. 2001. Evolução do comércio exterior do complexo automotivo. *BNDES Setorial* 13: 205–18.

Schattschneider, Elmer Eric. 1957. Intensity, Visibility, Direction and Scope. *The American Political Science Review* 51, no. 4: 933–42.

————. 1960. *The Semisovereign People: A Realist's View of Democracy in America.* New York: Holt, Rinehart and Winston.

Schmitter, Philippe C. 1971. *Interest Conflict and Political Change in Brazil.* Stanford, Calif.: Stanford University Press.

Schor, Miguel. 2003. The Rule of Law and Democratic Consolidation in Latin America. Paper presented at Latin American Studies Association Meeting, Dallas, Texas, March 2003.

Scribner, Druscilla. 2003. "Limiting Presidential Power: Supreme Court—Executive Relations in Argentina and Chile." Ph.D. dissertation, University of California, San Diego.

Segal, Jeffrey A., and Harold J. Spaeth. 1993. *The Supreme Court and the Attitudinal Model.* New York: Cambridge University Press.

Sen, Amartya. 1999. *Development as Freedom.* New York: Alfred A. Knopf.

Shapiro, Martin. 1981. *Courts: A Comparative and Political Analysis.* Chicago: University of Chicago Press.

————. 2004. Judicial Review in Developed Democracies. In *Democratization and the Judiciary: The Accountability Function of Courts in New Democracies,* eds. Siri Gloppen, Robert Gargarella, and Elin Skaar. London: Frank Cass.

————. 2005. Law, Courts and Politics. In *Institutions and Public Law: Comparative Approaches*, eds. Tom Ginsburg and Robert A. Kagan, 275–97. New York: Peter Lang.

Shapiro, Martin, and Alec Stone Sweet. 2002. *On Law, Politics, and Judicialization*. Oxford: Oxford University Press.

Sieder, Rachel, Line Schjolden, and Alan Angell, eds. 2005. *The Judicialization of Politics in Latin America*. New York: Palgrave Macmillan.

Silva Martins, Ives Gandra da. 13 April 1996. Decisão foi eminentemente técnica. *Folha de São Paulo*, p. Brasil 5.

Skidmore, Thomas E. 1988. *The Politics of Military Rule in Brazil, 1964–85*. New York: Oxford University Press.

Smith, Rogers M. 1988. Political Jurisprudence, The "New Institutionalism," and the Future of Public Law. *American Political Science Review* 82, no. 1: 89–108.

Sola, Lourdes. 1998. *Idéias econômicas, decisões políticas: Desenvolvimento, estabilidade e populismo*. São Paulo: Editora da Universidade de São Paulo.

Sola, Lourdes, and Laurence Whitehead, eds. 2006. *Statecrafting Monetary Authority: Democracy and Financial Order in Brazil*. Oxford: Centre for Brazilian Studies.

Sola, Lourdes, Christopher Garman, and Moisés Marques. 1998. Central Banking, Democratic Governance and Political Authority: The Case of Brazil in a Comparative Perspective. *Revista De Economia Política* 18, no. 2: 106–31.

Souza, Celina. 1997. *Constitutional Engineering in Brazil: The Politics of Federalism and Decentralization*. New York: St. Martin's Press.

————. 2001. Federalismo e descentralização na constituição de 1988: Processo decisório, conflitos e alianças. *Dados—Revista De Ciências Sociais* 44, no. 3: 513–60.

————. 2003. Federalismo e conflitos distributivos: Disputa dos estados por recursos orçamentários federais. *Dados—Revista De Ciências Sociais* 46, no. 2: 345–84.

Spiller, Pablo T., and Mariano Tommasi. 2003. The Institutional Foundations of Public Policy: A Transactions Approach with Application to Argentina. *The Journal of Law, Economics, & Organization* 19, no. 2: 281–306.

Staton, Jeffrey K. 2004. Judicial Policy Implementation in Mexico City and Mérida. *Comparative Politics* 37: 41–60.

Stein, Ernesto, Mariano Tommasi, Koldo Echebarría, Eduardo Lora, and Mark Payne, coordinators. 2006. *The Politics of Policies: Economic and Social Progress in Latin America. 2006 Report*. Washington, D.C.: Inter-American Development Bank.

Steinmo, Sven, Kathleen Thelen, and Frank Longstreth. 1992. *Structuring Politics: Historical Institutionalism in Comparative Politics*. New York: Cambridge University Press.

Stepan, Alfred. 2000. Brazil's Decentralized Federalism: Bringing Government Closer to the Citizens? *Daedalus* 129, no. 2: 145–69.

Stone, Alec. 1992. Abstract Constitutional Review and Policy Making in Western Europe. In *Comparative Judicial Review and Public Policy*, eds. Donald W. Jackson and C. Neal Tate, 41–57. Westport, Conn.: Greenwood Press.

Stone Sweet, Alec. 2000. *Governing with Judges: Constitutional Politics in Europe.* Oxford: Oxford University Press.

———. 2005. Judicial Authority and Market Integration in Europe. In *Institutions and Public Law: Comparative Approaches*, eds. Tom Ginsburg and Robert A. Kagan, 99–140. New York: Peter Lang.

Supremo Tribunal Federal. 1989. *Revista Trimestral de Jurisprudência do Supremo Tribunal Federal.* Vol. 127–forward. Brasília: Supremo Tribunal Federal.

———. 2005. *A Justiça em Números: Indicadores Estatísticos do Poder Judiciário 2003.* Brasília: Supremo Tribunal Federal. Available online at www.stf.gov.br.

———. 2006. *Banco Nacional de Dados do Poder Judiciário (BNDPJ).* Brasília: Supremo Tribunal Federal. Available online at www.stf.gov.br.

Tapia Palacios, Paulo. 2003. "El nuevo papel de la Suprema Corte de Justicia en México." Licénciate thesis. México City: CIDE.

Tate, C. Neal. 1992. Comparative Judicial Review and Public Policy: Concepts and Overview. In *Comparative Judicial Review and Public Policy*, eds. Donald W. Jackson and C. Neal Tate, 3–13. Westport, Conn.: Greenwood Press.

Tate, C. Neal, and Torbjörn Vallinder. 1995. The Global Expansion of Judicial Power: The Judicialization of Politics. In *The Global Expansion of Judicial Power: The Judicialization of Politics*, eds. C. Neal Tate and Torbjörn Vallinder. New York: New York University Press.

Taylor, Matthew M. 2004. El partido de los trabajadores y el uso político del poder judicial. *América Latina Hoy* 37: 121–42.

———. 2005. Citizens Against the State: The Riddle of High-Impact, Low-Functionality Courts in Brazil. *Revista De Economia Política* 25, no. 4: 418–38.

———. 2006a. Courts, Policy Contestation and the Legitimation of Economic Reform Under Cardoso. In *Statecrafting Monetary Authority: Democracy and Financial Order in Brazil*, eds. Lourdes Sola and Laurence Whitehead, 205–36. Oxford: Centre for Brazilian Studies.

———. 2006b. Veto and Voice in the Courts: Policy Implications of Institutional Design in the Brazilian Judiciary. *Comparative Politics* 38, no. 3: 337–55.

———. 2006c. Beyond Judicial Reform: Courts as Political Actors in Latin America (book review). *Latin American Research Review* 41, no. 2: 269–80.

Taylor, Matthew M., and Vinicius Buranelli. 2007. Ending Up in Pizza: Accountability as a Problem of Institutional Arrangement in Brazil. *Latin American Politics and Society* 49, no. 1: 59–87.

Tocqueville, Alexis de. 1969. *Democracy in America*, ed. J.P. Mayer. New York: Harper Perennial.

Trevisan, Claudia. 1 February 1995. OAB faz hoje sua eleição mais disputada. *Folha de São Paulo*, p. Brasil 10.

Tsebelis, George. 1995. Decision Making in Political Systems: Veto Players in Presidentialism, Parliamentarism, Multicameralism, and Multipartyism. *British Journal of Political Science* 25: 289–325.

———. 2002. *Veto Players: How Political Institutions Work*. Princeton, N.J.: Princeton University Press.

Ungar, Mark. 2002. *Elusive Reform: Democracy and the Rule of Law in Latin America*. Boulder, Colo.: Lynne Rienner.

Uprimny, Rodrigo. 2004. The Constitutional Court and Control of Presidential Extraordinary Powers in Colombia. In *Democratization and the Judiciary: The Accountability Function of Courts in New Democracies*, eds. Siri Gloppen, Robert Gargarella, and Elin Skaar. London: Frank Cass.

Vanberg, Georg. 2001. Legislative-Judicial Relations: A Game-Theoretic Approach to Constitutional Review. *American Journal of Political Science* 45, no. 2: 346–61.

———. 2005. *The Politics of Constitutional Review in Germany*. Cambridge: Cambridge University Press.

Vasconcelos, Frederico. 17 November 2004. Pelo menos o STF deve melhorar, diz pesquisadora. *Folha de São Paulo*.

———. 2005. *Juízes no Banco dos Réus*. São Paulo: PubliFolha.

Veiga da Rocha, Jean Paul Cabral. 2004. "A capacidade normativa de conjuntura no direito econômico: O déficit democrático da regulação financeira." Ph.D. dissertation, University of São Paulo.

———. 2006. Direito e política econômica: Os poderes do Conselho Monetário Nacional e do Banco Central na jurisprudência do STF. Paper presented at the 2006 Meeting of ALACIP, Campinas, September 4–6.

Veja. 9 June 2004. O febeapá da OAB.

Velloso, Carlos Mario. 1999. Judicial Management Information Systems. In *Judicial Challenges in the New Millenium: Proceedings of the Second Ibero-American Summit of Supreme Courts and Tribunals of Justice*, eds. Andrés Rigo Sureda and Waleed Haider Malik. Washington, D.C.: The World Bank.

———. 2005. Poder Judiciário: Reforma. A Emenda Constitucional No. 45, de 08.12.2004. *Revista Forense* 101, no. 378: 11–26.

Velloso, Raul. 2 June 2003. Reforma da Previdência vai fundo nos problemas da área. *Agência Estado*.

Venâncio Filho, Alberto. 1982. *Notícia histórica da Ordem dos Advogados do Brasil: 1930–1980*. Rio de Janeiro: OAB.

Verner, Joel G. 1984. The Independence of Supreme Courts in Latin America: A Review of the Literature. *Journal of Latin American Studies* 16, no. 2: 463–506.

Vilhena Vieira, Oscar. 2002. *Supremo Tribunal Federal: Jurisprudência Política,* 2nd ed. São Paulo: Malheiros Editores.

Volcansek, Mary L. 1992. The European Court of Justice: Supranational Policy-Making. *West European Politics* 15, no. 3: 109–21.

Weber, Max. 1978. *Economy and Society: An Outline of Interpretive Sociology,* eds. Guenther Roth and Claus Wittich. Berkeley, Calif.: University of California Press.

Werneck Vianna, Luiz, ed. 2002. *A democracia e os três poderes no Brasil.* Belo Horizonte: Editora UFMG.

Werneck Vianna, Luiz, and Marcelo Burgos. 2002. Revolução processual do direito e democracia progressiva. In *A democracia e os três poderes no Brasil,* ed. Luiz Werneck Vianna. Belo Horizonte: Editora UFMG.

Werneck Vianna, Luiz, Maria Alice Rezende de Carvalho, Manuel Palacios Cunha Melo, and Marcelo Baumann Burgos. 1997. *Corpo e alma da magistratura brasileira,* 2nd ed. Rio de Janeiro: Editora Revan.

———. 1999. *A judicialização da política e das relações sociais no Brasil.* Rio de Janeiro: Editora Revan.

Whittington, Keith E. 2005. "Interpose Your Friendly Hand": Political Supports for the Exercise of Judicial Review by the United States Supreme Court. *American Political Science Review* 99, no. 4: 583–96.

Wiarda, Howard J. 1973. Toward a Framework for the Study of Political Change in the Iberic-Latin Tradition: The Corporative Model. *World Politics* 25, no. 2: 206–235.

———. 1981. *Corporatism and National Development in Latin America.* Boulder, Colo.: Westview Press.

———, ed. 2004. *Authoritarianism and Corporatism in Latin America, Revisited.* Gainesville: University Press of Florida.

Wilson, Bruce M. 2005. Changing Dynamics: The Political Impact of Costa Rica's Constitutional Court. In *The Judicialization of Politics in Latin America,* eds. Rachel Sieder, Line Schjolden, and Alan Angell. New York: Palgrave Macmillan.

Wilson, Bruce M., and Juan Carlos Rodríguez-Cordero. 2006. Legal Opportunity Structures and Social Movements: The Effects of Institutional Change on Costa Rican Politics. *Comparative Political Studies* 39, no. 3: 325–51.

Wilson, Bruce M., Juan Carlos Rodríguez-Cordero, and Roger Handberg. 2004. The Best Laid Schemes . . . Gang Aft A-Gley: Judicial Reform in Latin America—Evidence from Costa Rica. *Journal of Latin American Studies* 36: 507–31.

Wilson, Frank L. 1983. Interest Groups and Politics in Western Europe: The Neo-Corporatist Approach. *Comparative Politics* 16, no. 1: 105–23.

Wilson, James Q. 1995. *Political Organizations.* Princeton, N.J.: Princeton University Press.

Wolthers, Gabriela. 27 October 2000. O tráfico e a OAB. *Folha de São Paulo,* p. Opinião A2.

INDEX